The Laskin Legacy

The Laskin Legacy:
ESSAYS IN COMMEMORATION OF
CHIEF JUSTICE BORA LASKIN

edited by
Neil Finkelstein & Constance Backhouse

The Laskin Legacy: Essays in Commemoration of Chief Justice Bora Laskin
© Irwin Law Inc., 2007

All rights reserved. No part of this publication may be reproduced, stored in a retrieval system, or transmitted, in any form or by any means, without the prior written permission of the publisher or, in the case of photocopying or other reprographic copying, a licence from Access Copyright (Canadian Copyright Licensing Agency), 1 Yonge Street, Suite 800, Toronto, Ontario, M5E 1E5.

Published in 2007 by

Irwin Law
14 Duncan Street
Suite 206
Toronto, Ontario
M5H 3G8

www.irwinlaw.com

ISBN-13: 978-155221-140-3

Library and Archives Canada Cataloguing in Publication

[tk]

The publisher acknowledges the financial support of the Government of Canada through the Book Publishing Industry Development Program (BPIDP) for its publishing activities.

We acknowledge the assistance of the OMDC Book Fund, an initiative of Ontario Media Development Corporation.

Printed and bound in Canada.

1 2 3 4 5 11 10 09 08 07

ALL ROYALTIES FORM THE PUBLICATION OF
THIS BOOK WILL BE DONATED TO THE
LAWYERS FEED THE HOMELESS PROGRAM
OF THE LAW SOCIETY FOUNDATION

Contents

CONTRIBUTORS

1 **Introduction** 1
Constance Backhouse

PART ONE: PERSONAL PHILOSOPHY

2 **Some Memories of My Father** 13
John I. Laskin

3 **Comments on My Dad** 27
Barbara Laskin

PART TWO: EDUCATOR

4 **Laskin and the University** 33
Martin Friedland

5 **Laskin and the University Crisis of 1949** 41
Horace Krever

PART THREE: IMPACT ON THE SUPREME COURT OF CANADA

6 **Laskin's Legacy to the Supreme Court** 51
Ian Binnie

7 **Laskin's Impact on the Supreme Court** 67
Peter W. Hogg

8 **Memories of Laskin at the Court** 77
Sheridan Scott

PART FOUR: SUBSTANTIVE CONTRIBUTIONS TO LAW

9 **Laskin's Legacy to National Unity and Patriation** 83
R. Roy McMurtry

10 Laskin's Legacy to Law   91
J.J. Michel Robert

PART FIVE: ADMINISTRATIVE AND LABOUR LAW

11 Chief Justice Laskin's Approach to Administrative Law   99
Stephen T. Goudge

12 Laskin's Contribution to Labour Law   109
Chris G. Paliare

PART SIX: CONSTITUTIONAL LAW, FEDERALISM, AND INDIVIDUAL RIGHTS

13 Laskin and the Constitutional Protection of Rights and Freedoms   117
Robert J. Sharpe

PART SEVEN: CONTRACT, TORT, AND FIDUCIARY OBLIGATIONS

14 The Laskin Legacy in Private Law: The Judge as Custodian of the Common Law   131
John D. McCamus

15 Laskin and Fiduciary Duties   149
Kathryn N. Feldman

PART EIGHT: LASKIN IN DISSENT

16 Chief Justice Bora Laskin: The Great Dissenter   159
Neil Finkelstein

PART NINE: REASSESSMENT: THE NEXT GENERATION

17 Bora Laskin: Lifting the Legacy from the Legend   173
Ellen Snow

Contributors

Constance Backhouse is a Professor of Law, Distinguished University Professor, and University Research Chair at the University of Ottawa. She obtained her B.A. from the University of Manitoba (1972), her LL.B. from Osgoode Hall (1975), and her LL.M. from Harvard Law School (1979.) She was called to the Ontario Bar in 1978. She teaches feminist law, criminal law, human rights, and labour law. She is the author of many award-winning legal history books, including *Petticoats & Prejudice: Women and Law in Nineteenth-Century Canada* (1991), *Colour-Coded: A Legal History of Racism in Canadian Law, 1900-1950* (1999) and *The Heiress vs. the Establishment: Mrs. Campbell's Campaign for Legal Justice* (2004). She received the Law Society Medal in 1998, and an Honorary Doctorate from the Law Society of Upper Canada in 2002. She has served as an elected Bencher of the Law Society from 2002. She became a Fellow of the Royal Society of Canada in 2004.

The Honourable Mr. Justice John I. Laskin is the son of Bora and Peggy Laskin. He is a graduate of the University of Toronto Law School. He maintained a litigation practice for over twenty years, mainly in the fields of administrative, constitutional and commercial law. He has been counsel to several commissions of inquiry. He was appointed to the Court of Appeal for Ontario in 1994. He is the chair of the annual CIAJ judgment writing seminar, and an instructor in advocacy and decision writing at numerous programs for lawyers, judges and members of administrative tribunals.

Barbara Laskin, the daughter of Bora and Peggy Laskin, was born in Toronto. Formerly a senior official with the Canada Council for the Arts, she has worked for over fifteen years as a consultant to organizations in the public and non-profit sectors, contributing expertise in strategic communications, policy and program design, public relations, and board governance. She has worked in various capacities with a range of federal, provincial and community-based boards, including the Law Society of Upper Canada, where she served as a lay Bencher from 1999–2003. She is President of Meta4 Creative Communications Inc., an Ottawa-based communications firm, and currently serves as a member of Ontario's Consent and Capacity Board.

Martin Friedland is a University Professor and Professor of Law Emeritus at the University of Toronto, where he was formerly the dean of law. He received his LL.B. from the University of Toronto with the Gold Medal in 1958 and an honorary doctorate in 2001. Professor Friedland was called to the Bar in 1960 with the Treasurer's Medal and was granted a Ph.D. from Cambridge University in 1967 and an LL.D. in 1997. He is the author or editor of seventeen books, including the prize-winning *The Trials of Israel Lipski* and *The University of Toronto: a History*. The recipient of numerous honours and awards, including the Criminal Lawyers Association's G. Arthur Martin Criminal Justice Award, the Canadian Bar Association's Ramon John Hnatyshyn Award, and the Canada Council's Molson Prize in the Humanities and Social Sciences, he was appointed an Officer of the Order of Canada in 1990 and became a Companion in 2003.

The Honourable Mr. Justice Horace Krever was called to the bar of Ontario in 1956, and practised civil and criminal litigation with the firm of Kimber and Dubin until 1964. From 1964 to 1968, he was a professor in the Faculty of Law and special lecturer in the Faculty of Medicine at the University of Toronto. From 1969 to 1974, he was a professor in the Faculty of Law and special lecturer in the Faculty of Medicine at the University of Western Ontario. In 1974, he returned to the University of Toronto where he was a professor in both faculties of Law and Medicine until 1975. From 1971 to 1975, he was an elected Bencher of the Law Society of

Upper Canada. In 1975, he was appointed to the High Court of Justice of the Supreme Court of Ontario. In 1986, he was appointed to the Court of Appeal for Ontario, where he served until his retirement in 1999.

The Honourable Mr. Justice Ian Binnie, B.A., LL.B., LL.M., LL.D., was appointed to the Supreme Court of Canada on January 8, 1998. Prior to his appointment, he was a senior partner of McCarthy Tétrault from 1986 to 1998, an Associate Deputy Minister of Justice for Canada from 1982 to 1986, and practised litigation in Toronto from 1967 to 1982. He studied law at the University of Toronto and at Cambridge University (where he was the first Canadian elected President of the Cambridge Union). He has been called to the Bar of Ontario, the English Bar, and the Bar of the Yukon Territory. He received occasional calls to appear in the courts of British Columbia, Alberta, Saskatchewan, Manitoba, and Newfoundland. He received Honorary LL.D.'s from the Law Society of Upper Canada and from McGill University in 2001. He was elected a Fellow of the American College of Trial Lawyers in 1992, and is a Member of the Middle Temple Inns of Court (England). In April 2003, he was appointed a Commissioner of the International Commission of Jurists based in Geneva, Switzerland.

Peter W. Hogg, C.C., Q.C., L.S.M., F.R.S.C., is a scholar in residence at the law firm of Blake, Cassels & Graydon LLP. He was the Dean of the Osgoode Hall Law School of York University from 1998 to 2003, and has been a professor at the Law School since 1970. He is the author of *Constitutional Law of Canada* (Carswell, 4th ed., 1997) and *Liability of the Crown* (Carswell, 3rd ed., 2000 with Patrick J. Monahan), as well as other books and articles. He has appeared as counsel in constitutional cases.

Sheridan Scott obtained an LL.B. from the University of Victoria in 1981, after which she served as law clerk to the Chief Justice of Canada, the Right Honourable Bora Laskin. From 1983 to 1992, she worked as Legal Counsel and Senior Legal Counsel at the Canadian Radio-television and Telecommunications Commission. From 1992 to 1994, she worked as Assistant Vice-President, Planning and Corporate Development, and Vice-President of Planning and Regulatory Affairs at the Canadian Broadcasting Corporation. She then worked as the Chief Regulatory Officer and Vice-President of Bell Canada, before becoming Canada's

Commissioner of Competition at the Competition Bureau in 2004. She has taught part-time at the University of Ottawa and Carleton University, and was named one of Canada's 100 Most Powerful Women in the Trailblazer category in 2005 by the Women's Executive Network.

The Honourable Chief Justice R. Roy McMurtry was called to the Bar in 1958 and practiced law as a trial counsel for seventeen years before being elected to the Ontario Legislature in 1975. Immediately upon his election, he was appointed to the Cabinet of the Premier, William G. Davis, as the Attorney General for Ontario, a position that he held until 1985. He played a major role in the patriation of the Canadian Constitution in 1982 and the creation of the *Canadian Charter of Rights and Freedoms*. During his years as Attorney General, the Ontario Legislature passed more than fifty law reform statutes, including the first major family law reform legislation in Canada and the creation of a bilingual court system. From 1978 to 1982, he also served as the Solicitor General for Ontario. In 1985, he was appointed Canada's High Commissioner (Ambassador) to Great Britain, a post he held until late 1988. Upon his return to Canada, he re-entered the practice of law and in 1991 he was appointed Associate Chief Justice of the Superior Court, Trial Division. He became Chief Justice of that court in 1994. In February 1996, he was appointed Chief Justice of Ontario.

The Honourable Chief Justice J.J. Michel Robert, P.C., Q.C., B.A., LL.L, was born January 29, 1938 in Montreal, Quebec, Canada. He was educated at College St. Marie, Montreal, B.A. (1958), University of Montreal, LL.L (1961) and McGill University (1962). He was called to the Bar of Quebec, July 3, 1962. He practised law as the senior partner, Robert Dansereau, Barre, Marchessault & Lauzon, Montreal, 1968-90, and partner, Langlois Robert, 1990–95. His political career included serving as President of the Young Liberals of Canada, 1963–65, as a member of the Royal Commission on the Economic Union and Development Prospects for Canada (Macdonald Commission), 1982–85, and as President, Liberal Party of Canada, 1986-90. He was sworn to the Privy Council December 5, 1991 (Right Honourable B. Mulroney). He was appointed as a Member, Security Intelligence Review Committee, December 5, 1991. He was appointed to the Court of Appeal of Quebec, May 9, 1995, and appointed Chief Justice of Quebec, June 25, 2002. He served as the President of the Quebec Bar Association, 1974–75 and Federation of Law Societies of Canada, 1976–77. He was a Member of Council, Canadian Bar Association, 1975–82. He served with the Canadian Officer Training Corps, 1956–60, and as Lieutenant, Royal Canadian Signal Corps, 1960. He is the co-author and author of numerous articles and books. He was appointed Queen's Counsel, 1982, and as a Fellow, American College of Trial Lawyers, 1987–present. He was a lecturer, faculty of Law, University of Montreal in civil liability and civil procedure 1970–1980.

The Honourable Mr. Justice Stephen T. Goudge obtained a B.A. (Political Science/Economics), University of Toronto, 1964, an M.Sc. (Econ.), London School of Economics, 1965, and an LL.B. (Awarded Dean's Key), University of Toronto, 1968. He was articled to the Hon. Ian G. Scott, Q.C., and called to the Bar of Ontario in 1970. He was appointed a Queen's Counsel in 1982. He practiced with the small litigation firm of Cameron Brewin and Scott until it merged with Gowling and Henderson in 1983. He became managing partner of the firm Gowling, Strathy & Henderson in Toronto where he engaged in a general litigation practice. He appeared before many administrative tribunals and Courts at all levels in Ontario and the Supreme Court of Canada. He served as a lecturer, University of Toronto Faculty of Law in both Labour Law and Native Rights 1974 to 1985. In 1989 he became Counsel to the Office of the Premier of Ontario. He was active in the Ontario Bar Association and the Canadian Civil Liberties Association. He was an elected Bencher of the Law Society of the Upper Canada from 1991 to 1996. He is a Judicial Fellow of the American College of Trial Lawyers. He was appointed to the Court of Appeal for Ontario in 1996.

Chris G. Paliare, LSM, received his LL.B. from Osgoode Hall in 1970, and his LL.M. from the University of Texas (Austin) in 1971. He was called to the Ontario Bar in 1973, with honours. He is certified as a specialist by the Law Society in civil litigation. He is a partner in Paliare Roland Rosenberg Rothstein LLP, where he practises in the areas of complex corporate and commercial litigation, shareholder disputes, securities litigation, administrative law, and white collar criminal law. He is engaged as counsel in trials and in appeals before the Divisional Court, Court of Appeal, and Supreme Court of Canada. He is a Fellow of the International Academy of Trial Lawyers, a Fellow of the American College of Trial Lawyers, and a former Ontario Provincial chair, as well as an Honorary Member of COMBAR. He was the recipient of the Law Society Medal in 2004. He is consistently listed in the *Lexpert Guide to the Leading 100 Canada/US Cross-Border Litigators; Lexpert Guide to the 100 Most Creative Lawyers in Canada; Lexpert/American Lawyer Media Guide to the Leading 500 Lawyers in Canada; Chambers Globe The World's Leading Lawyers; International Who's Who of Commercial Litigators; Mondaq's Employment Lawyers,* and *Euromoney's Expert Guide to Global Labour and Employment Lawyers.*

The Honourable Mr. Justice Robert J. Sharpe has been a member of the Court of Appeal for Ontario since 1999. He was formerly a member of the Superior Court of Justice and Professor and Dean of the Faculty of Law, University of Toronto. Robert Sharpe is the author of several books including *The Last Day, the Last Hour: The Currie Libel Trial* (1988); *Injunctions and Specific Performance* (3rd ed. 2000); *Brian Dickson: A Judge's Journey* (with Kent Roach) (2003); *The Charter of Rights and Freedoms* (with Kent Roach) (3rd ed. 2005)

John D. McCamus is a Professor of Law and University Professor at Osgoode Hall Law School of York University, a faculty which he served as Dean from 1982-1987. Prior to joining the faculty at Osgoode, he served as a law clerk at the Supreme Court of Canada for Chief Justice Laskin. At Osgoode, his principal areas of research and teaching have included private law, especially restitution and contract, and commercial law. His published work includes two texts, *The Law of Contracts* (2005) and *The Law of Restitution* 2d ed. (2004), the latter volume co-authored with P.D. Maddaugh. Professor McCamus served, from 1993 to 1996, as Chair of the Ontario Law Reform Commission. In 1998, he was appointed by the American Law Institute to the Advisory Committee for the Restatement of Restitution and Unjust Enrichment 3d. He was elected a Fellow of the Royal Society of Canada in 2006.

The Honourable Justice Kathryn N. Feldman received her B.A. from the University of Toronto in 1970 and her LL.B. from the University of Toronto, Faculty of Law in 1973. She was a partner in the firm of Blake, Cassels & Graydon until her appointment on December 24, 1990, to the Ontario Court of Justice (General Division), now called the Superior Court of Justice. She was appointed to the Court of Appeal for Ontario on June 11, 1998. It was as a friend of John Laskin that she had the privilege of knowing his dear parents, Bora and Peggy Laskin.

Neil Finkelstein obtained his B.A. and LL.B. from McGill (1973, 1979), and his LL.M. from Harvard (1980). He became a Chartered Accountant (1975). He was former law clerk to the Hon. Bora Laskin, Chief Justice of Canada (1980-81). He was admitted to the Ontario Bar in 1982. He served as senior policy advisor to the Attorney General of Canada (1985–86). He served as a Bencher of the Law Society of Upper Canada from 1991 to 2007. His practice at Blake, Cassels & Graydon LLP includes broad corporate, commercial, competition and public law (constitutional and administrative) litigation practice. He served as co-counsel for the Gomery Commission, and his national litigation practice includes seventy-three major trials and hearings at courts, tribunals and commissions of inquiry across Canada, thirty-eight appeals in five provinces and the Federal Court of Appeal, and twenty-two appeals in the Supreme Court of Canada. Publications include *Laskin's Canadian Constitutional Law* (5th edition) and *Finkelstein and Finkelstein, Constitutional Rights in the Investigative Process*.

Ellen M. Snow is an associate practicing in the litigation department of the Toronto office of Stikeman Elliott LLP. She obtained a B.A. (Hons) from McMaster University (2002) and a J.D. from the Faculty of Law, University of Toronto (2005). She was called to the Ontario Bar in 2006. Her practice focuses primarily on corporate and civil litigation. She has published several articles: "Enforceability of National Classes: The New Landscape" *Class Action Defence Quarterly* (September, 2006); "Protecting Canadian Plaintiffs in International Class Actions: The Need for a Principled Approach in Light of *Currie v. McDonald's Restaurants of Canada Ltd.*" *The Canadian Class Action Review* (December, 2005).

Introduction

CONSTANCE BACKHOUSE

BORA LASKIN, THE MAN who became one of Canada's most celebrated chief justices of all time, was born in Fort William (now Thunder Bay), Ontario, in 1912. The middle son of impoverished Russian immigrant Jews, he signalled his remarkable talents while still a youth. He graduated as class valedictorian, excelled in athletic competition, mastered Yiddish, English, and Hebrew, and took to debating as effortlessly as he did to the violin. After completing legal degrees at the University of Toronto, Osgoode Hall, and Harvard Law School, Laskin's career encompassed teaching law at the University of Toronto and Osgoode Hall, a distinguished labour arbitration practice, and the publication of a substantial body of constitutional law scholarship. His reputation as an influential public intellectual who took principled stands on civil liberties and equality rights brought him to the attention of powerful politicians at a time of growing public criticism over non-meritorious judicial appointments. In 1965 Laskin was appointed to the Ontario Court of Appeal, an appointment described as "virtually unprecedented [for] a non-partisan, an academic, and a Jew."[1]

Laskin's elevation to the Supreme Court of Canada in 1970, and his unanticipated appointment as Chief Justice of the Supreme Court in 1973, contributed to the building of the "Laskin legend."[2] He reshaped public law, legitimated a franker discussion of policy choices, persuaded his fellow judges to take their law from many sources, and stimulated both legal and social discussions about the concept of rights. His colleague Justice Brian Dickson attributed to Laskin a "moral grandeur without the slightest taint of self-righteousness."[3] The eulogies that flooded in on Laskin's death in 1984 described him as a man whose life was graced by a "creative approach to the law," an "independence of mind," and, most important, "compassion."[4] He was credited with taking the judiciary to the threshold of a "new public prominence and stature."[5] His successor as Chief Justice depicted him as a "great judge" who had "made a lasting impression on the jurisprudence of our country and a major contribution to Canadian social thought and action."[6]

Philip Girard has published the definitive biography in his *Bora Laskin: Bringing Law to Life*.[7] This volume of essays is not intended to compete with Girard's scholarly biography. Instead, it is something of a companion piece, a collection of short essays from family members, judges, law professors, and lawyers whose recollections about Laskin flesh out the life of a man "at the summit of Canada's political and legal life," with commentary from some whose paths crossed his.[8] With one exception, the essays were all originally delivered orally at a symposium hosted by the Law Society of Upper Canada on May 25, 2005, at Osgoode Hall. The final chapter, written by a third-year University of Toronto law student, was selected as one of the prize-winning essays submitted for adjudication in conjunction with the symposium.[9]

The first two authors, Laskin's children, offer their own views about Bora Laskin's personal philosophy. The Hon. John I. Laskin, a Judge of the Ontario Court of Appeal and Bora's older child, set the stage with his childhood memories of the private life of Bora Laskin. He describes what it was like to grow up in a household with a parent whose commitment to work drove him mercilessly, but who "enjoyed his work more" than anyone his son would ever know. He captures some of this father's rare leisure moments and conveys his intense loyalty to his family and his friends. John Laskin's comments also explain some of the ties and connections that bind Bora Laskin to the other authors whose recollections appear in this volume. Barbara Laskin is the only non-lawyer to contribute to this volume. Although her career path took her into the field of arts and culture, her contribution to the legal profession has been considerable. She served as a lay bencher appointed by the provincial government to the Law Society of Upper Canada and recalls with irony what her father would have thought of her connection to the professional body against which he had warred for so many years. She reminisces about her father's unswerving insistence on proper grammar, his lack of interest in the trappings of material success, and his amused forbearance when she breached the crusty Rideau Club's rule requiring females to enter by a separate women's entrance. She recounts that her father always attributed his success to "accident" and "serendipity" – that he seemed far too consumed with current responsibilities to spend time plotting his career elevation. She sheds some light on the social side of the private Bora Laskin, an aspect of his character mostly hidden from public view.

Laskin's role as an educator within the broader university is the context for the recollections of the next two authors. Professor Martin L. Friedland, whose legal career began in 1955 as a student of Bora Laskin's at the University of Toronto, describes the complicated hiring process that brought Bora Laskin to his first academic appointment in 1940 at the University of Toronto. He documents the haphazard route by which his professor moved from the University of Toronto to Osgoode Hall in 1945, the grand collective resignation in 1949, and the subsequent reinstallment at the University of Toronto. Friedland brings a unique voice to the collection when he recounts the "no-nonsense ... [no] chit-chat" but remarkably effective style of mentoring that Laskin brought to his professorial role. He also describes the memorable moment when Laskin was advised of his first judicial appointment, an evening Friedland unknowingly shared with his former professor over dinner in London, England, in early July 1965. Although Laskin died before the court could deliver any judgments under the new *Charter of Rights and Freedoms*, Friedland credits his "wise Solomon-like figure" as influential in bringing the public to an acceptance of the broadened judicial presence essential to the enactment of the *Charter*.

The Hon. Horace Krever, a retired judge of the Ontario Court of Appeal, recounts the momentous events of 1949 and their aftermath, when Bora Laskin, along with three other full-time members of the Osgoode Hall Law School, resigned over the heavy-handed interference of the benchers of the Law Society of Upper Canada. Laskin, Caesar Wright, and John Willis subsequently accepted appointment to the University of Toronto Faculty of Law, where they created the three-year LL.B. program that would become the model for Ontario law faculties across the province. For eight years, the Law Society refused to recognize the academic validity of the University of Toronto degree. Krever was a law student there at the time and remembers picketing Osgoode Hall in protest with other law students in 1952. With some sense of pride, he describes their official reprimand from the Law Society and the unofficial support they received from Bora Laskin. He also recounts how, after his own election as a bencher, Laskin asked him to find and pass along a copy of an unpublished bencher report that had provoked the faculty resignations. Krever's pleasure that he was able to provide Laskin with this report, and his fascination with the letters he received from his mentor reflecting on the report, are palpable even after the passage of so many years.

Laskin's impact on the Supreme Court of Canada is the topic examined by the next three authors: a judge, a law professor, and a former law clerk who is now a legal practitioner. The Hon. Ian Binnie, a judge of the Supreme Court of Canada, was a student of Laskin and has appeared as counsel before him in the Ontario Court of Appeal and in the Supreme Court of Canada. With his trademark wit and humour, Binnie tries to place Laskin among his judicial peers, rating the judges over such factors as birth place, religion, pre-judicial careers, time on the bench, academic brilliance, judicial writing style, and even official portraits. Sir Samuel Henry Strong's "mutton-chop whiskers," Sir Henri-Elzéar Taschereau's "patrician air," and the "bashful smiles" of the other ceremonially robed judges pale in front of Binnie's description of Laskin's "ferocious gaze," which he proclaims rivals in intensity "Rocket Richard zooming across the blue line." He suggests that Laskin's impact on the Supreme Court revolutionized the way litigation was conducted, enhanced the court's jurisprudential sophistication, staked out new directions in private law, restructured administrative law, and "torpedoed the Federal Court." Justice Brian Dickson will likely "have a more lasting impact on Canadian jurisprudence," he says, but concludes that it is our "collective tragedy" that Laskin, a "heretic in the temple of legal conformity," should have died at the threshold of the *Charter* era.

Professor Peter W. Hogg also appeared before Justice Laskin in the Supreme Court of Canada, and the two squared off occasionally over differing perspectives on constitutional law scholarship. Hogg describes the "Laskin Court" as a "court of change" and attributes to Laskin the transformative impetus that made the Supreme Court of Canada "recognizably modern." He notes how Laskin shifted the court from slavish adherence to English precedent and towards "a uniquely Canadian jurisprudence." Under Laskin, even Supreme Court of Canada precedents were overturned, as *stare decisis* came under the scrutiny of principled policy analysis. Hogg claims that the distinctively "Canadian" jurisprudence that began under Laskin has, ironically, been the spark that has attracted international interest and acclaim.

Sheridan Scott, the first female law clerk that Bora Laskin hired to work for him at the Supreme Court of Canada, recalls what it was like to meet the Chief Justice when she was freshly graduated from the University of Victoria law school. Her memories of talking with Laskin as they took daily walks around the grounds of the Court or of Parliament are stirring and enlightening. She describes his pride in the athletic achievements of his youth, his belief in the importance of university-based legal education, and his principled disagreement with acts of civil disobedience.

The volume next turns to a consideration of Bora Laskin's substantive contributions to law. In the section on his input to national unity and patriation of the Constitution, the Chief Justices of both Ontario and Quebec describe their shared experience, before their elevation to the bench, of appearing in the Supreme Court of Canada before Bora Laskin as the respective litigators for Ontario and the federal government. The Hon. R. Roy McMurtry, Chief Justice of Ontario, recollects wryly upon the hazards of appearing personally as attorney general in the anti-inflation legislation case and in the *Patriation Reference* case. On the *Patriation* file, he describes the behind-the-scenes lobbying with the British attorney general, Sir Michael Havers; the last-minute rallying of Department of Justice lawyers by the minister of justice, Jean Chrétien; and the finer points of the complex argument. From the vantage of hindsight, McMurtry considers Laskin's dissenting judgment and makes it clear that he still believes it was the only rational legal answer that could have been made in response to the constitutional issues at stake.

The Hon. J.J. Michel Robert, Chief Justice of Quebec, began his law career at the University of Montreal but also travelled to Toronto to take a course of lectures on constitutional law. He reflects on the gaping chasm between the visions of the Canadian Constitution promulgated by his Montreal professor, Jean Beetz, and his Toronto professor, Bora Laskin, marvelling that "Quebec and Ontario were living peacefully side by side but were not living under the same Constitution." Robert offers his personal reflections about what it was like to argue the *Patriation Reference* case before Chief Justice Bora Laskin. While he questions the outcome of the case in several respects, he also states that Laskin's decision allowed for the ultimate entrenchment of the *Charter* and the constitutional protection of Aboriginal rights – collectively, in his view, the "most important legal revolution" in the history of Canada.

Bora Laskin's contributions to administrative law are evaluated by the Hon. Stephen T. Goudge, a judge of the Ontario Court of Appeal. Goudge explains that he grew up in a family that maintained a close friendship with the Laskins. He describes with some amusement the surprise he felt on discovering as a law student and litigator that "John and Barbie['s] parent" enjoyed enormous stature as a jurist. Goudge explores the two themes that he feels enshrine Laskin's administrative law decisions: the complementary concepts of deference and fairness. He concludes that Laskin played an unparalleled role in shaping "the modem framework of administrative law."

Chris G. Paliare, a highly-respected Toronto barrister, explores Bora Laskin's contributions to the substantive field of labour law. He depicts Laskin as simultaneously a "labour relations visionary" and a "pragmatist." Paliare considers Laskin's desire to craft an efficient and fair mechanism for alternative dispute resolution in industrial strife. He explains how Laskin's penchant for practical, balanced solutions found favour with both labour and management, and he heralds Laskin as a "revolutionary" theorist, a "ground-breaking" arbitrator, and a "powerful and passionate" judge.

The Hon. Robert J. Sharpe of the Ontario Court of Appeal addresses Laskin's contribution to the constitutional protection of rights and freedoms. According to Sharpe, although Laskin was always a "passionate defender of civil liberties," his ideas witnessed a dramatic change after he proceeded from the academy to the bench. While still a legal scholar, Laskin saw a limited role for the courts and resisted the idea of an entrenched charter of rights. While a judge, his decisions (often in dissent) elevated the *Canadian Bill of Rights* above federal legislation to give it "quasi-constitutional status." Throughout both roles, however, Sharpe explains that Laskin continued to respect the central role of Parliament. Sharpe traces the evolution of Laskin's analysis and suggests that it paralleled broader shifts in Canadian thinking. He credits Laskin with having a "significant influence" on Canada's decision to entrench the *Charter*. Sharpe concludes that Laskin laid the foundation for the *Charter* and made it possible.

Professor John McCamus, from Osgoode Hall Law School, considers the Laskin legacy in the private law areas of tort and contract. He begins with some humorous anecdotes from his time as a law clerk to Bora Laskin, recounting his linguistic proficiency in English but not in French and reflecting on his congeniality and "consummate professionalism" towards law clerks and colleagues. McCamus points out that Laskin's knowledge of common law was "prodigious" and notes that many of his torts and contracts decisions still retain pride of place in Canadian casebooks. He documents the ways in which Laskin "opened the Canadian judicial door widely to the richness of American jurisprudence" and other academic writing, despite marked resistance from some of his brothers on the bench. He suggests that Laskin understood the appellate courts to be the guardians of the common law of obligations, with the responsibility to monitor and "refresh" doctrines that were no longer defensible. McCamus examines Laskin's vision of the judiciary as the "architect" of the common law, and he contrasts that with other perspectives that positioned the legislature as the principal instrument of private law reform. He argues that Laskin's gifts as a public lawyer rest on the "strong and analytical conceptual foundation he developed as a private law scholar and jurist."

The Hon. Kathryn Feldman of the Ontario Court of Appeal explores Laskin's contribution to the substantive law of fiduciary duties. She considers the 1974 decision in *Canadian Aero Service (Canaero)*, in which Laskin identified the defendants as "faithless fiduciaries" and issued a ruling that "set the tone for the corporate behaviour of directors and officers." Despite the increasingly short "shelf-life" of many judicial opinions, Feldman notes that *Canaero* remains the "leading authority" in Canada, while highly influential in England and Australia too, on the nature and extent of the duty owed by corporate directors and officers not to appropriate corporate opportunities. Feldman compares the strict corporate ethic that Laskin promulgated in *Canaero* with his famous dissent in *Murdoch*. She describes Laskin's creative use of the doctrine of constructive trust to award a wife her rightful share of the family property as a "testament to Justice Laskin's judicial courage."

Neil Finkelstein, another former law clerk to Bora Laskin and now an eminent Toronto barrister, reviews Laskin's dissenting judicial decisions to portray the impact that he made on Canadian jurisprudence as Canada's "great dissenter." Finkelstein emphasizes that Laskin's dissents enunciated legal standards before they existed in any written instruments and proclaimed civil liberties using vocabulary that had not existed before. He notes that 24 percent of the judgments that Laskin penned on the Supreme Court of Canada were issued in dissent, but he argues that Laskin's influence on his fellow judges increased substantially over time. He suggests that, by the second half of his term, Laskin's perspectives had begun to persuade his colleagues substantially more often, and they would subsequently evolve into majority decisions under the *Charter*, "casting beams that lighted the subsequent ways of the law."

Ellen Snow, a law student at the University of Toronto at the time she wrote her essay, represents the response of a new generation of lawyers to Bora Laskin. Clearly bemused by the vast scholarship written by more senior practitioners and academics, she concludes that the precise scope of Laskin's legacy remains debatable. She chooses to focus on the divergent assessments of Laskin's career offered by Ian Bushnell and Peter McCormick. Bushnell has suggested that Laskin was highly influential at the Supreme Court in his early years but, by the late 1970s and early 1980s, had been relegated to a "marginal position." McCormick, in contrast, argues that Laskin became most influential in shaping the holdings of the court after 1979. After her own thoughtful examination of Laskin's decisions and scholarly writing, Snow concludes that neither Bushnell nor McCormick is completely correct. In her assessment, Laskin's legacy lies somewhere in-between. She argues that Laskin's early reforming zeal was not maintained throughout his judicial tenure but that he continued to effect substantial change, albeit of a more moderating sort, throughout his last days on the bench. Her final conclusion presages the ongoing assessments of future generations of lawyers and judges who will, undoubtedly, continue to debate and disagree but will always remain drawn to, and fascinated by, the legacy of Bora Laskin.

NOTES

1 Philip Girard, *Bora Laskin: Bringing Law to Life* (Toronto: University of Toronto Press, 2005), 317.
2 For reference to this term, see ibid., 392.
3 Robert J. Sharpe and Kent Roach, *Brian Dickson: A Judge's Journey* (Toronto: University of Toronto Press, 2003), 141.
4 Girard, *Bora Laskin*, 536, citing the anglophone press, while noting that the francophone media was equally positive.
5 Sharpe and Roach, *Brian Dickson*, 287.
6 Ibid., 141.
7 Girard, *Bora Laskin*.
8 Ibid., 535.
9 Two student essays were selected to share this distinction. Brent Arnold, M.A. (Queen's University), LL.B. candidate (Osgoode Hall Law School), whose paper is not included in this collection, wrote the other impressive prize-winning essay.

◀ PART ONE ▶

Personal Philosophy

◀ 2 ▶

Some Memories of My Father

JOHN I. LASKIN

LIKE MANY CHILDREN, I find it difficult to talk publicly about my dad. We were a close-knit family, but also a private family. Although cast into the public eye, my father remained a modest and reserved person.

So I will begin with something much easier: thanking all of the contributors to this book, who have so graciously taken time from their busy lives to pay tribute to my father. My sister, Barbara, and I are so appreciative of their willingness to do so. Although they have been asked to write about our father's legacy, I hope that they have not felt the occasion precludes them from being critical of his record. My dad always encouraged rigorous debate. The last thing he would have wanted was a love-in of his work.

Each of the contributors has, in one way or another, intersected with my dad – some, of course, more directly than others. I will mention these connections as I share a few of the many memories I have of my dad and my mom.

My father had two great loves in his life: the law and his family. I will talk a little about each.

My father was passionate about law and about its importance as an instrument for change in our society. He worked enormously hard, without seeming to tire of doing so. For him, law was very much a labour of love. He loved what he did – and he enjoyed his work more than anyone I have ever known.

He also had a remarkable capacity to work long hours. While we were growing up, most days he worked far into the night. Luckily for him, he needed little sleep. Luckily for us, his "after-hours" work took place at home in Toronto, in our basement, which we affectionately called "the Dungeon." We always had dinner together; he would come up for air during the evening to spend some time with us.

I think the hardest he ever worked was on his constitutional law casebook. I was barely eight years old when he finished the first edition of that book. Even today, I remember him working into the wee hours of the morning, night after night, to finish it. If he got to bed at 2 a.m., that was an early night for him. Of all the many things he wrote, none was dearer to his heart than that casebook. He completed a third revised edition in 1969, but when he went to the Supreme Court of Canada he felt that it was inappropriate to continue to work on it. His friend and teaching colleague Albert Abel did the fourth edition, and then my dad asked his former law clerk Neil Finklestein to take it over. It is a mark of his respect for Neil and for his scholarship that he entrusted him with the book that meant so much to him.

If my father began the serious study and teaching of constitutional law in Canada, Peter Hogg has become the acknowledged master. They did not always see eye to eye on the distribution of legislative powers – the section 91 and 92 issues. When I was young, my dad often told me that "the whole is greater than the sum of its constituent parts." That simple sentence summed up his view of legislative power. He firmly believed in a strong central government. Peter, I think, takes a more expansive view of provincial power.

These two constitutional scholars intersected in the 1978 *Agricultural Products Marketing Act Reference*. As a law professor, my dad was not enamoured of some of the Privy Council's constitutional decisions. He had written critically of their marketing-board decisions, especially the *Crystal Dairy* case decided in 1933. In the 1978 *Reference* he got a chance to set things right. The Court overruled *Crystal Dairy*. Peter Hogg presented the winning argument.

My father always combined his hard work with doing things right away. Whether they were things he had to do, or felt he ought to do, he never let them accumulate. Procrastination was not part of his vocabulary. When he was appointed to his various judicial posts, he received hundreds of congratulatory letters. To my utter amazement, he personally answered every one right away. Over the years, many people I hardly know have come up to me and given me a photocopy of a handwritten note they received from my dad.

On the bench, he immediately tackled his judgments, too, which was why he was able to write so many. In most cases, he had a clear idea of where he was going. He wrote quickly and he had what I would call a sharp pen. He wrote very few drafts – often just one. Try as we did, my sister and I never persuaded him to use the new technology of the day, not even a Dictaphone. He gave dictation to his secretary. In Ottawa he had two secretaries: his long-time secretary Micheline Rochon, to whom he was devoted, and Suzanne D'Aoust. He wrote his judgments in longhand, a habit he passed on to me. That was how he thought through his reasoning.

My father never sought judicial office. He believed strongly in "accidentalism," the word he used to describe his appointments to the bench. He thought he was lucky and happened to be in the right place at the right time. Had he never been appointed to the court, he would undoubtedly have happily remained a university professor. He loved students and he loved the university life. The University of Toronto Law School had a small but extraordinary faculty, which included his hero, Caesar Wright, and the modest John Willis, the founder of administrative law in Canada. My dad used to say that to have John Willis as a colleague was to have the best postgraduate education you could ever get.

In the early days of the law school, classes were very small. The faculty and their spouses got to know the students in a way that is no longer possible. My father always considered finding articling jobs for his students to be one of his mandates. Martin Friedland and Horace Krever were among my parents' favourite students, and the friendships between the Krevers, the Friedlands, and the Laskins endured long after law school. The university itself was smaller and closer back then. My dad had many friends in the university outside the law school. One was my colleague Steve Goudge's father, a distinguished professor of philosophy. The association between the Laskin family and the Goudge family goes back to the time we boys were born and then went to nursery school together.

As much as my dad loved the university and teaching, he relished the challenge of his new job, judging – first at the Court of Appeal in 1965, and then at the Supreme Court in 1970. He especially looked forward to judging in the two main areas in which he had taught: constitutional law and labour law. The Supreme Court had a heavy dose of each while he was there. The *Patriation Reference* was undoubtedly the most important constitutional case he heard, but the *Anti-Inflation Reference* was a close second.

Roy McMurtry, then attorney general of Ontario, argued both cases for our province. As he always is with everyone, Roy was exceptionally kind to my parents, and they, in turn, were fond of him. This friendship helped him not a whit in the *Anti-Inflation Reference*, where, on one of the two main issues in the case, he lost 9–0. He was, however, one of the architects of the *Canadian Charter of Rights and Freedoms*, in which my father believed strongly. Michel Robert argued the *Patriation Reference* for the federal government. By then, I was a young litigator, interested not just in the result of the case but in who were the best advocates. Many lawyers argued in that *Reference*, some very well, but, according to my dad, none better than Michel Robert.

During these years at the Supreme Court, the standard of review emerged as a dominant issue in labour law. Chris Paliare juniored to Ian Scott in one of my dad's most important standard-of-review decisions, *McLeod v. Egan*. Although he graduated from that "other" law school, Osgoode Hall, he had been taught by the two professors my father considered his real protégés: Harry Arthurs and Paul Weiler. Chris went on to become a protégé of Ian Scott, who was always on my dad's list of the top five advocates to appear before him.

Even after my father left teaching for judging, much of the teacher remained in the judge. When asked to compare the two, he often commented that, as a judge, he simply had fewer students to contend with. Few things made him happier than having one of his former students argue a case before him. One of those students was Ian Binnie, class of 65, along with my colleague and friend Robert Armstrong. That class was the last one my dad taught before his appointment to the Ontario Court of Appeal. Ian had been a student in his constitutional law class and, before Ian's own appointment to the Supreme Court of Canada, he became one of our country's great advocates. He argued several public law cases before my dad. For me, two stand out. The first, decided in 1976, was the *Committee for Justice and Liberty v. The National Energy Board*, which established our test for bias. Binnie and Robert Sharpe won that case in

Bora & Peggy Laskin,
Honeymoon at Kekebeka falls, near Thunder Bay

Bora & Peggy Laskin

Above, clockwise from left, Peggy, Bora, John, & Barbara Laskin

Above left, John & Bora Laskin

L–R, John, Bora, & Barbara Laskin, summer vacation

*Above, front row: Barbara, Bora, Peggy, & John Laskin,
back row: Tim Plumptre*

*Below, L–R: John, Barbara, Bora, & Peggy Laskin
at Bora & Peggy's 70th birthday party*

the Court, and, although the test for bias comes from Justice DeGrandpré's dissenting judgment, my father wrote the majority decision.

The other case was *Borowski*, the third case in the so-called standing trilogy, and a case that caused much discussion in our family. Joseph Borowski, an anti-abortion crusader, challenged the existing abortion provisions of the *Criminal Code*. Ian Binnie acted for the government, and Borowski was represented by a Regina lawyer, Morris Shumiatcher. He had been a founding member of the Co-operative Commonwealth Federation, had studied under my dad, and, with his wife, Jackie, had become close family friends. In this case, he had become a convert to his client's cause. Although in *Thorson* and *McNeil* my dad had expanded the right of ordinary citizens to challenge the validity of legislation, he drew a line in *Borowski*. He had no sympathy for Borowski's position and held that he had no right to sue – others with a more direct interest could do so. The majority on the Court, however, gave Borowski standing.

My father and the Court of his day did not favour appointments to the Supreme Court of Canada directly from the bar. Back then, the Court thought that Supreme Court appointees should have previous judicial experience. Were my dad alive today, I have no doubt he would retract that view. Ian Binnie and another of my dad's favourite students, John Sopinka, have shown that appointees don't need to have previous judicial experience to be great judges on our highest court. Ian Binnie is a towering intellect on the Supreme Court, a brilliant writer, and a spectacular public speaker.

At times, my dad found the Supreme Court to be an isolating place, as many of the judges went their separate ways. Interaction was limited. Perhaps that is why he considered that establishing a judges' lunchroom in the building was one of his most important contributions to the Court.

For intellectual sustenance and vigorous challenge to his views, my father turned to his law clerks. Neil Finklestein, John McCamus, and Sheridan Scott were three of his favourites. I have already talked about Neil. John McCamus and I articled together at the old Fasken, Calvin law firm, but he decided not to stay in practice and chose, instead, to clerk. Sheridan Scott was the first female clerk my dad hired. He developed a real affection for her and greatly admired her work. When her first son, Richard, was born, he got him a little T-shirt with the words "Supreme Court of Canada" on it.

Along with his work, family was very important to my dad. His own parents had made extraordinary sacrifices so he could get a university education, sacrifices he never forgot. Like many Jewish families, my grandparents believed above all else in education. Unfortunately, these were the 1930s, and they had very little money. So they moved out of their house in Fort William and rented it to pay for the education of my dad and his older brother, Charles. My grandfather moved into a local hotel for four years, while my grandmother came to Toronto and rented a small place on Markham Street, where she kept house for her three boys. The youngest son, my Uncle Saul, never had the opportunity to go to university; after finishing high school, he had to return to the Lakehead to help run my grandfather's furniture store. But he made his own mark: distinguished war service, followed by public service as the mayor of Port Arthur and the first mayor of Thunder Bay.

My mother's dad died before I was born, but her mother lived to a good age in a little apartment on Clinton Street, in Toronto, along with her son, Sam, who never married but was like a second father to his nieces and nephews. My dad had great respect for my mother's family and, because he could speak both Hebrew and Yiddish, he carried on lively conversations with my grandmother. She even figured in one of his favourite stories. There used to be a program on CBC television called *Viewpoint*, which came on right after the 11 o'clock news. Each night, some speaker would give his or her views on a topic of interest. One night, while my dad was still teaching, he was asked to give his viewpoint on some constitutional issue. My grandmother usually went to bed around 9 o'clock and got up at 4 or 5 in the morning. But this night my uncle kept her up to watch her son-in-law. When the talk was over, he turned to her and asked, "Well, what do you think?" "He spoke very nicely," she replied, "but what did he say?" My dad told this story as a constant reminder of the importance of humility.

My parents had what we would call a traditional marriage. Although university educated herself, my mother left the workforce to raise her two children and never returned to it. She generally ran the household while her husband was the wage earner. She devoted herself, at considerable personal sacrifice, to our well-being. We knew, as did our dad, that much of what he achieved he could not have accomplished without her support and forbearance.

My parents' relationship worked for them. Though they divided responsibilities, they also helped each other – even with cooking. My mother was a superb cook, a graduate of the University of Toronto Honours Course in Household Science and Economics, now abolished. She made most of the meals, but my dad chipped in. He made us breakfast most school days and, on weekends, French toast or kippers, a favourite of his. On Saturdays he made himself a special sandwich: sardine and onions. He also sought and took my mother's advice on many aspects of his professional life, including his speeches (for which she was often his harshest critic), personnel problems he had to resolve at the court, and the myriad social demands that went with the job.

My parents always had a wide circle of friends, none closer than Anne and Charles Dubin – CL, as we called him. CL and Anne, a formidable lawyer in her own right, came to our home many times, frequently to play bridge. I have good empirical evidence that there is no correlation whatsoever between great judges and great bridge players. Most of the time, Anne and my mother won easily. My one regret is that I did not tape some of the legal discussions between CL and my dad.

One of CL's prize stories – which became legendary in our family – is the one of how he lost both sides of the same case in the Supreme Court of Canada. When he was a young lawyer he acted for a tobacco producer named Robbins, who challenged the right of the Tobacco Board to delegate regulatory authority over quotas. He lost the case all the way to the Supreme Court. Several years later, now more established, he was retained on the same issue – this time not by the producer but by the board. The case was *Brant Dairy*, and the product was milk. Relying on his previous losses, CL figured victory was assured. And so it was in the Ontario courts.

By the time the case got to the Supreme Court of Canada, however, my father was on the Court, and CL lost 5–4. My father wrote the majority opinion. CL naturally felt somewhat aggrieved – what advocate wouldn't? Finally, he decided to express his annoyance to my dad. One night, when the Dubins came over for dinner, CL broached the subject. "Bora, how could you do this to me?" he asked. My dad was a little taken aback but then replied, "Charlie, I don't know why you are so upset. After all, we vindicated you." I am not sure that CL or his client saw it quite that way.

Like many in our profession today, my father found it difficult to balance the demands of his work and his home life. Still, he always managed to find time for us. His family was his outlet from the demands of his professional life. Growing up, we did not often talk about law. He was more interested in what was going on in our lives. He watched me play basketball and my sister dance. We took many wonderful family vacations together, invariably car trips with my dad doing all the driving. He was not a good swimmer, but he loved to be near water, which he found soothing.

Although demanding of himself, he rarely made demands of me or my sister, Barbara. He tended to guide us more by example than by words. He neither encouraged nor discouraged me from going into law. And I am sure he would have been proud of us no matter what we did. Barbara – whom he affectionately called "Little One" – followed a different career path into the arts, and he was enormously proud of her accomplishments.

My dad never mastered French. He often turned to Barbara, who is perfectly bilingual, to help him obtain the minimum grasp of our other official language that he needed to get by. The year he had to double as acting governor general because Jules Léger had been stricken ill, Barbara spent hours tutoring him so he could get through the Speech from the Throne.

Over the years, my parents also embraced our friends. One was Harvey Strosberg. Another was Kathy Feldman, whom they met when she was just a law student, when Harvey and I took her to Ottawa for a case we argued in the Supreme Court. Not surprisingly, they liked Harvey and Kathy instantly and asked about each often over the years.

My father had neither the time nor the inclination for athletic hobbies. His family and his work were all he needed to make him happy. He had been a very good athlete in school, and for many years he held the record for having hit the longest home run in the City of Port Arthur – a record he was quite proud of. He rowed at university. But he never took up golf or tennis or any other "social" sport. What exercise he got came mainly from walking our dog, a miniature French poodle named Sucre, or more often, Sukie.

Sukie came into our lives because my mother, who had grown up on a farm, loved animals, and Barbara desperately wanted a dog. My father resisted at first, but he adored Barbara so much he didn't resist for long.

We got the dog, and he fell in love with it – so much so that he insisted on walking her every night. That was how he unwound. During those nightly walks, he talked through his judgments with his confidante, little Sukie.

Although my dad didn't play sports, he maintained a keen interest in them, especially baseball. He was always a great New York Yankee fan, an allegiance he passed on to me. But his favourite player was not Joe DiMaggio or Mickey Mantle or any of the other great stars who populated the team. Instead, it was Hank Bauer, a decent right fielder but by no means a household name, who came from a working-class family and who, without fanfare, played hard every night. One of my most cherished memories is of my dad taking me to New York in the fall of 1961, after I had finished grade 13, to watch the Yankees and the Detroit Tigers play a crucial three-game series that would decide the American League pennant. I should record that the Yankees won all three games.

Although my father accomplished much and received many honours, he did not like to dwell on his honours or his achievements. He preferred to live in the present and look to the future, to the next challenge. Still, he would have appreciated the tribute of this symposium and this volume from so many friends, students, and people he admired.

◀ 3 ▶

Comments on My Dad

BARBARA LASKIN

AS A NON-LAWYER CONTRIBUTING to a book of reminiscences by lawyers and judges, I feel somewhat conspicuous, the way I did back in the late 1970s and early 80s when Dad occasionally phoned me up, spur of the moment, to ask me to lunch at Ottawa's famed Rideau Club, where we liked to share the oyster special. Oysters weren't on his diet, but he knew his secret was safe with me, as long as he didn't overdo it. In those bad old days, the Rideau Club, still in its original location opposite the Parliament Buildings, had strict rules about women – they were to use a separate entrance and confine themselves to the ground-floor dining room lest they quicken too many geriatric pulses and cause mass cardiac arrest. My father used to stand, arms folded and with an amused expression, behind the main entrance, which he knew very well I would choose over the women's entrance; he would wait while I brazenly waltzed through, causing the doorman to choke on his dentures. My entrances were grander than my exits, and I always enjoyed the vaguely triumphant, illicit feeling of it all. The oysters, too, were excellent.

I want to share with you here some of my dad's characteristics and personality traits that I have come, over the last twenty years, to treasure even more than I did when he was alive. First, and most important, he was committed to living in the present. Not that the past didn't interest him – he was, in fact, a great student of history and read widely on a whole variety of topics, from ancient Greek philosophy to contemporary political theory, from historical fiction to biographies of all kinds. Nor was he unconcerned about the future; had he not been, he would never have taken on the enormous extracurricular load he did, whether it was serving as president of the Canadian Association of University Teachers, chair of the board of the Ontario Institute for Studies in Education, or president of his synagogue, among the many other tasks he undertook in service to the community.

These pursuits aside, my father was focused to a remarkable degree on the here and now. In his personal life, he did not believe in looking back, except to reminisce fondly about his family. He held no grudges and had no regrets about paths not taken or opportunities missed. He used the past almost exclusively as an instrument to inform the present. He was completely uninterested in writing or having others write his memoirs. He saw no reason why anyone would want to read them, and, besides, he gave absolutely no thought to retirement, the time when autobiographies are usually written. Alas, he never got to that stage.

During my father's latter years, many were the nights he and Max Cohen, the former McGill University Law Dean who lived in the apartment next door, would come together for some companionship after dinner and to discuss current events and legal affairs; the conversations were always lively, often riveting. Although I regret we have none of that rich material on tape – and many other things besides – I am grateful for the heightened awareness he gave me of the importance of *now*.

Speaking of *now*, Dad was something of a stickler for language. My brother, John, and I have both inherited his interest – in my case fed by a steady supply of books and dictionaries that my father liked to bring back from business trips. Nothing peeved him more than the sloppy use of English. He used to groan whenever he heard the phrase "between you and I" or when some unsuspecting litigator appearing before him had the misfortune to say "at this point in time." Dad would lower his glasses on his nose, arch one eyebrow, and fix the poor blighter with a steely glance. "Do you mean NOW?" he would ask. Whichever way you cut it, *now* was an important construct.

The daily manifestation of Dad's appetite for living in the present was his prodigious capacity and enthusiasm for work. No sooner was a job conceived than it was done. Bills to pay? They were out the door the moment after they arrived. Letters to write? No fuss, they were written at once. Judgments to dispatch? I can still see him coming down the hall in his dressing gown, rubbing his hands together with glee while announcing that he had just "knocked off another one." Until his final illness, he regularly worked until 11 p.m. or midnight, and that was a significant concession to age and Supreme Court responsibilities. While we were growing up, his bedtime was more like 2 or 3 a.m.

In 1980, on a magnificent summer day that my brother and I will never forget, we found ourselves assembled on the green outside the Ivy-covered walls of Harvard, where Dad was to receive an honorary doctorate along with Helmut Schmidt, Jacques Cousteau, Milton Friedman, and Desmond Tutu. It was my first time in Boston and, in the excitement of anticipation, I had suggested to Dad that, before the ceremony, he might show us around the city. Imagine my surprise on learning that he knew the city as little as I did – his entire time as a student at Harvard had been spent in the law library, the classroom, and his rooming house. There was no time, and certainly no extra money, for anything else. When he returned home to visit his girlfriend (our mother) in December, his one meal a day, supplemented by chocolate bars, had taken its toll and he had lost 20 pounds.

The all-consuming nature of his work was something we all came to regard as normal, although to others it could appear something of a distortion. I recall one occasion when, on learning my father had turned down the opportunity to spend a beautiful July weekend in the country, my husband, Tim, said, "What's the matter, Bora, don't you like nature, trees, country life?" To which my dad replied, thoughtfully, "Trees are all right, I suppose, in their place ..." Tim's various attempts, over the years, to appeal to the outdoorsman or the handyman that he assumed lurked within my father were doomed to fail. Dad was resolutely urban and barely knew one end of a hammer from the other. Nevertheless, they had a genuine affection for each other, and Tim was a great support to all of us during my parents' Ottawa years.

My father was a workhorse, to be sure, but underlying all that midnight oil was a driving passion for his profession, for doing work well – something I always thought made him one of the luckiest of people. He knew from an early age that law was what he wanted – although how he ever imagined he would get there, coming as he did from such humble circumstances, I will never know. I have spent the better part of my career working in the field of arts and culture, and this passion is something I come across regularly in artists. It is why they tend to go on working at their craft despite being so poorly paid and, often, so little recognized or respected. I wonder how many of us can truly say we are so committed to the lives we lead that we never have a moment's doubt about the course our careers have taken. Other than his participation in sports as a young man, our father had no hobbies – simply because he had no need of them. His work and his family were the source of all contentment, the well-spring from which he derived all his energy.

The path to his career was a brilliant mind, a golden pen, and a lot of hard work. My father would dispute the brilliant mind, an attribute he ascribed readily to others but never to himself. The golden pen was another story. Dad loved the English language – he cared deeply about using it well and took great pride in his work. When a high school English teacher of his wrote to say she had used one of his judgments as an example of good writing, he considered it the greatest of compliments. So yes, he might have conceded the golden pen, but the brilliance belonged to others.

The final quality I want to speak about is my father's modesty – his lack of ego. Coming from the background I do, I have the greatest respect for the legal profession, for the fine minds and exceptional people who are among its greatest servants. But it is a profession in which the temptation is strong to succumb to overbearing pride and a preoccupation with material things – the trappings of success. Anyone who knew my father would agree that he was remarkably free of such traits.

He was at heart a very simple person, with simple needs and responses. He never consciously climbed any ladder or social scale because he was unaware they were available to him (and, given the times, perhaps they weren't). He never plotted his career path, the way people do today, because it never occurred to him that another pasture might be greener. Had he remained a professor of law, I am convinced he would have been perfectly content. His only ambition was to get done the things that mattered to him, whether it served his career or not. At least some of the things he did were contrary to good sense – his resignation, along with Caesar Wright and John Willis, from Osgoode Hall Law School was hardly a judicious move for a man with a young family. His pro bono defence of a friend who, in a highly charged political skirmish, was falsely accused of embezzlement was not career enhancing.

Each of my father's three judicial appointments – the first to the Ontario Court of Appeal, the second to the Supreme Court, and the third as Chief Justice – came as a complete surprise to him, not to say shock. In those days, you didn't apply to become a judge. If there were some who actively sought appointment, my father was not among them. He was always happy with his lot, too consumed with his current workload to worry about what might come next. Dad always contended that everything that happened to him was a result of what he called "accidentalism." He might have grudgingly admitted that his hard work played a role, but he didn't like to dwell on it. He preferred to think it was all serendipitous.

Dad's unassuming nature endeared him to many people in addition to his family. Our parents had a wide circle of acquaintances, mostly nurtured by my mother, who was an incomparable hostess, a fantastic conversationalist, and a sympathetic ear to many. Their friends included university people, artists, lawyers and judges of course, and many working people whom they had met in their youth and to whom they remained attached throughout their lives. To this day, there are people who come up to me to recount stories I have never heard about a chance encounter, an unexpected kindness, a touching incident. It is a measure of my father's exceptional character, I feel, that, twenty years after his death, I am still learning about sides of him I did not entirely know.

As a young girl, I always marvelled at how many people Dad knew. I remember walking in the port of Le Havre, age eleven, where our ship had unexpectedly docked late at night because of labour unrest in Southampton. We were on our way to an exciting year in England, the only sabbatical year my father took in twenty-five years of teaching and our parents' first foray outside North America. The docks were populated by streetwalkers, ladies of the night, all of whom approached my father as if they were old acquaintances. I saw nothing *too* strange in this – I was quite used to my father being accosted by former students, no matter where we travelled – but I did notice that they looked a bit different and that all of them were women. "How come all these women know Dad?" I asked my mother. I never did get the answer, but I remain secure in the knowledge that my father probably never even noticed them, fixated as he was on the welfare of his family and the interesting work ahead of him.

◀ PART TWO ▶

Educator

◀ 4 ▶

Laskin and the University[1]

MARTIN L. FRIEDLAND

ALL TOLD, BORA LASKIN spent more than thirty years at institutions of higher education and fewer than twenty years as a judge. He first entered the University of Toronto as a student in September 1930, graduating with a B.A. in law three years later. Given the stock-market crash of the previous year, it was not a carefree time to go to university, and his family had to sacrifice to send him to Toronto. Because of his high marks at Fort William Collegiate Institute, he was able to enter directly into the second year of W.P.M. Kennedy's honour law course, an undergraduate program that Kennedy had begun in 1927. In future years, all students would have to study for four years, rather than three, to get their degrees.

Laskin's undergraduate life is well documented in Philip Girard's fine biography. As a Jew, Laskin automatically enrolled in University College – the non-denominational "godless" college. He got involved in student politics, became the literary director of the University College Literary and Athletic Society, and was active in debating and sports, particularly in rowing and track and field. He also joined a Jewish fraternity, Sigma Alpha Mu.

Laskin had lectures from some of the leading figures of the period – in philosophy from George Brett, history from Frank Underhill, and political science from Alex Brady. The law side of the program was dominated by Kennedy, who, surprisingly, was not trained as a lawyer. He had come to the university as a professor of English literature, then switched to history, then to political science, and finally to law. He was an impressive scholar. By the end of the 1920s he had published ten books. He was also a sparkling teacher. J.J. Robinette, who was taught by Kennedy in the 1920s and became one of Canada's greatest lawyers, recalled that he "was one of those brilliant Irishmen who could dazzle you ... a performer as much as a teacher."

The program attracted students who became leaders of the profession – Charles Dubin, William Howland, G. Arthur Martin, and Sydney Robins, to name only some who later became members of the Ontario Court of Appeal. Perhaps they were inspired by Kennedy's view that legal education should "create a body of citizens endowed with an insight into law as the basic social science, and capable of making those examinations into its workings as will redeem it from being a mere trade and technique and ... make it the finest of all instruments in the service of mankind." Another fine scholar was Larry MacKenzie, who taught international law. Jacob Finkelman, a graduate of the honour law program and the first Jew to be appointed to a full-time position at the university, began teaching the year that Laskin arrived and no doubt influenced Laskin's lifelong interest in labour law.

The Law Society of Upper Canada gave no credit for Kennedy's law course. Laskin therefore had to enroll in Osgoode's law program, which combined lectures and articling. Before he was permitted to register, however, he had to find someone who would give him employment and sign his articles. In his first year at Osgoode, he was "employed" by his fraternity brother Samuel Gotfrid, who had received his call the year before but could not offer his articling student either much work or remuneration. The following year, Laskin articled for a non-Jewish lawyer in the same building who had a busy real-estate practice – an experience that probably accounts for Laskin's later interest in land law. He graduated near the top of his class at Osgoode, just as he had done in Kennedy's honour law program.

While at Osgoode, he obtained an M.A. in law from the University of Toronto and, after his call to the bar, went to Harvard Law School on a scholarship. There he came under the influence of some of the greatest names in academic law – Felix Frankfurter in administrative law, Roscoe Pound in jurisprudence, and Zechariah Chafee in equity. Two of the seventeen LL.M. students at Harvard that year received their degree *cum laude* – Bora Laskin and his best friend at Harvard, Albert Abel. In 1955 Laskin persuaded Dean Caesar Wright to bring Abel to the University of Toronto from the University of West Virginia. Abel diligently and effectively taught legal writing, and he had an important influence on legal scholarship in Canada.

After Harvard, Laskin returned to Toronto, but he could not find a job teaching or practising law. In those years, there was a great divide between Jewish and non-Jewish lawyers, so joining an established non-Jewish firm was out of the question. He was also unsuccessful in obtaining satisfactory work with a Jewish firm and filled his time doing summaries of legal cases for the *Canadian Abridgment* – a job that paid twice as much as he later earned as an academic.

When Larry MacKenzie resigned in 1940 to become the president of the University of New Brunswick, Kennedy had the opportunity to hire a replacement. He considered two candidates for the position: J.K. Macalister and Bora Laskin. Macalister had graduated from his law course in 1937 with the highest marks ever recorded – an A in every subject in every year – and then went to Oxford on a Rhodes scholarship, where he obtained a first and later topped the standings for the English bar exams. MacKenzie initially offered the job to Macalister, who cabled back, "IN ARMY SINCE YESTERDAY SORRY MANY THANKS." He then offered the appointment to Laskin. How much Laskin knew of the story is not known, but he would obviously have known that Macalister was a serious competitor for the position. The Canadian infantry assigned Macalister to British intelligence, and, in June 1943, he was parachuted behind enemy lines in France to act as a secret agent. He was captured, tortured, and executed at Buchenwald concentration camp in September 1944.

Laskin taught at the University of Toronto until he left for Osgoode Hall Law School in 1945. His move may have been part of a plan by Caesar Wright, then a professor at Osgoode Hall, and his friend Sidney Smith, the new president of the University of Toronto, to have legal education in Ontario shift from the Law Society of Upper Canada to the University of Toronto. Smith wanted to establish "a Law School that would rank first in Canada, and be among the leading schools of the North American continent." He had already offered the deanship to Wright, but the offer was not accepted.

The plan was that Laskin would join Wright at Osgoode and then, at an appropriate time, they would move with a few others to the University of Toronto. First, though, they had to convince Kennedy that the plan made sense. Laskin and Wright therefore went to Kennedy's summer place, "Narrow Waters," north of Huntsville and west of Algonquin Park and, as the three men walked along a lakeside trail, Wright attempted to convince Kennedy of the wisdom of his plan. Kennedy grudgingly agreed, and Laskin left the university for Osgoode.

Four years later, Wright and Laskin, along with John Willis, found an opportune time to leave Osgoode and start a new three-year postgraduate law school at the University of Toronto, with Wright as dean. They had resigned from Osgoode because of the Law Society's reactionary proposal to increase the articling experience at the expense of the academic program. Most people expected that the Law Society would quickly recognize the new program at the university – it had an outstanding faculty that also included Jim Milner and Wolfgang Friedmann. But the Law Society was reluctant even to discuss that possibility and agreed to give students credit for only two of the three years they had completed at the University of Toronto. Students therefore had to spend an extra year at Osgoode after articling. Willis resigned, telling Wright that "just two years after it started up as a professional school, the School of Law is to all intents and purposes dead."

I entered first-year law at the University of Toronto in 1955, thinking, as did my classmates (who included soon to be notable lawyers Harry Arthurs, Jerry Grafstein, Julius Isaac, and John Sopinka), that we would later have to spend an extra year at Osgoode. As it turned out, on February 14, 1957, in our second year of law school, the Law Society recognized the University of Toronto Law School as equal to its new Osgoode program.

We had Laskin for three subjects – real property in first year, constitutional law in second, and labour law in third. Today, most professors concentrate on one area of law, perhaps two. Laskin specialized in all three areas. His property course was the most technical one we had in all of law school. We learned in great detail such arcane subjects as future interests and shifting and springing uses. Although Laskin was more open to questions than Wright, he always had a tremendous amount of material to cover, so lectured most of the time. He left the Socratic Method to Milner and Abel.

Although Laskin's door was always open and he would deal with whatever you wanted to discuss with him, he never had time for much chit-chat at the law school. Many of us went to see him about where we should article. We were in and out of his office in less than five minutes. He was a no-nonsense professor. One day, when he remarked critically on the Queen's Counsel list that had just been published in the *Globe and Mail* and a voice from the back shouted "sour grapes," Laskin walked out, but he soon came back. Nor was he amused in his upper-year labour law class when someone secretly brought in a record player and opened the class with Pete Seger's "There once was a union maid." Laskin did not want to be identified with one side in labour-management relations. He mellowed over the years, particularly after he became a judge. He was also more relaxed when not teaching or at his desk. During my two years as a student at the law school's temporary quarters at the Glendon estate, he sometimes walked with us down in the Don Valley forests between classes. He also attended my wedding at the end of third year, and, like many others over the years, I often turned to him for advice.

In early July 1965, my wife and I were having dinner with the Laskins at an Italian restaurant in London, England, when Laskin was called to the telephone. He said nothing about the call when he returned to the table, although it was clear that it had been an important conversation. We later found out that the call had been from the solicitor general, Larry Pennell, telling him that the Cabinet had appointed him to the Ontario Court of Appeal. Jerry Grafstein, who had close ties with the Liberal Party and had played an important role in the appointment, had tracked Laskin down at the restaurant. Laskin's acceptance was a great loss to the university because he was the clear choice to succeed Wright as dean.

As an academic, Laskin had always been busy with outside assignments, giving opinions, conducting labour arbitrations, being involved in faculty association matters, participating in civil liberties issues, and writing government reports. He also wrote headnotes for the *Dominion Law Reports*, the case-law series edited by Wright. His appointment to the Court no doubt allowed him to slow down a bit.

Perhaps Laskin's most important non-legal contribution to the University of Toronto was chairing an influential committee, established in 1964, on graduate studies. The committee had twelve members, including Northrop Frye, John Polanyi, and Ernest Sirluck, the dean of the graduate school. President Claude Bissell later called it "the strongest internal committee in the history of the University." Laskin wrote its unanimous report: it recommended a centralization of graduate studies in the university and reflected his constitutional view that a strong central presence was best. There is no doubt that, in the years since, the graduate school has been a major factor in the high reputation of the University of Toronto.

After his appointment to the bench, Laskin continued his involvement in higher education. He chaired the board of directors at the Ontario Institute for Studies in Education, which was established in 1966, and joined the board of York University in 1967. Like Wright, he produced important casebooks and wrote a large number of articles and notes, particularly for the *Canadian Bar Review*, though he never produced a major text in any of his fields of expertise. Moreover, he died just before the development of jurisprudence by the Supreme Court of Canada based on the *Canadian Charter of Rights and Freedoms*, so his judgments are not as frequently cited today as they otherwise would have been. Nevertheless, I believe that his approach to adjudication influenced other members of the Court, particularly Brian Dickson, in their readiness to give a broad interpretation to the *Charter*. He also indirectly influenced the enactment of the *Charter*, not because he was active behind the scenes but because he looked and acted like a wise Solomon figure whom the public could trust to deliver sound judgments under a new *Charter*.

Bora Laskin was a powerful force in the law and in higher education. He was also an inspiration to his students, fellow judges, and law clerks – and, altogether, a great Canadian.

NOTES

1 This paper draws on the author's *The University of Toronto: A History* (Toronto: University of Toronto Press, 2002); Philip Girard, *Bora Laskin: Bringing Law to Life*, (Toronto: University of Toronto Press, 2005); C. Ian Kyer and Jerome E. Bickenbach, *The Fiercest Debate: Cecil A. Wright, the Benchers, and Legal Education in Ontario 1923–1957* (Toronto: The Osgoode Society, 1967); and Irving Abella, 'The Making of a Chief Justice: Bora Laskin, The Early Years,' (1990) 24 *Law Society of Upper Canada Gazette* 187.

◀ 5 ▶

Laskin and the University Crisis of 1949

HORACE KREVER

IN THE PROGRAM FOR the opening ceremony for the Bora Laskin Law Library at the University of Toronto, Bruce Dunlop, one of Laskin's teaching colleagues, wrote:

> After all, Bora Laskin was a law teacher for longer than he was a judge. The University of Toronto was his intellectual home .... Bora was a workhorse. He taught more different courses than any other teacher. He was the one we automatically turned to for assistance in obtaining articling positions. His classes were inspiring. His belief in the importance of the legal process, of human rights, of a strong federal presence in the constitutional field infected us all.

Until January 1949, Bora Laskin had been a full-time member of what the Law Society of Upper Canada called "the staff" – not the faculty – of the Osgoode Hall Law School, the only professional law school in Ontario. The three-year course consisted of a combination of lectures and service under articles – a lecture first thing in the morning and another late in the afternoon, and attendance between lectures at the law office of each student's principal. The dean, Dr. C.A. "Caesar" Wright, was editor of the *Canadian Bar Review*, and, together with Laskin, wrote almost all the case comments published in the journal. In his scholarly writing, Wright often advocated the establishment of a full-time law school. Finally, in 1946, a special committee of the benchers was struck to examine and report on legal education. It reported to Convocation on January

20, 1949 – a majority report and two dissenting, or minority, reports. The majority report was adopted by Convocation that same day. It contained nine recommendations, the most important of which for Bora Laskin's future career was the subordination of the "academic" instruction to the "practical," or articling, component of the law school's program. The flavour or tone of the majority report can be gleaned from a few extracts:

> It is unfortunate that for a good many years there have been differences of opinion between the Legal Education Committee and the full-time Law School staff. These, in the opinion of your Committee, have been detrimental to the work of the School by making impossible the full and harmonious co-operation which must exist between all those concerned in the work of legal education if the best results are to be obtained. These differences are, we think, largely due to the attitude of the full-time staff in regard to the present system of concurrent Law School and practical training. There are other factors contributing to the misunderstandings which have from time to time arisen between these two bodies but your Committee is satisfied that the fundamental cause is the difference in viewpoint as to the respective merits of the concurrent system of training and a full-time Law School. The members of the full-time Law School staff are advocates of a full-time School and some of them have given public expression to their opinions. This is, we think, regrettable, as the Legal Education Committee is charged by Convocation with the task of directing the work of legal education under the concurrent system, and must be able to count on the loyal co-operation of the staff appointed by Convocation on their recommendation. Unfortunately, the opinions of the staff have become known to the students and this has had an unsettling effect, as those who are finding it difficult to keep up with their work are prone to blame their troubles on what they visualize as a struggle between two conflicting schools of thought. During his years at the Law School a hard-pressed student who is in daily contact with a lecturer whom he knows to be an advocate of a full-time school is likely to adopt the views of the lecturer and, in most instances, it is not until a student has graduated and embarked on practice that he appreciates the value of the training he has received under the concurrent system. It is the opinion of your Committee that whatever system of Legal Education Convocation sees fit to adopt, all persons entrusted with the

task of carrying that system into effect must bend every effort towards making it a success. This they obviously can not do if they are ready to criticize openly the very institutions under which they are working.

A later extract from the adopted majority report is also illuminating:

> Before setting out our recommendations we feel compelled to comment on certain matters of general concern which have come to our notice in the course of this enquiry. One is that we think it doubtful whether under present conditions students are being taught to have a proper respect for the Bench.... The second matter is that a tendency appears to have developed in the Law School to follow American systems of training and the opinions of American Judges and writers rather than those in England.... This situation may in time be remedied to some extent by the establishment of scholarships, but in the meantime your Committee suggests for the consideration of Convocation the possibility of adding to our staff a lecturer who is a member of the English Bar. We feel that if the right type of man could be engaged, this would be a most desirable step.
>
> Before making our recommendations, we feel that we should again stress a matter which we deem of paramount importance. We feel that no matter what decision is reached by Covocation as to the system of Legal Education which is to be prescribed, the members of the staff who are charged with the administration of certain duties under that system must fulfil those duties loyally and without public criticism of the very system under which they are working....

The "staff" of the law school learned of the report and its adoption only when they read a summary of it in the newspaper. This insult prompted a mass resignation of all four members of the full-time staff, and the incident quickly became not a matter "of a merely local or private Nature in the Province" but a national cause célèbre. The bold headline on the front page of the *Globe and Mail* on Saturday, January 22, 1949, in letters extending across six columns, read, "Hall Pushed Back 25 Years, Osgoode Dean Says, Quits." The sub-headline added, "3 Lecturers Join Protest Over Policy." Immediately under the main headline were diplayed, across four columns, the four photographs of these staff members: Stanley Edwards, Bora Laskin, Dean Wright, and John Willis. The caption below the photographs summarized the story, which continued in two columns on page 2.

At the mid-winter meeting of the Ontario Branch of the Canadian Bar Association two weeks later, on February 4, 1949, what was, in effect, a vote of want of confidence in the benchers was passed. That prompted the lead editorial in the *Globe and Mail* on February 8, 1949, under the headline, "The Lawyers' Vote of Censure." The first two paragraphs read as follows:

> The question of legal education in Ontario is now wide open for discussion. When the Benchers of the Law Society last month ordered changes which would make the training course less "academic" and more "practical," it looked like their decision would be final because an Ontario statute gives them absolute control. Now it seems certain that they will have to think again. The legal profession itself for which the Benchers are supposed to speak, evidently does not approve of their new educational Plan.
>
> In convention last week, three hundred members of the Canadian Bar Association, Ontario branch, voted unanimously that the Benchers' proposals are "inadequate" and should be "reconsidered." This voluntary Association does not include all practicing lawyers but it is fairly representative of those with public spirit and an interest in keeping professional standards high. Their motion last week was, in effect, a vote of censure and no confidence. It was the more impressive in that it was carried without a dissenting vote. The Benchers cannot possibly ignore it.

Within months, Wright, Laskin, and Willis were appointed full professors at the University of Toronto, where they created the three-year LL.B. course. It became the model for all the other Ontario law faculties when, in 1957, the benchers recognized the right of the universities to teach law as a qualification for admission to the bar. In the meantime, however, the University of Toronto's course was not so recognized – providing yet another reason for Laskin to feel bitter towards the Law Society of Upper Canada. This inequality provoked a public demonstration in February 1952, when students of the University of Toronto Law School, of whom I was one, picketed Osgoode Hall. Officially, we were reprimanded; unofficially, Laskin, who knew something about picketing, was anything but critical.

As a result of the vote of censure, the benchers reconsidered their decision and adopted the minority report of D. Park Jamieson, KC. It had recommended a four-year course consisting of two years of full-time lectures, followed by a year of articling and another year of concurrent lectures and articling. Not long afterwards, the benchers recognized the University of Toronto's law course, in part, by admitting its graduates to the third year of the four-year course. Laskin did not consider this response a principled concession.

The report of the special committee was not given to the members of the staff. Wright went to his grave without ever having seen it. In his Cecil A. Wright Memorial Lecture of March 10, 1982, now to be found in the *University of Toronto Law Journal* for 1983, Laskin remarked:

> A précis of the report, substantially its recommendations, was published in the morning Toronto press on 21 January, 1949. The report itself was not published, nor was it made available; certainly I could not get it and did not see its text until more than twenty years later when I asked a former student, who had become a Bencher, to get me a copy.

I am that former student. After my election as a bencher, Laskin asked me to do two things: to get a copy of the report for him and to try to persuade the benchers to eliminate the $100 fee that a student was obliged to pay to the Law Society on entering into articles. The second request was out of the question, but the first was done. I also sent a copy to John Willis, who had never seen it. That Bora Laskin, though by then Chief Justice of Canada, still had strong feelings about the entire experience can be discerned from two letters he wrote to me, the first dated August 19, 1975, and the second, October 7, 1976:

> Some things pass belief but I do congratulate you of course on assuming the chairmanship of the Legal Education Committee of the Law Society of Upper Canada. I am very happy to have, at last, a copy of the famous unpublished report. It is certainly the one that I had in mind. I regret that only Percy Wilson is shown to have taken a sensible position but I do admire his courage in standing out. [Wilson, though chair of the special committee, had submitted one of the two minority reports in which he recommended a full-time law school.] I have not yet read the report through but there is certainly no hurry at this date.
>
> It must be many months ago now that you presented me with a copy of the famous report of the Special Committee on Legal Education which

was considered by the Benchers of the Law Society at its meeting on January 20th, 1949. I had laid the report aside at the time and it was only yesterday and to-day that I sat down to read it. It does produce a culture shock of a kind that would have even excited Alvin Toffler. The minority view of Percy Wilson is the only light in the total darkness that pervades the report of the majority. I know how much he suffered as a result of presuming to submit a minority report when he was the Chairman of the Special Committee. Without going into detail about the narrative I think the loudest sound that I emitted in reading the report was at Recommedation No. 9 that consideration be given to the establishment of a post-graduate course in law. Some of my colleagues here have indicated their interest in looking at the report and I am presuming to give them copies of it.

The significance of Laskin's comment about his astonishment at the recommendation for consideration of a postgraduate course may be better understood in the context of a paragraph in Wright's remarkable letter of January 21, 1949, to the treasurer in which he submitted his resignation:

> The suggestion in the report that consideration be given to the establishment of a post-graduate course in law is, if you will forgive me, under the circumstances laughable. A post-graduate course in law can only be founded on a sound undergraduate course. The props for such a course have now been removed by the recommendations in this report and, therefore, it must follow that a post-graduate school falls with it. This means, of course, that our students must continue, as they have in the past, to seek post-graduate work in a professional school of law outside the confines of this country. I believe that Canada is of an age where it should be able to supply the educational requirements of its own citizens and it is this amongst other reasons which compels me to resign as Dean of your Law School.

After all these years, I still find the story fascinating. It is surely evidence that we live in a more enlightened age, one in which institutions and even nations are exerting efforts to make amends for past hurts. So far as Laskin is concerned, the cataclysmic events of 1949 may have been one of the best things that ever happened to him. They had a lifelong influence on him and profoundly affected his career. Given Laskin's passionate devotion to the cause of legal education, his attitude to the Law Society of Upper Canada was often bitter. It is therefore of no little interest that, more than a half-century later, the symposium to honour the legacy of Bora Laskin – and which gave rise to this volume – was sponsored by this same Law Society.

◀ PART THREE ▶

Impact on the Supreme Court of Canada

◂ 6 ▸

Laskin's Legacy to the Supreme Court

IAN BINNIE[1]

BORA LASKIN WAS AND continues to be a heroic figure, and it is useful to remind ourselves why this is so. In terms of judges of the Supreme Court of Canada, Ivan Rand was a more memorable writer. Antonio Lamer wrote more judgments. Sir Lyman Duff served more years on the Court – thirty-seven years compared to Laskin's fourteen, of which the last five or six were beset with serious health problems. Beverley McLachlin has already served longer on the Supreme Court than Bora Laskin did and has almost as long to go again before reaching mandatory retirement age. And, from the present perspective, especially given the importance of the *Canadian Charter of Rights and Freedoms*, Brian Dickson will likely have a more lasting impact on Canadian jurisprudence.

What, then, made Bora Laskin unique? It was, I think, the fateful conjunction of a prodigious mind and the soul of a rebel. He was a proverbial "disturber" in a legal culture that, at the time, put excessive emphasis on form and precedent. He was a heretic in the temple of legal conformity. When he became Chief Justice, it was as though the medieval church had made Martin Luther its pope.[2]

By the time Laskin got to the Supreme Court, he looked every inch the establishment figure. In the hallways of the judges' chambers, where the portraits of all the Chief Justices hang, Bora Laskin does not look out of place with the mutton-chop whiskers of Sir Samuel Henry Strong or the patrician air of Sir Henri-Elzéar Taschereau, each of whom put in twenty-seven years of work as judges of the Court, almost double the time span allotted to Laskin. The only clue in Laskin's portrait to the underlying personality is his ferocious gaze, an expression of such armour-piercing intensity that it recalls Rocket Richard zooming across the blue line rather than the usual judge smiling bashfully from behind the ceremonial red robes. Viewed among the portraits of his peers, Laskin is the eagle in the dovecote. He was, in fact, a profoundly anti-establishment member of the establishment. He had more in common with the rebellious William Lyon Mackenzie or the sceptical Northrop Frye than he did with his predecessors John Robert Cartwright or Joseph-Honoré-Gérald Fauteux.

His anti-establishment credentials are not wholly explained by his origins at the far end of Thunder Bay. After all, Canada's first Chief Justice was born in Brockville, and he was succeeded by judges from Annapolis, Nova Scotia, and Sainte-Marie de Beauce. Our present Chief Justice was born in Pincher Creek, Alberta. Nor, I think, can his highly individualistic attitude be explained by the fact that he was the first Jewish judge appointed to the Supreme Court. Lord Reading, the first Jewish Lord Chief Justice of England, also overcame considerable barriers in the law because of his religion, but Lord Reading was profoundly clever and profoundly conformist. In fact, it is difficult to think of a single new legal idea associated with his seven-and-a-half years in office, albeit in his case the First World War and other responsibilities intervened. Nor does Laskin's academic brilliance explain his radicalism. His benchmate Ronald Martland edged out Sir William Holdsworth to become the prestigious Vinerian scholar at Oxford, yet a more traditional mind is hard to imagine. Nor would Laskin's background as a law teacher explain his unique perspective.[3] Louis-Philippe Pigeon taught for a few years at Laval University but he preferred the safety of black-letter law to the stormy waters into which Laskin wanted to lead the Court.[4] It is an observable fact that members of the legal profession, regardless of their background, tend to buy into the values of the establishment as they swarm up the greasy pole to the bench.

Whatever the reason for his radicalism, and it is probably a result of all of these factors, Bora Laskin was always able to avoid the embrace of orthodoxy and to take a fresh and sometimes withering look at the system of which he increasingly became a central figure. His attitude was nicely summed up by the style in which he accepted the appointment as Chief Justice of Canada on December 27, 1973, leaping over seven more senior colleagues and earning some criticism for not being a "team player." Of course he was not, in that respect, a team player. Had that been in his nature, he would not have accomplished what he did.

Laskin was a judicial activist before the epithet became a term of abuse. Writing in the *Canadian Bar Review* in 1951, in the aftermath of abolition of appeals to the Judicial Committee of the Privy Council, he stated:

> It will be unfortunate if the Court's vision is limited by the range of existing case-law, whether it be English, or Australian, or whether it comes from the United States or some civil law country. A final court, *like a legislature,* may be expected to make its own assessments of our *current social problems* and give us its own solutions.[5]

If judges today were to link the policy-making function of courts and the legislature with respect to "current social problems," the conservative element of Canadian society would suffer a collective stroke. Indeed, Laskin's rallying cry of 1951 would not have seemed out of place in Justice Louise Arbour's envelope-pushing Baldwin Lafontaine Lecture fifty-three years later.[6]

Laskin advocated a "purposive" approach to law decades before the idea became fashionable. At a convocation address given two years after his appointment to the Supreme Court, he said:

> [I]mportant as it is to know what the law is, it is at least equally important to know what the law is for. The distinction I draw is between a purely formal, mechanical view of the law, antiseptic and detached, and a view of the law that sees it as purposive, related to our social and economic conditions, and serving ends that express the character of our organized society.[7]

Bora Laskin's reinvigorating presence on the bench was seen as a judicial parallel to the rise to power of Pierre Elliott Trudeau two years earlier.[8] In both cases, the country wanted some relief from the apathy and lack of imagination that permeated our national life. Things were so pedestrian in the courts that even the practitioners were complaining. When Laskin was appointed, Earl Warren had just stepped down as Chief Justice of the United States. The storm surrounding *Brown v. Board of Education*[9] was still raging south of the border. *Roe v. Wade*[10] lay in the future, but groundbreaking decisions such as *Gideon v. Wainwright*[11] and *Miranda v. Arizona*[12] were already on the books. By way of contrast, the juices of creativity of the Rand era in the Supreme Court of Canada had dried up. In 1971 the Court handed down *Regina v. Wray*,[13] ruling that trial judges had no discretion to exclude evidence even if they considered it to have been unjustly obtained or if its admission was calculated to bring the administration of justice into disrepute. Outside Quebec, Canadian courts were generally mired in the search for English precedent, the more obscure the better, after the fashion of the Dead Poets' Society.[14] Of course, the fact the new judge bore the fabulous name "Bora" signalled some sort of breakthrough in the ranks of Supreme Court judges, but Télesphore is also a great name, and Justice Télesphore Fournier never achieved iconic status, despite putting in twenty years on the Supreme Court bench.

In this essay, my role is to consider Bora Laskin from the perspective of an itinerant practitioner who sat through his lectures at the University of Toronto, appeared occasionally before him when he was in the Ontario Court of Appeal, and argued almost a dozen appeals where he presided in the Supreme Court of Canada. If some of these recollections are personal, it is because I was asked to take that approach.

From a practitioner's point of view, it is important to recall that, before Laskin's tenure, a hearing in the Supreme Court of Canada was much like a hearing in the Ontario Court of Appeal except that the judges were more polite and there were more of them. They frequently wrote reasons without reference to each other, and all of them generally focused on error correction. In Laskin's vision, however, the Supreme Court was not just another level of appellate review. It was to become a great engine to move the jurisprudence forward. He practically reinvented Supreme Court hearings to create the conditions he considered conducive to the sort of debates he thought necessary for issues of serious public importance. To this end, as Chief Justice, Bora Laskin inherited two important prerogatives. The first was his discretion to settle both the composition of a panel to hear each appeal and the way in which hearings would proceed.[15] The second was the power to designate the judge who would write the principal set of reasons for the outcome he supported. (If the Chief is in the minority, the practice is to let the majority pick their own spokesperson.)

Girded with this procedural authority, Laskin threw open the doors to interveners. In *R. v. Morgentaler*,[16] to counterbalance the ranks of the attorneys general, he let in no fewer than six interveners supporting women's choice. In *Canada (Attorney General) v. Lavell*,[17] dealing with the right of an Indian woman to stay on the reserve if she married a non-Indian, he let in no fewer than twenty interveners, including the University Women's Club of Toronto. Justice Bertha Wilson is sometimes criticized for expanding the role of interveners in the Supreme Court, but it was Laskin who led the way. Opening up the judicial debate to interveners was just a start. In *Thorson v. Attorney General of Canada*,[18] and *Nova Scotia Board of Censors v. McNeil*,[19] he more or less invented the concept of a public-interest plaintiff to get his hands on issues that he thought interesting and that otherwise might have escaped scrutiny. In doing so, he blew away a precedent written by Sir Lyman Duff that had stood for more than fifty years.[20]

At the same time, Laskin viewed law strictly as the interplay and expression of rational argument. He was prepared to extend the playing field to facilitate rational debate, but he was not prepared to turn the courts into a platform for emotional protest. Thus, in *Borowski*, he drew the line at granting public-interest status to an anti-abortion crusader who, in Laskin's view, was simply suffering "an emotional response" to the operation of the abortion law.[21] I had the misfortune to argue that appeal for the federal government, and throughout the hearing Justice Martland kept nagging, "What about *Blaikie*, Mr. Binnie, what about *Blaikie*?"[22] I suggested that there seemed to be a world of difference between the situation of Peter Blaikie, a Quebecer whose language rights were said to have been violated, and Joe Borowski, an indisputably male politician who stood in no danger of becoming pregnant and requiring the services of an abortionist, but Martland was unimpressed. He wrote for the majority, declaring that almost anyone with "a genuine interest" in a subject should be given standing if, in the Court's view, there was no other practical way to have a serious legal question adjudicated. Only Justice Lamer signed on to Laskin's dissent.

Having created a vehicle for the cases he wanted to hear and expanded intervener status to let in the people he wanted to hear from, Laskin then, in the *Anti-Inflation Act Reference*,[23] enlarged the range and scope of out-of-court evidence he thought judges should be able to hear about. All these changes were accomplished in little more than five years. Laskin put the Court on the procedural path it more or less follows today, including the introduction of television in the courtroom. It was our collective tragedy that he died at the threshold of the *Charter* era. At that point, the debating forum that Laskin had envisaged as desirable became absolutely essential.

In substantive terms, as well, Bora Laskin set to work to reform the law to achieve what he considered to be its underlying purpose, just as he said he would. Famously, in *Harrison v. Carswell*,[24] he squared off against his successor, Brian Dickson, in contending that the law of trespass had to move with the times. In that case a Dominion store employee had picketed her employer's store, which was located in a privately owned Winnipeg shopping centre. The owner (not the employer) asked her to take up her picket sign and leave. She refused and was charged with trespass. Laskin recognized that, in modern society, shopping centres are one of the great gathering places for people. For him, the controlling legal issue of the case was picketing, not property. In upholding her right to do what she did, he was prepared to overrule a recent case of the Supreme Court on the same point, saying that "this Court, above all others in this country, cannot be overly mechanistic about previous decisions, whatever be the respect it would pay such decisions." Justice Dickson was not prepared to follow such a bold lead and held for the majority that, if the effect of the Court's earlier decision were to be reversed, it would have to be done by the Manitoba legislature.

Laskin was in the vanguard of many of the Court's later positive private law initiatives. As is well known, in *Rathwell v. Rathwell*,[25] Dickson's plurality opinion that accepted, in the area of domestic arrangements, a doctrine of unjust enrichment enforced by a constructive trust based itself explicitly on Laskin's earlier solo dissent in *Murdoch v. Murdoch*.[26] A measure of how far the Laskin Court had moved beyond its predecessors was exposed for all to see in *Pettkus v. Becker*,[27] where a majority of the judges endorsed Laskin's original analysis in *Murdoch*, leaving Justice Martland to protest in a bad-tempered way that the majority had descended into "palm tree justice."[28]

In *Canadian Aero Service Limited v. O'Malley*,[29] Laskin, assisted by Charles Dubin as counsel, raised the bar on corporate governance. The issue of fiduciary duties had been used in a corporate context before, but, if anything, the forceful analysis set out in Laskin's judgment, combined with his sense of moral outrage at corporate self-dealing, has more impact today than it did when the case was decided thirty years ago.

More cerebrally, Laskin rewrote the law on the recovery of "pure" economic loss in tort in *Rivtow Marine Ltd. v. Washington Iron Works*.[30] He was, in dissent, joined only by Justice Hall, but four years later his dissent was accepted as the better opinion on this issue by the House of Lords in *Anns v. Merton London Borough Council*,[31] a development that may have softened Laskin's earlier dismissal of the wisdom of that body.[32] The Laskin view was eventually repatriated to our shores by the Supreme Court of Canada in *Winnipeg Condominium Corp. No. 36 v. Bird Construction Co*.[33] We now take for granted the so-called LSD trio of Justices Laskin, Spence, and Dickson. But it was not always thus. Brian Dickson was a successful corporate lawyer from Winnipeg who had climbed a judicial hierarchy more respected for soundness than for creativity. The early Dickson was not the judge who took hold of the *Charter* ten years later and fashioned it into one of the cornerstones of modern Canadian society. Dickson's transition from a very good judge to a very great judge was, in its way, even more astonishing than Laskin's performance on the Court.[34] Laskin was and remained a radical thinker. Dickson, during Laskin's tenure as Chief Justice of Canada, became one, a transformation in which Laskin played a pivotal role.

This transition is most clearly evident in the impact of Laskin's energetic proselytizing in support of the *Canadian Bill of Rights*, usually in dissent. Over the course of more than a dozen opinions beginning with *R. v. Appleby* in 1972[35] and ending with *R. v. Shelley* in 1981,[36] Laskin gradually brought the Court back to a Rand-like commitment to civil rights. For whatever reason, probably just the vagaries of the judicial calendar, many of these decisions were written in the context of drunk-driving offences. Nevertheless, case by case, Laskin exposed the impoverished state of the Court's civil-rights thinking. The fact that neither the profession nor the public were impressed with the Court's record on the *Canadian Bill of Rights* was in part fuelled by Laskin's vision of what it might have become.[37] This dissatisfaction likely contributed to the resolve of a renewed Court led by Chief Justice Dickson to make the *Charter* a truly powerful instrument for justice.

Although Laskin was not prepared in *Morgentaler* (1976) to invalidate the criminalization of abortion as being in violation of the *Canadian Bill of Rights*, he demonstrated an appetite for *Charter*-like results in a series of subsequent decisions, including *R. v. Hogan*,[38] where Laskin would have precluded the use of evidence obtained in violation of the *Bill of Right* in order to sustain a conviction. Similarly in *MacKay v. The Queen*,[39] Laskin denounced the cosiness of military procedures when conducting a trial on charges of a breach of the ordinary criminal law. While Justice Dickson, still the old soldier, joined in the majority to uphold this application of military justice, Laskin seemed to share the view attributed to French prime minister Georges Clemenceau that "military justice is to justice what military music is to music."

Again, in the Indian cases *Canada (Attorney General) v. Lavell*[40] and *Canada (Attorney General) v. Canard*,[41] Laskin advanced a number of propositions that are still a mainstay of equality jurisprudence. For example, to establish inequality, a claimant does not have to show conflicting treatment between two federal statutes but only that the impugned statute is in conflict with the equality guarantee itself.[42]

Other essays in this volume will consider Laskin's revolutionary impact on administrative law in general and on procedural fairness in particular.[43] His decision in *Nicholson v. Haldimand Norfolk (Regional) Police Commissioners*,[44] has been cited over thirty times by the Supreme Court itself and in hundreds of lower-court decisions. It allowed the Court's writ to penetrate far deeper into the bureaucracy than had ever been possible before. Other authors will also talk about Laskin's great constitutional differences with Justice Jean Beetz,[45] disagreements that resulted in a series of judgments wonderfully argued on both sides. Perhaps never in the Court's history have the opposing views of federal-provincial power been represented with such erudition. This clash of perspectives eventually gave way to the middle path of Brian Dickson, which, it must be admitted, was closer to Beetz than to Laskin.

As an aside from all these labours, Laskin dashed off a series of decisions in the late 1970s that effectively crippled the aspirations of the Federal Court of Canada. He thought the Canadian judicial structure centred on the superior courts of the provinces was infinitely preferable to the dual court system in the United States, and he was not impressed with the American theory of "pendent" jurisdiction. In *Quebec North Shore*[46] and *McNamara Construction*,[47] he showed that, although Parliament had the power to require claimants to sue the federal Crown in the Federal Court, it could not give the Federal Court jurisdiction to hear any counterclaims the Crown itself might want to bring under provincial law. This decision made the exclusive jurisdiction of the Federal Court much less attractive to the federal government. Indeed, Laskin's judicial blows rendered the Federal Court's ability to deal with claims against the Crown somewhat dysfunctional[48] and led one judge to suggest that Laskin had made the Federal Court into the "Rodney Dangerfield of the Canadian court system."[49] Eventually Parliament bowed to the inevitable and restored concurrent jurisdiction in the provincial superior courts to hear claims against the federal Crown.

How, then, are we to summarize Bora Laskin's impact on the institution of the Supreme Court? Between his appointment to the Court on March 19, 1970, and the onset of serious health problems less than a decade later, he had revolutionized the way in which litigation was conducted before the Court, lifted its jurisprudence to a level of sophistication that had only sporadically been achieved before, laid the basis for much of the future *Charter* jurisprudence with his bold initiatives under the *Canadian Bill of Rights*, staked out seminal doctrines in areas of private law such as unjust enrichment and corporate governance, reordered administrative law, and, during his spare time, torpedoed the Federal Court.[50]

Of course Laskin had his critics. His judgments, bristling with insights, were not always written in a way that was user friendly. Whereas Justice Martland wrote with engaging directness, and Justice Judson covered no more ground than was absolutely necessary to make his point, Laskin spared his readers none of the complexities. He paid the legal profession the compliment of thinking that its members were as interested in the issue at hand as he was, and in that respect, perhaps, he overshot much of his potential audience.

So far as substance is concerned, some critics fault Laskin for what they see as an overly centralist view of Canadian federalism, for his *leben und leben lasen* attitude to administrative tribunals, and for other matters that can be picked apart with the benefit of three decades' worth of hindsight.[51] My own criticisms, such as they are, are those of a lawyer who, for better or worse, appeared before him with some frequency in the early eighties. While Laskin threw open the Supreme Court to litigation and to stakeholders not previously heard from, and while he listened attentively during oral argument, it was not at all clear if anything any counsel ever said actually changed his mind. He seldom asked questions. Two instances may illustrate the point. When his panel heard our leave application in the *Marshall Crowe* case,[52] where we were attempting to unseat the chairman of the National Energy Board in the middle of the hearing of the Canadian Arctic gas pipeline, he opened the session by asking if anybody among the twelve lawyers assembled seriously supported the test for apprehension of bias adopted and applied by the Federal Court of Appeal. Dr. Bob Sharpe and I, as counsel for the upstart public-interest appellant, were pleased to have Chief Justice Laskin on board so early, but his opening salvo sat poorly with learned counsel for the gas companies, who were puffing up to soar on flights of oratory.

A few years later, David Scott and I were sitting at the end of the list of leave applications waiting our turn in what became *The Queen v. Beauregard*.[53] Scott, acting for the respondent and understandably counting on the fact that we were about number 14 on the morning list, went up to the library to polish the finer points of his oral argument. A few seconds later, Laskin entered the courtroom and announced, "Well, there is one case where clearly leave has to be given. Who's on *Beauregard*?" I stood up and identified myself, but explained that my opponent had gone upstairs to the library. Laskin made an irritated comment about where were lawyers when they were needed, indicated that leave ought to be given, but sent me upstairs to advise Mr. Scott that, if he really felt he had something significant to say, he should come back at the end of the day to explain why members of the Court ought to change their mind. Scott prudently declined the opportunity and, like Elvis, left the building. (Unfortunately, Chief Justice Laskin died before the *Beauregard* case, which became one of the great authorities on judicial independence, could actually be heard.)

Occasionally, too, Laskin could be quite dismissive of lawyers in oral argument, especially as he grew older and the effect of his illnesses became more pronounced. I recall responding in one case where the Court had granted leave, and Laskin tore a strip off a fairly senior lawyer saying, "Well, Mr. X, you'll have to do better than that in this Court." He was equally dismissive as the lawyer soldiered through his remaining points. Afterwards, in the robing room, learned counsel was understandably seething: "If they didn't like my goddamn arguments," he said, "why did they give me leave?"

It was not always thus. In earlier times, when he was still in good health, Laskin was considered by the bar to be a joy to appear before. He was every practitioner's favourite appellate judge. No matter how thin the argument, lawyers could be heard consoling themselves in the robing room, "Well, at least Laskin understood my point." But that was in the 1960s and 1970s. By 1980, things were more difficult. Even then, however, Laskin's irritability seemed confined to the courtroom. After one harrowing morning in his grip, as I was walking along the Sparks Street Mall comforting myself with a large ice-cream cone, I was embarrassed to bump into the Chief Justice as he walked out of his bank. "Good," he beamed warmly, "I like to see a man enjoying himself."

There is also, I suppose, the suggestion that he overreacted in his criticism of Thomas Berger when Berger, then a judge of the British Columbia Supreme Court, wrote an article in the *Globe and Mail* in 1981 protesting the governments' short-lived decision to drop Aboriginal rights protection from the 1982 constitutional reform. Although Berger suggests in his book that Laskin's initial criticism grew into something of a vendetta, Laskin's approach was consistent with his view that judicial independence was a two-way street.[54] Politicians should keep out of the way of the judges, but the courtesy should be reciprocated. Judges had no business wading into the middle of constitutional talks. The authors of the recent biography of Brian Dickson also seem to criticize Laskin for taking a hard line against the grandstanding of headline-hunting lawyers, in particular those who acted for the appellants in *Operation Dismantle*.[55] However, Laskin's wrath was consistent with his belief that law was a process of rational debate. He did not believe that lawyers should harangue the media from the front steps of the Supreme Court building. I happen to think Laskin was right on this point.

In many cases, Laskin's abruptness was a function of his intellectual strength. He had thought long and hard about the state of the law throughout his professional life. He had undoubtedly put more reflection into legal points than most of the lawyers trying to change his mind. He cared deeply about the direction the law should take and could not easily abide a lawyer trying to persuade a majority of his colleagues on the Court to take it elsewhere. He prepared his cases meticulously and was impatient with those who didn't. Taking the good with the bad and recognizing the increasingly debilitating effects of his illnesses, it is difficult to see Laskin's "faults" as anything more than personal idiosyncracies of little lasting importance (unless you were the lawyer involved) in the overall scheme of things.

Some years ago, on being asked to deliver a eulogy after the death of the Right Honourable Brian Dickson, I recalled the words of George Bernard Shaw that became something of a mantra for Robert F. Kennedy: "You see things; and you say, 'Why?' But I dream things that never were; and I say, 'Why not?'"[56] Dickson, I suggested, fell into the latter camp. Laskin, working in an earlier state of our legal evolution, was necessarily more concerned with the world as he found it.[57] The difference is evident in their writing styles. Dickson's elegant, sweeping prose was addressed not only to us but to future generations. Laskin's style was focused intensely on the problem at hand, usually seeking to demonstrate the illogic or inadequacy of the existing jurisprudence. But in terms of looking at the way things were and asking why, Laskin raised the level and sophistication of legal debate to the point where the whole Supreme Court, including Dickson, was lifted on a rising tide largely of Laskin's making. Dickson was indeed a visionary and, building on Laskin's work on the *Canadian Bill of Rights*, he fashioned the *Canadian Charter of Rights and Freedoms* into a far more formidable weapon for justice than had generally been expected. Dickson's reassuring public image as the old soldier who, in times of peace and war, dedicated himself to a better life for his fellow citizens was eventually able to carry the Canadian public towards his vision of what "things ought to be." But though Dickson's skills and uplifting vision allowed him to see so far, he would certainly have shared the sentiment of Sir Isaac Newton: "If I have seen further, it is by standing on the shoulders of giants." In particular, Brian Dickson was able to stand on the shoulders of the great rebel at the heart of the Canadian legal establishment, the Right Honourable Bora Laskin.

NOTES

1 Of the Supreme Court of Canada. I would like to thank my former law clerk Cara Faith Zweibel for her helpful research into aspects of the paper.
2 Writing shortly after appeals to the Privy Council were abolished, Laskin's assessment of the work of the Supreme Court of Canada was not flattering: "[S]uch a dissociation, whether formally expressed or not, is imperative if the Court is to develop a personality of its own. It has for too long been a captive court so that it is difficult, indeed, to ascribe any body of doctrine to it which is distinctively its own, save, perhaps, in the field of criminal law." Bora Laskin, "The Supreme Court of Canada: A Final Court of and for Canadians," *Canadian Bar Review* 29 (1951): 1038 at 1075.
3 His acceptance of a judicial appointment seemed in part due to his despair of exercising significant influence in Canadian courts through academic writing. In "The Institutional Character of the Judge," *Israel Law Review* 7 (1972): 329 at 344–45, he commented:

> Legal writings are proper reference material for submission to courts in argument, and they ought, according to their materiality and persuasiveness, to have as direct an impact as reported cases which are cited to the court, other than those that are binding upon the particular court. I cannot say, so far as Canada is concerned, that they have so direct an impact, save in isolated cases. Their effect has been discernible only in a long-term sense of the improved education of the bar, and, consequently, of the bench.

4 In 1951 Laskin wrote that "Empiricism not dogmatism, imagination rather than literalness, are the qualities through which the judges can give their Court the stamp of personality." Laskin, "The Supreme Court of Canada," 1076.
5 Ibid., 1046–47. Emphasis added.
6 Available online at http://www.lafontaine-baldwin.com/lafontaine-baldwin/e/2005_speech-1.html.
7 Bora Laskin, "The Function of the Law," *Alberta Law Review* 11 (1973): 118 at 119.
8 Trudeau became prime minister on April 20, 1968.
9 *Brown v. Board of Education* 347 U.S. 483 (1954).
10 *Roe v. Wade* 410 U.S. 113 (1973).
11 *Gideon v. Wainwright* 372 U.S. 335 (1963).
12 *Miranda v. Arizona* 384 U.S. 436 (1966).
13 *Regina v. Wray*, [1971] SCR 272.

14 Justice Schroeder of the Ontario Court of Appeal would occasionally spell *show* as *shew* and always rejoiced to hear the odd scrap of legal Latin in his courtroom. By contrast, in the place of what he regarded as an antiquated reliance on Britain, Laskin advocated a global perspective:

> Now that the Supreme Court is a free court subject only to self-imposed limitations, it is reasonable to expect that it will explore the entire common law world and not only that part which is called Great Britain. Moreover, the stock in trade of this world includes not only decisions of courts but also the conclusions of scholars whose meditations on particular problems are not the result of the chance of litigation but the product of attempts to see the legal system as a integrated whole. This is the Supreme Court's task today in relation to Canada.

Laskin, "The Supreme Court of Canada," 1046–47.
15 In theory, every judge is entitled to sit and write in every case, but in practice the bench generally goes along with the Chief Justice. In any event, Laskin's policy was to *increase* the number of judges sitting on a case.
16 *R. v. Morgentaler*, [1976] 1 SCR 616.
17 *Canada (Attorney General) v. Lavell*, [1974] SCR 1349.
18 *Thorson v. Attorney General of Canada*, [1975] 1 SCR 138.
19 *Nova Scotia Board of Censors v. McNeil*, [1976] 2 SCR 265.
20 *Smith v. Attorney General of Ontario*, [1924] SCR 331.
21 *Minister of Justice v. Borowski*, [1981] 2 SCR 575 at 585.
22 *Blaikie v. Attorney General of Quebec*, [1979] 2 SCR 1016.
23 *Anti-Inflation Act Reference*, [1976] 2 SCR 373 at 388.
24 *Harrison v. Carswell*, [1976] 2 SCR 200.
25 *Rathwell v. Rathwell*, [1978] 2 SCR 436.
26 *Murdoch v. Murdoch*, [1975] 1 SCR 423.
27 *Pettkus v. Becker*, [1980] 2 SCR 834.
28 Ibid., 859.
29 *Canadian Aero Service Limited v. O'Malley*, [1974] SCR 592.
30 *Rivtow Marine Ltd. v. Washington Iron Works*, [1974] SCR 1189.
31 *Anns v. Merton London Borough Council*, [1978] AC 728.
32 Lord Wilberforce said: "On the question of damages generally I have derived much assistance from the judgment (dissenting on this point, but of strong persuasive force) of Laskin J. in the Canadian Supreme Court case of *Rivtow Marine Ltd. v. Washington Iron Works*," above note 30 at 759.
33 *Winnipeg Condominium Corp. No. 36 v. Bird Construction Co.*, [1995] 1 SCR 85 at para. 30.

34 The story is told by Robert Sharpe and Kent Roach in *Brian Dickson: A Judge's Journey* (Toronto: University of Toronto Press in association with the Osgoode Society, 2003).
35 *R. v. Appleby*, [1972] SCR 303, in which Laskin in a concurring judgment anticipated the Court's later *Charter* approach to reverse onus provisions.
36 *R. v. Shelley*, [1981] 2 SCR 196.
37 Those who consider that the *Canadian Bill of Rights* was doomed by its non-constitutional status should look at what has been accomplished under the *Quebec Charter*.
38 *R. v. Hogan*, [1975] 2 SCR 574.
39 *MacKay v. The Queen*, [1980] 2 SCR 370.
40 *Canada (Attorney General) v. Lavell* [1974] SCR 1349.
41 *Canada (Attorney General) v. Canard*, [1976] 1 SCR 170.
42 Ibid., 178.
43 Laskin took pride in the fact that, in Canada, due process was "a social norm, implying both a right of individuals and groups in our society, who have grievances to air, or demands to press, or claims to litigate, to make themselves heard; and, correlatively, an obligation to advance their causes through rational procedures which, after painful experience, have displaced naked force as the means through which the case is made for change or for the redress of wrongs." Bora Laskin, "The Judge and Due Process," *Manitoba Law Journal* 5 (1972): 235 at 236–37.
44 *Nicholson v. Haldimand Norfolk (Regional) Police Commissioners*, [1979] 1 SCR 311.
45 Their disagreement is illustrated by *Construction Montcalm v. Minimum Wage Commission*, [1979] 1 SCR 754. Spence joined Laskin in the dissent. Laskin also dissented from Beetz's majority judgments in *DiOrio v. Montreal Jail*, [1978] 1 SCR 152, and *Four B Manufacturing Ltd. v. United Garment Workers of America*, [1980] 1 SCR 1031.
46 *Quebec North Shore Paper Company v. Canadian Pacific Limited*, [1977] 2 SCR 1054.
47 *McNamara Construction (Western) Ltd v. The Queen*, [1977] 2 SCR 654.
48 The final indignity was inflicted by Justice Pigeon in *Queen v. Thomas Fuller Construction*, [1980] 1 SCR 695.
49 The wit was Justice Robert Reid of the Ontario Supreme Court, as it then was.
50 As early as 1975, Laskin was expressing some satisfaction that the Court had already shown

> in its recent decisions a willingness to expand the law as to standing to challenge the constitutionality of legislation; it has opened to a degree the door to intervention by responsible and interested organizations in litiga-

tion raising issues under the *Canadian Bill of Rights*; it has expanded tort liability in the matter of hazardous products and in respect of recovery for economic loss unattended by physical injury; it has given more flexibility to the law of occupiers' liability.

Bora Laskin, "A Judge and His Constituencies," 11.

51 See generally Philip Girard, *Bora Laskin, Bringing Law to Life* (Toronto: Osgoode Society for Canadian Legal History, 2005).
52 *Committee for Justice and Liberty v. National Energy Board*, [1978] 1 SCR 369.
53 *The Queen v. Beauregard*, [1986] 2 SCR 56.
54 Tom Berger, *One Man's Justice: A Life in the Law* (Vancouver: Douglas & McIntyre, 2002) at 160–64.
55 *Operation Dismantle*, [1985] 1 SCR 441. See Sharp and Roach, *Brian Dickson*, 332.
56 George Bernard Shaw, *Back to Methuselah*.
57 It is easy to forget the length of the journey Laskin himself travelled. Some of his early crusades sound like pre-history – for example, his advocacy that the Supreme Court should free itself from its self-imposed deference to the jurisprudence of the Privy Council. As he wrote: "It seems so pointless today to comment on these utterly pathetic suggestions for the long-delayed recognition of a country's final court as its ultimate judicial expositor. The Privy Council never was a Canadian Court; there was only the formal legal pretense." Laskin, "The Institutional Character of the Judge," 333.

◂ 7 ▸

Laskin's Impact on the Supreme Court

PETER W. HOGG[1]

THE SUPREME COURT OF CANADA IN 1970

IN 2005 THE LASKIN Award in Labour Law was presented to Paul Weiler, formerly a professor at the Osgoode Hall Law School and now at the Harvard Law School. In accepting the award, Weiler spoke of his admiration for and debt to Bora Laskin. Several of the speakers talked about Weiler's scholarly work, which owed much to Laskin, and especially of Weiler's great study of the Supreme Court of Canada, *In the Last Resort*.[2] That book painted a most unflattering picture of the Court, and it was bitterly resented by members of the Court and by many in the legal profession. Reviewing the work of the Court in the 1960s, Weiler identified a highly formalist style – short judgments that adhered strictly to English precedent, ignored the rich jurisprudence of the United States, rarely cited academic writing (and never a "living author"), showed no interest in the policies (or even the principles) that the law was supposed to serve, and never considered whether doctrine developed in England was appropriate for Canada. The Court saw no larger role for itself than resolving the dispute between the parties, and it never claimed any ambition to develop a distinctively Canadian jurisprudence. It had a low reputation in the rest of the world and was rarely cited outside Canada.

Fast forward to 2005, and we find a Court that is the precise opposite of the one Weiler depicted. The formalist style has been abandoned in favour of a rich, discursive style that is firmly anchored in the Canadian social context: it emphasizes principle and policy, seeks to formulate the just rule, and often refers to the jurisprudence of other countries and to academic writing. Adherence to precedent is still the rule, but the automatic deference to English decisions has gone, and the doctrine of precedent is mitigated by the Court's power to overrule its own decisions and those of the Privy Council. The Court now has a very high reputation outside Canada, where its judgments are frequently cited and its members are flooded with invitations to visit and speak.

LASKIN'S APPOINTMENT

HISTORIANS HAVE NEVER SETTLED the debate about whether great individuals shape events or impersonal forces alone provide a full explanation. We know intuitively, however, that individual agency is of huge importance. In his book, Weiler identified the appointment of Bora Laskin to the Supreme Court in 1970 as a harbinger of change. And he was even more pleased with Laskin's elevation to the position of Chief Justice in 1973, in defiance of the seniority conventions that then prevailed. Both the initial appointment and the elevation were highly controversial, as was his earlier appointment to the Ontario Court of Appeal in 1965. Not only was he the first Jew to be appointed, but he was also the first judge who had never practised law. That had never happened before. Moreover, as an academic, he had been a harsh critic of the Court and a strong advocate of judicial activism and law reform. Could such a person really be a "sound" lawyer?

Laskin served as Chief Justice from 1973 to 1984. These turned out to be watershed years for the Court, and his leadership was a key influence. In fact, it was only with Laskin that we began to speak of the various incarnations of the Court by the name of the Chief Justice. And the "Laskin Court" was, indeed, a court of change. He led his peers in their rejection of formalism; in their relaxation of the doctrine of precedent; and in their attention to policy, to social and economic context, and to academic and international sources. By the end of his tenure, the Supreme Court had become a recognizably modern court that was starting to develop a uniquely Canadian jurisprudence. And it certainly did not hurt that his brilliant successor, Brian Dickson, was an admirer of Laskin and carried forward Laskin's values during his tenure from 1984 to 1990. After that, no reversion to the era of formalism would be conceivable.

STRUCTURAL CHANGE

THE LASKIN COURT WAS marked by two significant structural changes: larger panel sizes and greater unanimity of decisions.[3] In 1970, Laskin's first year as a puisne judge, the Supreme Court of Canada usually sat as a panel of only five judges (five being the statutory quorum). This custom contrasted with the Supreme Court of the United States, which sat as a full court of nine judges in most appeals. One of the duties of the Chief Justice is to decide on the composition of the Court's panels for its hearings. After Laskin became Chief Justice in 1973, he immediately began to allocate appeals to larger panels. By 1976 the proportion of appeals being heard by a panel larger than five had nearly doubled (from 27 percent to 53 percent), and by 1979 had reached 69 percent.[4] The Court now routinely sits as a full court of nine judges on most appeals.

In 1975 an amendment to the *Supreme Court Act* eliminated the appeal as a right for civil cases involving more than $10,000. This right had loaded the Court's docket with cases that were unimportant except to the parties. Since that amendment, most cases come to the Court only with leave of the Court, and the Act stipulates that leave should be granted only in "important" cases. Obviously, this reform would not have been enacted without the support of the Chief Justice. It greatly increased the Court's control over its own docket, and it reinforced the trend to sitting in larger panels. If a case had been declared by the Court itself to be important, should it not be considered by more than a bare quorum of five judges?

Not only did the judges sit more often in the Laskin Court but they agreed more often. This fact may appear to be counterintuitive, because Laskin was famous for his strong dissents, often with the support of Justices Spence and Dickson – the so-called LSD group. But Laskin's dissents were never seen as simple contrariness; rather, they emerged from his commitment to principle, and they only increased the respect for his intellect and integrity that developed in the legal community and among the other members of the Court. The number of unanimous decisions steadily increased during his tenure. In 1974 the Court delivered unanimous judgements in 65 percent of reported cases, and by 1984 that number had increased to 88 percent.[5] This unanimity is a great compliment to the leadership of the Chief Justice.

PRECEDENT

THE FORMALISM OF THE pre-Laskin Court was characterized by an adherence to precedent, especially English precedent. Apart from the Privy Council and the House of Lords, the decisions of English courts were not literally binding on Canadian courts, but they were treated with great deference by the Supreme Court. The Court did not consider whether the social and historical context of Canada might sometimes call for changes in common law rules that had developed in a different time and place. Moreover, it regarded itself as bound by its own prior decisions and by the decisions of both the Privy Council (although appeals had ended in 1949) and the House of Lords ("the supreme tribunal to settle English law").[6]

Laskin's role in shifting the Court away from its adherence to English precedent and towards its own distinctively Canadian jurisprudence was foreshadowed in his 1951 article, "The Supreme Court of Canada: A Final Court of and for Canadians."[7] In that article he criticized the Court as having remained a "captive court" for too long after appeals to the Privy Council had ended. After his appointment to the Court, Laskin followed his own advice, though with limited success at the beginning. In the early days on the Court his voice was often opposed by a chorus chanting – to borrow the words of Frank Scott – "the old sing-song" of *stare decisis*. It was not that he was unfaithful to precedent, but that he was more willing than his colleagues to review an earlier decision that had been shown to be contrary to principle or policy, leading to an unjust result. After he became Chief Justice, however, the Court for the first time ever explicitly refused to follow one of its own prior decisions, and it did so again on at least four other occasions. The Court continues to review its own previous decisions and occasionally refuses to follow them.[8]

I was fortunate to be the counsel who, in 1978, urged the Laskin Court to refuse for the first time to follow a decision of the Privy Council. In *Re Agricultural Products Marketing Act* (1978),[9] I had been appointed by the Court to make the constitutional argument on behalf of Ontario egg producers opposed to marketing levies that had been imposed on them by federal law. Parliament had acted on the assumption that the levies were indirect taxes. My argument was that they were regulatory charges that could only be imposed by the provinces. The difficulty with my argument was that the Privy Council had held that such levies were indirect taxes; moreover, that decision had been affirmed in a later case by the Supreme

Court itself, and Parliament had then enacted the levies in reliance on the two decisions. The only authority in support of my argument was an article published in 1959 in the *University of Toronto Law Journal*, in which the author asserted that the two decisions were wrongly decided.[10] However, all was not lost: the author of the article was Bora Laskin! When I cited the article to the Court over which he was presiding, he smiled and said, "We'll have to see if I've learned anything in the last twenty years." Fortunately he hadn't, and the Court struck down the marketing levies. That became the first case in which the Court explicitly refused to follow a decision of the Privy Council.[11] (There have been two subsequent overrulings of the Privy Council, both after the retirement of Chief Justice Laskin.)[12]

POLICY

THE FORMALISM OF THE pre-Laskin Court also manifested itself in an unwillingness to examine the policy that a legal doctrine was supposed to serve. This separation continued into the 1970s. An excellent example is *Rivtow Marine v. Washington Iron Works* (1974)[13] on the recovery of economic loss for negligence. Justice Ritchie for the majority of the Court, denying recovery, accepted English precedents and refused to "follow the sometimes winding paths leading to the formulation of a 'policy decision.'"[14] Laskin's dissent, which was explicitly based on policy considerations, was quickly appreciated as the better view, and in a case in 1995 was adopted by a unanimous Supreme Court.[15] In the latter case, the changed attitude of the Court to policy was articulated by Justice La Forest, who, writing for the Court, started his discussion with the traditional characterization of economic loss, but went on to add that he found it "more congenial to deal directly with the policy considerations underlying that classification."[16] By 1995 there was nothing surprising about that statement. Indeed, counsel before the Court now know very well that they will succeed only by showing that the doctrine on which they rely produces results that are sound in policy and principle. That standard started with Laskin.

ACADEMIC SOURCES

THE FORMALISM OF THE pre-Laskin Court also manifested itself in a reluctance to cite academic literature. The Court followed the English rule that the citation of living authors was forbidden.[17] But the distaste for academic writing seemed to go deeper than that. As Chief Justice Rinfret pointed out in 1950, refusing to listen to counsel reading from an article by Vincent MacDonald (admittedly a living author), "the *Canadian Bar Review* is not an authority in this Court."[18] Of course, there were not many academic sources to cite before the massive growth of university law schools in the 1960s. The small number of full-time academics carried heavy teaching loads that limited their time for scholarly inquiry. Laskin himself was unusual in the quantity and quality of his scholarship. In his article on the Supreme Court,[19] he bemoaned the unwillingness of the Court to look at sources outside English and Canadian cases. Even the decisions of courts in the United States and Australia were treated with utmost suspicion. On academic writings, he pointed out that the late development of university law schools was at last leading to "free inquiry grounded in Canadian experience." And he also pointed out that, in civil cases from Quebec, the Court made the customary civil law references to academic writings, which contrasted markedly with its approach in common law appeals.

A few academic citations slipped under the wire even in the 1950s and 1960s. An article by Black and Richter in the *Dalhousie Law Journal* shows that, in 1957, ten of sixty-six decisions (15 percent) made reference to an academic source, and in 1967 the rate declined slightly to twelve of ninety (13 percent).[20] The Laskin Court abandoned the silly prohibition on the citation of living authors, which was no longer accepted even in England, and academic writing, now much more voluminous than ever before in Canada, started to find its way routinely into the factums filed by counsel, who knew it would be respectfully considered by the Court. The Black-Richter study does not provide numbers for the Laskin Court, but it shows that, between 1985 and 1990, academic authority was cited in 298 of 620 decisions (48 percent), and in terms of opinions (majority, concurring, or dissenting) in 397 of 993 opinions (40 percent).[21] The authors observe that "in the span of a generation the frequency of reference to scholarly writing has more than tripled."[22] Of course, this was the natural outcome of introducing a wider set of considerations into the Court's decision making, and it started with Laskin.

ACCESSIBILITY

THE PRE-LASKIN COURT WAS one known only to lawyers, and its style of opinion writing was one that only lawyers could appreciate. (Weiler wrote in the *Last Resort* that even lawyers were starting to be uncomfortable with the sparse reasons and narrow range of sources that characterized the formalist style.) By the time Laskin was appointed as Chief Justice, the public had begun to show an interest in the Court. Public debate in the United States about the activism of the Warren Court led to comparison with the *Canadian Bill of Rights* of 1960 and awakened Canadians to the fact that a supreme court could wield considerable power. Then Prime Minister Trudeau's appointment of Laskin in defiance of seniority conventions attracted the news. And Trudeau's efforts to secure amendments to the Constitution, including the adoption of a new *Canadian Charter of Rights and Freedoms*, which finally succeeded in 1982, was the subject of intense public debate, much of it centred on the increased powers of judicial review that would be invested in the Supreme Court of Canada.

It has been suggested that the evolution in judicial style during Laskin's era may have been motivated in part by a desire to reach out to a broader public.[23] Whether or not that is correct, the frank articulation of relevant policy considerations, the more discursive style of writing, and the generous citation of a wide variety of sources undoubtedly made the Court's decisions more accessible to the media and the public. This transformation became very important when, immediately following Laskin's departure, the Dickson Court started to receive appeals under the new *Charter of Rights and Freedoms*. Many of these decisions were truly newsworthy, addressing a host of issues formerly the exclusive domain of elected politicians and including abortion, pornography, hate propaganda, Sunday shopping, mandatory retirement, and due process for persons accused of crime. The Dickson Court maintained and indeed expanded on the style of the Laskin Court, and also made efforts to assist the different media in informing themselves on the Court's reasons as decisions were released. Once again, Laskin had prepared the way.

INTERNATIONAL PROFILE

IN 1970 THE SUPREME Court of Canada was widely regarded as weaker than the final courts of the United States, the United Kingdom, and Australia. The formalist style had long been rejected in the United States, and the decisions of the Warren Court, however controversial at home, were widely applauded for their efforts to eliminate racial discrimination and to protect the rights of criminal defendants. The formalist style still prevailed in the United Kingdom and Australia, but the elegant craftsmanship of the leading judges in the United Kingdom (Lord Reid, for example) and Australia (Chief Justice Dixon, for example) was rightly regarded as superior to that of the Canadian judges.

Laskin raised the bar. In the first place, he had an international reputation as a teacher and scholar when he was appointed to the Ontario Court of Appeal in 1965. The combination of his name and the unusual appointment of a full-time academic attracted attention in the legal communities of the other common law countries. His appointment to the Supreme Court of Canada in 1970, and then his elevation to Chief Justice in 1973, were also watched outside Canada. His opinion writing did not disappoint. His dissent in *Rivtow Marine v. Washington Iron Works* (1974)[24] was adopted by the House of Lords in *Anns v. Merton London Borough Council* (1978),[25] long before it was adopted by the Supreme Court of Canada. Significantly, it was Laskin's policy reasoning that influenced the House of Lords. The majority opinion, simply following the English precedents that denied recovery for economic loss, had no insights for international onlookers. Ironically, it was by developing a uniquely Canadian jurisprudence that the Supreme Court started to attract international interest.

Laskin's standards and his values were carried forward by Chief Justice Dickson and the judges of his Court, who had the challenge of developing the exegesis of the new *Charter of Rights and Freedoms*. The judges of the Lamer Court and the McLachlin Court continued in the same tradition. The contextual style is now uncontroversial. The Court's jurisprudence under the *Charter* and in the other areas of its work is admired all over the world. The judges of the Court are in constant demand to attend international conferences and to receive informal visitors. The international reputation of the Court could not be higher. How proud Laskin would be were he able to see the completion of the transformation of the "captive court" he criticized in 1951 and the triumph of the vision he articulated as an academic and acted on as a judge.

APPENDIX I
SUPREME COURT OF CANADA
PANEL SIZES AND UNANIMITY RATES, 1970–84[26]

Year	Total Number of Reported Decisions	Number of Unanimous Decisions	Percentage of Decisions That Were Unanimous	Number of Reported Decisions with Panels of More Than Five Justices	Percentage of Reported Decisions with Panels of More Than Five Justices
1970	86	55	64.0	23	26.7
1971	81	57	70.4	20	24.7
1972	73	47	64.4	9	12.3
1973	63	43	68.3	12	19.0
1974	94	61	64.9	24	25.5
1975	125	82	65.6	49	39.2
1976	108	69	63.9	57	52.8
1977	163	120	73.6	91	55.8
1978	162	118	72.8	107	66.0
1979	143	107	74.8	99	69.2
1980	155	125	80.6	98	63.2
1981	108	95	88.0	63	58.3
1982	122	103	84.4	79	64.8
1983	88	73	83.0	47	53.4
1984	65	57	87.7	37	56.9

NOTES

1. I gratefully acknowledge the excellent research of Jennifer Marston, my colleague in the Litigation Group of Blake, Cassels & Graydon, LLP.
2. P. Weiler, *In the Last Resort: A Critical Study of the Supreme Court of Canada* (Toronto: Carswell/Methuen, 1974).
3. P. McCormick, *Supreme at Last: The Evolution of the Supreme Court of Canada* (Toronto: James Lorimer, 2000), 88.
4. The numbers are tracked in the "Statistical Analysis" published annually in the *Osgoode Hall Law Journal*. For details, see Appendix A, "Panel Sizes and Unanimity Rates, 1970 to 1984," a table prepared by Jennifer Marston.

5   J.G. Snell and F. Vaughan, *The Supreme Court of Canada: History of the Institution* (Toronto: Osgoode Society, 1985), 231; "Statistical Analysis of [1984] S.C.R.," *Osgoode Hall Law Journal* 30 (1992): 851, 860. For details, see Appendix A.
6   P.W. Hogg, *Constitutional Law of Canada*, 4th ed. (Toronto: Carswell, Toronto, 1997, annually supplemented), sec. 8.7.
7   Bora Laskin, "The Supreme Court of Canada: A Final Court of and for Canadians," *Canadian Bar Review* 29 (1951): 1038, 1075–76.
8   The cases are listed in Hogg, *Constitutional Law of Canada*, sec. 8.7, note 104.
9   *Re Agricultural Products Marketing Act*, [1978] 2 SCR 1198.
10 B. Laskin, "Provincial Marketing Levies: Indirect Taxation and Federal Power," *University of Toronto Law Journal* 13 (1959): 1.
11 *Re Agricultural Products Marketing Act*, [1978] 2 SCR 1198, 1234, 1291.
12 *Re Bill 30 (Ontario Separate School Funding)*, [1987] 1 SCR 1148, 1190–96; *Wells v. Newfoundland*, [1999] 3 SCR 199, para. 47.
13 *Rivtow Marine v. Washington Iron Works*, [1974] SCR 1189.
14 Ibid., 1215.
15 *Winnipeg Condominium Corp. No. 36 v. Bird Construction Co.*, [1995] 1 SCR 85.
16 Ibid., para. 13.
17 G. Bale, "W.R. Lederman and the Citation of Legal Periodicals by the Supreme Court of Canada," *Queen's Law Journal* 19 (1994): 36, 51–52.
18 Ibid.
19 Laskin, "The Supreme Court of Canada," 1045–46.
20 V. Black and N. Richter, "Did She Mention My Name? Citation of Academic Authority in the Supreme Court of Canada, 1985–1990," *Dalhousie Law Journal* 16 (1993): 377.
21 Ibid., 383.
22 Ibid., 382.
23 P. McCormick, "Second Thoughts: Supreme Court Citation of Dissents and Separate Concurrences, 1949–1966," *Canadian Bar Review* 81 (2002): 369, 382.
24 *Rivtow Marine v. Washington Iron Works*, [1974] SCR 199, para 47.
25 *Anns v. Merton London Borough Council*, [1978] AC 728 (HL). Ironically, the English courts have since resiled somewhat from the *Anns* decision, but it remains good law in Canada. See *Winnipeg Condominium Corp. No. 36 v. Bird Construction Co.*, [1995] 1 SCR 85.
26 The values incorporated into this table were borrowed from the *Osgoode Hall Law Journal*, which, during the relevant period, published an annual statistical analysis of Supreme Court of Canada decisions. See, for example, "Statistical Analysis of [1970] S.C.R.," *Osgoode Hall Law Journal* 10 (1972): 487.

◀ 8 ▶

Memories of Laskin at the Court

SHERIDAN SCOTT

I FIRST MET BORA Laskin in 1980, when he interviewed and hired me to be his law clerk. I will never forget how he made me feel at ease, that day some twenty-five years ago, with his natural warmth and sympathy for a young law student. My job description, he declared, was to help him out. I blush to this day to recall that I actually believed I could do so. I know now that it was a bit like thinking I could help A.Y. Jackson paint, Karen Kain dance, or Steve Nash play basketball.

My capacity for self-delusion in those days knew no bounds. In my first weeks in the Chief Justice's employ, I met his wonderful wife, Peggy. "I'm worried about Bora," she confided. He's got to be pushed on the constitutional front. He's not the self-starter he once was. That's where you can make a huge contribution." And, with that suggestion, my fantasies were launched. I, Sheridan Scott, fresh out of the University of Victoria Law School, was to be no mere gopher of a clerk. I would become the prime mover behind the Chief Justice of Canada's constitutional thinking. The time was September 1981. The constitutional referendum decision was just days ahead, the *Charter* loomed, the scope for creating a just society appeared limitless. And I was to be the person who put the words into the mouth of the nation's leading legal voice.

If I may borrow a stock line from the comedian Dave Broadfoot, "When I regained consciousness," (pause) the reality turned out to be somewhat different from the dream. My constitutional mandate had nothing to do with the fundamental law of the land. My job was to ensure that every day, rain or shine, I persuaded the Chief Justice to take a half-hour of aerobic exercise – a walk around the Supreme Court of Canada or the parliamentary grounds. You see, Peggy Laskin had been talking about daily constitutionals. I had fancied myself as the reincarnation of John Dicey. She had cast me in quite another role, as Sheridan Scott, personal trainer.

Remarkably, this first great disappointment of my legal career turned out to be one of the most incredible experiences of my life. It was during these walks that I came to know and understand something of the qualities that made him so special as a jurist and as a person.

I learned to distinguish between strength and rigidity, between confidence and pride, between wisdom and mere intelligence. I learned that true modesty comes naturally to the lucky few born with clear vision and an acutely accurate sense of perspective. The Bora Laskin I came to know never saw himself as important. He knew that the job of Chief Justice was vitally important, but he never confused himself with the office he was privileged to hold.

Often, journalists or academics would try to get him to open up about his role in crucial Supreme Court decisions. A lesser person might have been tempted to indulge in a bit of self-promotion. Laskin never did. He always replied by saying that the decisions spoke for themselves. Sometimes his inquisitors would take another tack, asking instead what he considered the greatest achievement in his life. He had a stock response. Let me share it, as we lawyers love to do, with reference to authority. I will quote from the eulogy given in the House of Commons by Prime Minister Pierre Elliott Trudeau shortly after Bora Laskin died. Trudeau said: "His humility was as refreshing as it was genuine. I recall once asking him which of his many achievements he remembered most fondly. 'That's easy,' he replied. 'When I was young, back in Fort William, I played baseball. I still hold the record for the longest home run hit out of the local ballpark.'"

A final word on Laskin as heavy hitter must be added to the record on a life lived. Lest anyone think that the baseball story was merely Laskin's way of avoiding unwanted inquiries, let me tell you that he really did regard his home-run moment of fame as immensely fulfilling. When he told me the story, he augmented his narrative by letting me read some faded newspaper clippings recording the event. The Chief kept no scrapbooks, but someone had found those old cuttings and passed them on to him, and he couldn't bring himself to throw them away.

I also want to mention Bora Laskin's humanity, his sense of caring, and his deep commitment to fairness. I don't mean fairness as we lawyers define it. His was not an intellectual belief in an ancient doctrine of equity, but a sense of fairness rooted in old-fashioned notions of sharing and fair play. He told me a wonderful story about himself as a young man, about going down to the railway yards in the early hours of the morning looking for work loading grain elevators or something. He said all the men looking for work would gather, hoping to be called by the foreman. He was in great shape in those days and wanted to help his parents out by earning a few extra dollars. But when he saw all the other older men who were the sole supporters of their families, he decided he didn't want to take opportunities away from them, and he went home.

Bora Laskin was not without pride, but I only ever saw it surface when he spoke of the work of others. He admired Wishert Spence's clear thinking and clear writing. He was inordinately proud of the establishment of a university-based program for the teaching of law in Canada. Though he often spoke about this development during our so-called daily constitutionals around the Supreme Court building, he never focused on his role, at least not in my hearing. He gave the credit to his contemporaries, Cecil Wright and John Willis.

Laskin could be stubborn, but only to counter what he regarded as threats to the very underpinnings of the law and its foundation principles. He was extremely wary, for example, about the dangers of using civil disobedience as an instrument of change and insisted I read a speech he gave to a group of law students on this very topic – his favourite speech, he told me. His view was that disobeying the law might make a point, sometimes even effectively, but he saw the long-term threat it posed to the rule of law as too high a risk to take in pursuit of short-term goals, no matter how laudable.

The American philosopher Ralph Waldo Emerson once wrote: "Every hero becomes a bore at the last." To borrow one of Laskin's most used lines, "With respect, I disagree." I am uncomfortable with absolute pronouncements, even when they are the products of great minds. Perhaps if Emerson had said "most heroes" or "many heroes become bores at the last," I could concur. The Bora Laskin I knew, and I knew him very near to what Emerson called "the last," never stopped searching for better solutions. He remained true to his ideals, wrote his dissents when he could not convince his fellow judges, and laughingly cherished as a badge of honour his membership in the triad his critics dismissed as the LSD gang – Laskin, Spence, and Dickson.

How he would have loved to be a part of today's Supreme Court, to have played a role in weaving the *Charter of Rights and Freedoms* into the ancient fabric of the common law. Instead, his legacy remains that of a prophet, pointing to the road not yet taken and setting the course for the next generation of justices to follow.

The legendary American jurist Oliver Wendell Holmes Jr. once said of the profession of the law and those who embrace it as their life's pursuit: "… to think great thoughts, you must be heroes as well as idealists." That formula sums up the Bora Laskin I was privileged to know.

The Chief Justice whose decisions I read as a student, whom I clerked a year for, then counted as a friend for too short a time afterwards was a hero – an idealist and a great thinker. He was blessed with a wonderful mind, a truly generous heart, and a capacity to look forward and understand how all high-court rulings touch not only the parties to an appeal but, eventually, everyone.

Pierre Elliott Trudeau, who appointed Laskin as Chief Justice, coined the expression "a just society." Bora Laskin allowed us to believe that it could be more than a rallying cry, that it could become the birthright of all Canadians. All things considered, that's not a bad legacy – right up there with the mother of all home runs.

◀ PART FOUR ▶

Substantive Contributions to Law

Laskin's Legacy to National Unity and Patriation

R. ROY McMURTRY

I BELIEVE THAT I was the first attorney general to appear personally in the Supreme Court of Canada in many years when I argued on behalf of Ontario in support of the constitutionality of the anti-inflation board legislation. Chief Justice Laskin welcomed the renewal of this tradition, but I also learned the inherent risks associated with a politician's appearance in the Supreme Court.

My argument supporting the constitutionality of the legislation was accepted by the Court. However, a unanimous Supreme Court struck down the triggering mechanism employed by our government for the implementation of the federal legislation in Ontario because it was done by order-in-council and not by a provincial legislation. That part of Ontario's submissions was argued very well by David Mundell, my senior constitutional adviser. Nevertheless, when the decision was released, my opposition colleagues in the legislature of Ontario were determined that I get full credit for the loss. For some weeks I was bombarded with taunts of "nine–zero ... nine–zero."

I had not forgotten this experience when my senior colleagues in the ministry suggested that I argue the *Patriation Reference* case on behalf of Ontario. I have to admit that I was somewhat apprehensive, given the importance of the case and the obvious fact that I did not have any pretensions to constitutional scholarship. At the same time I recognized that it might well be a once-in-a-lifetime opportunity. I also had great confidence in my constitutional advisers, again David Mundell, John

Cavarzan, and Lorraine Weinrib, now Justice Cavarzan of the Superior Court and Professor Weinrib of the University of Toronto.

I had been urging the federal government to accept the political reality that the British government would continue to be reluctant to introduce the patriation legislation in its Parliament when the constitutionality of the legislation was still being tested in the Canadian courts and that the issue should be determined by the Supreme Court of Canada as soon as possible. In fact, I had had a long discussion with the English attorney general, Sir Michael Havers, in London in January 1981 over his government's concern about the legal challenges in the Appeal Courts of Quebec, Manitoba, and Saskatchewan. Immediately on my return to Canada, I wrote to him in part as follows: "My fear is that these worthy goals (i.e. Patriation, an amending formula and an entrenched *charter of rights*) may be put in jeopardy if an approach is pursued by the federal government which, in its haste, does appear insensitive to legitimate questions that some provinces have posed as to its legality."

I therefore suggested to Sir Michael Havers that the legislation in Westminster should await a decision of the Supreme Court of Canada. While I became somewhat unpopular with my federal colleagues when they learned of my intervention with Attorney General Havers, the federal government finally accepted the political reality a few weeks later that London would not act until the legal issues had been decided in Canada. Prime Minister Trudeau in particular was not happy because he clearly had mixed views about the role of the courts in relation to major political issues. His government had lost the *Senate Reference* case in 1980 when it had attempted unilaterally to change the structure of the Senate. There was clearly a high degree of nervousness in government legal circles about the issue being determined by the Supreme Court of Canada.

I believe both Trudeau and I were present at a meeting in the Ministry of Justice boardroom the day before the *Patriation* case was to commence in the Supreme Court. I still recall the room literally being crammed with federal justice lawyers who had worked on the file. Justice Minister Jean Chrétien had joined the meeting, and I remember that he soon tired of the legal chatter, slammed his fist on the table, and, glaring around the room, said, "Roy, I tell you this. If we do not win this Goddamn case, it will be Jonestown revisited around here!"

While the constitutional legality of the federal proposals was of paramount importance, the more controversial issue in the *Patriation* case was whether the lack of provincial support for the federal proposals breached a constitutional convention. When the issues were argued in the Supreme Court of Canada, eight provinces were still opposed to the federal proposals. The majority of the Supreme Court ruled that the lack of substantial provincial support did breach a constitutional convention, although Chief Justice Laskin, together with Justices Estey and McIntyre, dissented. Their dissent was, in fact, the result that had been urged on the Court by the federal government and the provinces of Ontario and New Brunswick. We were concerned that a legal requirement of unanimous support of the provinces, as urged by seven of the eight opposing provinces, would make patriation virtually impossible.

In this respect I would like to quote briefly from the notes of my argument as follows: "The many submissions made to the Court to establish a convention requiring the consent of the provinces indicate, in my view, simply that while consensus has been regarded as practically desirable, as a matter of law such consent has not been necessary." I went on to state, "The fact that the provinces have no legal status or powers with respect to amendments to the *BNA Act* is not a happy circumstance for the provinces; it was clear on the law that the provinces are subordinate in this respect. This colonial vestige or gap in our sovereignty remains as a unique historical anomaly. It is an anomaly with both legal and political dimensions." "The legal position as we see it does *in theory* make possible the extreme position, namely, that Parliament could by joint address request the abolition of the provinces and the establishment of a unitary state. In Ontario's view, however, political realities render the possibility of such action completely unrealistic. A joint resolution requesting legislation to establish a unitary state in Canada is simply unthinkable." I further stated that "the proposed joint resolution promises a way out of the impasse and provides that the provinces will have in future a legal role in the amendment procedure which will eliminate their present subordinate powerless position."

Although the historical record does not reveal the extent to which each of the dissenting judges contributed to the dissent, it is generally assumed by constitutional scholars, including my own colleague Justice Robert Sharpe, that it was written by Chief Justice Laskin.

In any event, it has always been my opinion that the dissent on the convention question was principled and well reasoned. First, the Chief Justice pointed out "that the majority who found the breach of a constitutional question did so in reasons that were not responsive to the actual questions before them." The question posed was as follows: "Is it a constitutional convention that the House of Commons and Senate will not request an amendment without first obtaining the agreement of the provinces?" This question was interpreted by almost all the governments as meaning the consent of all the provinces, whereas the majority of the Court found a constitutional convention that required only the substantial agreement of the provinces.

The Laskin dissent continued: "[T]he majority answered the convention question by responding to a question that was not actually before them: the Court may answer only the questions put and may not conjure up questions of its own which in turn would lead to uninvited answers." The following brief quotations are also from the dissent:

> The sanction for non-observance of a convention is political in that disregard of a convention may lead to political defeat, to loss of office, or to other political consequences.
>
> It is not for the courts to raise a convention to the status of a legal principle.
>
> Can it be said that any convention having such clear definition and acceptance concerning provincial participation in the amendment of the Canadian Constitution has developed?
>
> It is abundantly clear, in our view, that the answer must be no. The degree of provincial participation in constitutional amendments has been a subject of lasting controversy in Canadian political life for generations. In cannot be asserted, in our opinion, that any view on this subject has become so clear and so broadly accepted as to constitute a constitutional convention.
>
> Its effect (i.e., the joint resolutions before Parliament and the Senate) is to complete the formation of an incomplete Constitution by supplying its present deficiency, i.e., an amending formula, which will enable the Constitution to be amended in Canada as befits a sovereign state. We are not here faced with an action which in any way has the effect of transforming this federal union into a unitary state. The *in terrorem* argument raising the spectre of a unitary state has no validity.

What I will continue to refer to as the Laskin dissent clearly had the greater appeal to Pierre Trudeau. I well recall the former prime minister's address at the opening of the Bora Laskin Library at the University of Toronto Law School in 1991. While praising Chief Justice Laskin, it also contained an almost venomous attack on the majority of the Court that had found a breach of a constitutional convention. Trudeau's memorable address included these quotations:

> I never talked politics with Bora Laskin, and I have no idea how he voted before he was on the bench, nor how he might have voted had he not become a judge.
>
> I suppose he could be called a conservative in that he showed great respect for our laws and established public institutions. Or a liberal because of his faith in the individual as a rational being and a free agent in society. Or a radical, since he tempered freedom with justice and tended to empower the under-privileged.
>
> What drew me to him when I knew nothing of him except his writings was his great intelligence, combined with a concern for human beings and an apparent desire to live in a society which permitted self-fulfilment to all. Those qualities characterized much of his teaching and many of his judicial decisions. In particular, they contributed mightily to the wisdom of the dissent he formulated along with Justices Estey and McIntyre in the *Patriation Reference*.
>
> That dissent, I shall argue in this address, was not only the better law, but the better common sense.
>
> Indeed, the various judicial opinions that were handed down in the *Patriation Reference* went to the very roots of the Constitution, determining at a particular point in time the nature of the constituent power for Canada, and therefore defining – albeit indirectly – the essence of Canadian sovereignty.
>
> What I find most remarkable about the majority judgment is the number of times their lordships chose to turn a deaf ear and a blind eye to the legal arguments which might have led them in another direction.
>
> First, they had to find that that aspect of the reference dealing with conventions was justiciable. Courts had often in the past refused to answer questions deemed unsuitable for judicial determination. In this case, because conventions are enforceable through the political process, the courts should not have engaged even in declaring their existence. In

choosing to answer the question there is little doubt that the Supreme Court allowed itself – in Professor Hogg's words, "to be manipulated into a purely political role" going beyond the law-making functions that modern jurisprudence agrees the Court must necessarily exercise.

Further, having ignored the uniqueness of the joint address before them, the majority judges had to find some other way of breaking out of the box of unanimity in which their selection of evidence had put them. So they blatantly decided to *invent* a convention calling for "a substantial degree of provincial consent."

But alas! This Court was intent on pressing the political players to accept as binding a rule that only politicians can create and that only the political process should sanction.

They blatantly manipulated the evidence before them so as to arrive at the desired result.

And my purpose in returning to the *Patriation Reference* today is to point out – with the benefit of hindsight – that the minority judgment, couched in what Professor McWhinney has described as Chief Justice Laskin's "clearly identifiable drafting style," was not only the better law but also the wiser counsel.

Finally, the minority's more strictly legal approach lends itself far less to political manipulation of the courts than does the majority. By refusing to go beyond its role as interpreter of the law, the minority avoided the temptation to which the majority succumbed, that of trying to act as political arbiter at a time of political crisis. While there are no doubt differing views of how well the Court performed this role in the *Patriation Reference* it is not a role to which a court of law striving to remain above the day-to-day currents of political life should aspire.

Despite Trudeau's anger in relation to the majority decision on the convention question, he still remained committed to the principle of a dramatic increase in the role of judges in their interpretations of an entrenched *Charter*. The tradition of parliamentary supremacy was being replaced by the principle of the supremacy of the Constitution.

I often wonder what Pierre Trudeau would have thought about the debate over same-sex marriage, where it is alleged that the courts have not remained, in his words, "above the day-to-day currents of political life."

In any event, while I still believe that the Laskin dissent on the convention question was the better law, the majority decision did create the political climate that led to further negotiations and the patriation of the Canadian Constitution.

I also believe that the Laskin dissent on the convention question was influenced by his conviction that a strong federal government was essential to the unity and best interests of our nation. For Bora Laskin, it was only through a strong central government that Canada would be more than a community of communities and more than a mere sum of its individual parts.

◀ 10 ▶

Laskin's Legacy to Law

J.J. MICHEL ROBERT

IN 1961, WHEN I was studying law at the University of Montreal, Professor Jean Beetz taught me constitutional law. He was a meticulous and thorough professor, just as he was a meticulous and thorough judge in his judgments. So, after beginning with the Murray Proclamation in 1763, we moved on to the *Quebec Act* of 1774, the *Constitutional Act* of 1791, the *Union Act* of 1840, the *Colonial Laws Validity Act* of 1865, and, finally, we reached the *Constitution Act* – which was then known as the *British North America Act* of 1867. By the time I finished my law course, we still had not reached the division of powers. Over the next thirty years, I learned that topic on my own while practising constitutional law.

During my studies in Montreal, however, a group of us from the Faculty of Law came to Toronto for a series of lectures in constitutional law given by Professor Bora Laskin. To my great surprise I realized that Quebec and Ontario, though living peacefully side by side, were not living under the same constitution.

I had never heard the expression POGG, or peace, order, and good government. Somehow, the idea of a national dimension in Canada did not create much enthusiasm in Professor Beetz. But I realized the importance of the lesson I learned from Professor Laskin – an expression, really, of the two solitudes of those years – and it served me well for the remainder of my career as a lawyer and a judge.

Move ahead twenty years to September 28, 1981 – the date of the release of the Supreme Court judgment on the *Patriation* case. With great anticipation, the parties involved all went to the courtroom, where we were read not the entire long decision, in both English and French, but just the constitutional questions and the answers to those questions. Nobody understood at all what the decision was! The sound system was poor, so we couldn't catch the words. Even if we could have heard, we couldn't understand the meaning of the words. They ran in this kind of format: "To question (a) of the *Manitoba Reference* case, the answer is positive." "To question (b) of the *Quebec Reference*, the answer is positive in a legal way but negative in a constitutional way."

As we left, the press pushed forward, waiting for our comments. It was, after all, a period in the history of this country when we were very divided politically. My client, Minister of Justice Jean Chrétien, asked me in French, "Have we won?" "Well, we have won and we have lost," I replied. He was very nervous, very tense and he did not appreciate my legal niceties. He answered back in a French phrase I won't repeat, but it showed he had a good Catholic education at "Le Séminaire de Shawinigan" because he knew all the proper words of the Catholic liturgy. So I said to him, "Jean, probably you could tell the press that we have won." "That's okay," he shot back. "I don't want any more" – and he left to meet the crush of reporters. He told the press that we had won, which was true, but it was not the complete truth. We had won probably 60 percent of it and lost 40 percent.

In April 1981, when the case was argued in the Supreme Court, it was especially tense because this case was probably the first of such importance and involved national unity. I counted thirty-one lawyers in the courtroom in all. The clerks were sitting along the wall, and there were no seats for the public. The first lawyer to speak was the one acting for the government of Manitoba. His name was Kerr Twaddle, and he later became a judge of the Manitoba Court of Appeal.

As Justice Bertha Wilson remarked, "Mr. Twaddle was a member of an audible minority." He had a very pronounced Scottish accent, and he began to argue in a thorough, meticulous, but not very eloquent or interesting manner. The Supreme Court justices had just had their microphone system installed and, after a few hours, Justice Estey leaned towards Justice Martland and said in a very low voice, which was captured by the microphones, "We have to find a way to shut down this guy." These words put what we call in French a *douche froide* – a cold shower

– in the courtroom, but it didn't disturb Kerr Twaddle. He kept on arguing for another two hours.

Eight provinces – "the gang of eight" – opposed the federal side, and each one had its own lawyers to argue its case. Then it was the turn of the federal government. I was second in command, in the sense that the first speaker was Mr. Robinette. We had decided that he would make the introduction and I would make the legal argument. As Mr. Robinette spoke, I did not feel that there was total love between Mr. Laskin and him. Mr. Robinette was a bit more conservative than Mr. Laskin. Still, it went quite well because Mr. Robinette was, and probably still is, one of the greatest lawyers in this country. Then it was my turn.

There I was, forty-three years old, and English is not my first language. We had decided that I would argue the case partly in French and partly in English because, in those days, not all the judges of the Supreme Court were bilingual. Only a minority of those judges were bilingual, in fact, and they were not using the simultaneous translation service. So I started to argue, and I was very nervous. My argument had to be preceded by a historical overview of the different attempts to find an amending formula, beginning with the first dominion-provincial conference after the Balfour Declaration in 1927. Mr. Laskin knew the history of the Constitution much better than I did, and he helped me along. He was very kind to me, very sympathetic, and that gave me some assurance and some confidence, and I will always be grateful to him. He probably enabled me to make a good argument.

The argument had to be understood within the context of the constitutional history of Canada, but the question of amending the Constitution by a genuine Canadian amending formula was not possible before the Balfour Declaration. There were many dominion-provincial conferences between 1927 and 1980, but they all ended in failure. Right from the start, the participants took the view that, in order to find an amending formula, they had to follow a unanimity rule. There had to be unanimity between the provinces and the federal government, they claimed, even though it was clear that unanimity was a recipe for failure in finding this new amending formula.

I think this unanimity question triggered the legal decision, or the legal opinion, in this case because the eight provinces were all arguing that, in order to have an amending formula, it had to be unanimous.

And the historical facts all demonstrated that unanimity was probably impossible to achieve. Similarly, in the Meech Lake accord of the following years, even though many of the items in the package did not require unanimous consent, the parties decided to impose on themselves this same unanimity rule – with the resulting failure we all now know. In terms of a legal judgment, the *Patriation* case is unique in that there are two majority decisions. First, it's unique because it's both an appeal and not an appeal. In it, three provincial references were being appealed to the Supreme Court of Canada, so the federal government did not control the questions. The questions were drafted by three provincial governments, but they were acting in consultation with all eight provincial governments involved. They controlled the questions. Then there were three appeals, and the questions were not exactly the same.

There was a fourth, additional, question in the *Newfoundland Reference* which was based on the terms of union. This situation was unique both in itself and when the judgment was delivered. It had two majorities – one legal majority and one conventional (or constitutional) majority and, on close examination, those two opinions were somewhat contradictory. What's important, however, is the result: the compromise reached during the "Night of the Long Knives" – *la nuit des longs couteaux* – of November 1981.

One particularly significant passage may be found in the legal majority decision:

> THIS COURT IS BEING asked, in effect, to enshrine as a legal imperative a principle of unanimity for constitutional amendment to overcome the anomaly-more of an anomaly today than it was in 1867-that the *British North America Act* contain no provisions for effecting amendments by Canadian action alone. Although Saskatchewan has, alone of the eight provinces opposing the federal package embodied in the Resolution, taken a less stringent position, eschewing unanimity but without quantifying the substantial support that it advocates, the provinces, parties to the References and to the appeals here, are entitled to have this Court's primary consideration of their views. (1981) 1 S.C.R. 787.

In my opinion, for Mr. Justice Laskin and the other members of the legal majority, this consideration was very important. If the Court had denied the right of the federal government legally to move forward and request an amendment of the British Parliament, it would have meant that we would forever have needed unanimity in order to act. In all probability, that would have been a recipe for paralysis, and we would still be requesting the Imperial Parliament for modifications to our Constitution.

Between 1867 and 1981, without an amending formula, the Constitution of Canada was amended twenty-two times. The *Patriation* package made it twenty-three. Since then, the Constitution has been amended on only a few occasions, principally under the amending formula that deals with the consent of one province and the consent of the federal Parliament. It was done for the province of Newfoundland and the province of Quebec for linguistic legislation. The so-called general amending formula – seven provinces, 50 percent of the population, with or without financial compensation – has been used only once. I suspect it will not be used frequently because it is very impractical.

We should now look very briefly at the convention, or the constitutional judgment or opinion, on unaminous consent. In the twenty-two amendments that were made to the Constitution between 1867 and 1981, there was no proof that a constitutional convention existed requiring the consent of the provinces. In fact, the only amendment that really got the consent of all the provinces was the Unemployment Insurance amendment of 1940. All the others were made either without unanimous consent or without any consent at all from the provinces.

Although there is no evidence of any convention on unaminous consent, the majority found the origin of the so-called convention "in the principle of the Canadian federation" (*dans le principe de la fédération*). I suspect it was probably Professor Beetz who invented the *principe de la fédération*. And it was Bora Laskin who said, "No. We can move forward and amend our Constitution. There is no legal impediment to do it."

By these means we had the two majority decisions of the Supreme Court which led to the compromise of the night of November 1981. And, when we look at it very carefully, what was this compromise? It was very simple. Because of the majority judgment on the legal question, I suspect, Mr. Trudeau was able to tell his counterparts that he was determined to have a *Charter of Rights and Freedoms* and, also, to have the protection of Aboriginal rights enshrined in the constitutional map. In these decisions, he was able to prevail with his provincial premiers.

At the same time, he had to abandon the amending formula – the one that had been incorporated in the resolution based on some sort of a regional veto. He abandoned that formula, and we ended up with four amending formulas in the Constitution – two of which are very impractical.

What has happened since? Canadian federalism has continued to evolve, but through administrative arrangements and not through changes in the formal Constitution. We probably won't know for another twenty or thirty years whether that has been a positive or a negative change. Still, we owe to Chief Justice Laskin the legal judgment that permitted the entrenchment of the *Charter of Rights and Freedoms* as well as the protection of the Aboriginal rights in this country. To me, these two legacies are more important than all the amending formulas of the world because, aside from the creation of the Canadian confederation in 1867, they are, together, the most important legal revolution in the short history of this country.

We are a very different country from what we were in 1981, and we are progressing in the right direction.

◀ PART FIVE ▶

Administrative & Labour Law

◀ 11 ▶

Chief Justice Laskin's Approach to Administrative Law

STEPHEN T. GOUDGE

ANY DISCUSSION ABOUT CHIEF Justice Laskin's approach to administrative law will have to include his views on bias, so I must begin by making full disclosure. I have admired Bora Laskin for as long as I can remember. Like him, my father, too, was a professor at the University of Toronto – in philosophy, an area that has much in common with law. They were both involved in university affairs, so they saw a lot of each other, and the families became good friends. John Laskin and I have been lifelong friends, and we have been privileged to serve together as colleagues on the Court of Appeal for Ontario.

Turning now to my objective and impartial analysis of his administrative law, what do his judgments tell us about his view of the proper role of administrative decision makers within the broader justice system and the appropriate relationship between them and the courts that are tasked with supervising them? The answer comes in two parts. First, Chief Justice Laskin was one of the pioneers of the notion that, so far as possible, administrative tribunals should be given the freedom to do the work that the legislature set them up to do. Second, however, he felt strongly that they must be required to deal fairly with those affected by their decisions. Both deference and fairness are necessary if the machinery of administrative decision making is to best serve the public interest.

These views undoubtedly reflect many influences, but one suspects three as being of greatest importance. There was his time at the Harvard University of Felix Frankfurter and the New Deal, with its unbounded confidence in rational decision making by expert administrative actors as the best way forward in an increasingly complicated world. There was his fundamental belief in democratic institutions as the best navigator to set the directions that serve the public interest. And there was his own experience in labour law, which, at the end of the Second World War, had emerged as probably the first area of sophisticated administrative law in this country.

I don't think it's any accident that many of Chief Justice Laskin's important administrative law judgments arise in a context of labour law. While his approach to deference is evident in his judgments, his early work as a legal academic reveals that, even then, this idea was percolating in his mind. In his important 1952 article in the *Canadian Bar Review* entitled "Certiorari to Labour Boards: The Apparent Futility of Privative Clauses," his respect for the work of labour boards was clear. He wrote that

> [a]ny serious reading of the numerous labour board cases reported across Canada would establish that the boards are not mere inert pawns of labour unions (or of employers) and that, operating as they do in a controversial and not fully charted field, they take their administrative duties seriously. This is evident in the court cases in which unions have sought to challenge board action. Courts may well hesitate, therefore, before permitting the use of their standards of performance to measure the adequacy of labour board behaviour.[1]

Chief Justice Laskin also believed that the scope of judicial review must be driven by the intention of the legislature, and not the desire of the courts to control the justice system. His pungent words reflect a kind of iconoclasm and leave no doubt of his meaning:

> Buttressed by security of tenure not enjoyed by administrative boards, and surrounded by a tradition of impartiality, which is strong enough to make people accept from judges clichés and social and economic doctrine they would not accept from politicians, members of our superior courts are inhibited in their conduct only by their own sense of self-restraint; and, of course, by the threat of appeal to other judges in the same hierarchy if a right of appeal exists....
>
> We would not, of course, have it otherwise. It does not follow, however, that the sacred privilege of making mistakes, conferred on superior court judges, must be denied to any other tribunal with whose

opinions those judges disagree. Certainly it must not be denied when the legislature clearly (or as clearly as it can) indicates that it will assume the responsibility of checking board misbehaviour and will relieve the courts from that self-imposed duty.[2]

Moving now to a brief review of some of Chief Justice Laskin's important administrative law judgments, I am reminded of the number of towering figures who worked along with him in the legal profession. Not just his judicial colleagues, but counsel as well: in the early cases, John Robinette, Charles Dubin, David Lewis, Walter Williston, Sydney Robins, and the young Ian Scott. In the middle years, Claude Thomson, Frank Callaghan, Brian Crane, and an older Ian Scott. In the later cases, Roy McMurtry, Michel Robert, Mike Goldie, Ian Binnie, the young Robert Sharpe, the now very mature Ian Scott, and the young Chris Paliare.

With the nostalgia of hindsight, the twenty years Chief Justice Laskin spent on the bench seem to represent a truly golden age of litigation. The modern framework of administrative law owes much to his jurisprudence, and I will begin by outlining deference, that is, the scope that courts must give to administrative tribunals so they can do their intended work.

Judicial attitudes to the new decision makers emerging after the Second World War ranged from suspicion to downright hostility. In the mid-twentieth century, the concept of deference had not yet been fully accepted. Early in his time on the Court of Appeal for Ontario, however, Justice Laskin provided a harbinger of the change to come.

In *Regina v. Ontario Labour Relations Board, Ex parte Hannigan*,[3] a case about the board's power to determine the date at which union membership is assessed in a certification case, Justice Laskin was in dissent. He wrote, however, of the need for the board to exercise the powers given to it by the legislature so that it could do its job, and also of its right to be wrong in doing so. While his decision was phrased in the language of jurisdiction – the linguistic currency of administrative law in those days – there is no mistaking the bedrock notion that drove the dissent: where a tribunal is doing the job intended by the legislature, the courts should give it room to carry on.

Justice Laskin took a similar approach the next year in the famous case of *Regina v. Ontario Labour Relations Board, Ex parte Metropolitan Life Insurance Co.*[4] There the issue was the board's right to determine whether certain persons should be considered union members for the purposes of certification and, again, he found that the legislature intended that the court let the board call that issue as it saw it. This time he wasn't in dissent – he carried his colleagues on the Court of Appeal with him. However, the Supreme Court of Canada reversed the decision on the ground that the tribunal had asked itself the wrong question – a tool it borrowed from an infamous English case known as *Anisminic*.[5] This concept would divert administrative law for a number of years.

In 1970 we see another example of Justice Laskin's role in this struggle between deference and intervention. In *Regina v. Tarnopolsky, Ex parte Bell*,[6] Justice Laskin decided that the Ontario Human Rights Commission had been given the power under its legislation to determine whether a dwelling unit was self-contained, so that its owner could not discriminate in renting it out. He concluded that the court could not step in with its own answer and stop the proceedings before the commission had decided the question, and he carried all four of his colleagues on the Court of Appeal with him. Once again, however, the Supreme Court of Canada reversed the decision, finding that the court had every right to control the administrative proceeding and take this decision out of the hands of the commission.

By 1978 Justice Laskin had moved to Ottawa and had become the Chief Justice. In December of that year he wrote another administrative law judgment that signalled that the new era was imminent – *Bradburn v. Wentworth Arms Hotel Limited*,[7] a case involving a judicial review of a labour arbitration award. While he found review to be appropriate in that case, his language is prescient:

> [I]f the arbitration board has given the relevant words of the collective agreement an interpretation which those words could reasonably bear, [the courts] will not interfere with the arbitration board's determination....
>
> I think it is wrong for a court to turn an alleged error of law into a question of jurisdiction, based merely on the court's disagreement with the construction put upon words of the collective agreement by the board of arbitration. If the construction by the board of arbitration defies common sense, it is perforce a construction which the words in question cannot reasonably bear, and interference is warranted by reason of error of law without having to distort the issue by invoking excess of jurisdiction as the ground of interference.[8]

Here we see the modern language of judicial deference, a deference that applies unless the result is unreasonable or defies common sense.

Interestingly this decision was a concurring judgment in which he was joined by two of his colleagues, but not Justice Dickson. Why is that noteworthy? Because in March 1979, only three months later, Justice Dickson wrote the seminal judgment of *C.U.P.E. v. New Brunswick Liquor.*[9] He wrote for the full court. The issue involved the meaning given by the New Brunswick Public Service Labour Relations Board to the provision of the governing act preventing the employer from replacing striking employees with any other employee. In upholding the board's decision, Justice Dickson's reasons have strong echoes of the reasonableness approach of Chief Justice Laskin:

> I have discussed the possible interpretations of [the section] at some length only because, to some, the Board's interpretation may, at first glance, seem unreasonable if one draws too heavily upon private sector experience. Upon a careful reading of the Act, the Board's decision, and the judgments in the Court of Appeal, however, I find it difficult to brand as "patently unreasonable" the interpretation given to [it] by the Board in this case. At a minimum, the Board's interpretation would seem at least as reasonable as the alternative interpretations suggested in the Court of Appeal.[10]

Justice Dickson made it clear that the court should not brand as jurisdictional, and therefore subject to broader curial review, that which may only doubtfully be so. He offered a compelling justification for deference, one that no doubt resonated with the life experience of the Chief Justice. He said:

> The rationale for protection of a labour board's decisions within jurisdiction is straightforward and compelling. The labour board is a specialized tribunal which administers a comprehensive statute regulating labour relations. In the administration of that regime, a board is called upon not only to find facts and decide questions of law, but also to exercise its understanding of the body of jurisprudence that has developed around the collective bargaining system, as understood in Canada, and its labour relations sense acquired from accumulated experience in the area.[11]

This decision, as all administrative lawyers know, was quickly recognized as a watershed in administrative law. It established what Chief

Justice Laskin's judgments had been pointing towards for fifteen years – that expert administrative tribunals doing the tasks assigned to them by the legislature should be accorded judicial deference, provided they are not markedly unreasonable.

For the remainder of his time on the bench, in cases like *Teamsters Union v. Massicotte*[12] and *Canada (Labour Relations Board) v. International Longshoremen's Assn., Local 269*,[13] Chief Justice Laskin never missed an opportunity to underline the importance of this concept of judicial deference. Its patently unreasonable formulation held centre stage in administrative law for some twenty years, and, with its recognition of the importance of privative clauses, tribunal expertise, and, most important, the intention of the legislature, it can fairly be said to have provided the foundation for today's pragmatic and functional approach to the judicial review of administrative decision making.

Although this pioneering work in judicial deference is perhaps Chief Justice Laskin's most important legacy in administrative law, it is far from the only one. Other important judgments provide a slightly different window on his view of the importance of those decision makers in the broader justice system.

One example is *McLeod v. Egan*[14] in 1974, a case that involved an attack on an arbitration award which had interpreted a collective agreement to permit the employer to dictate the weekly hours of work required of employees while ignoring the limits placed on those hours by the *Employment Standards Act*. The Chief Justice, in concurring reasons, agreed that the award should be quashed. He held that although the arbitrator must be correct in doing so, that arbitrator has the right and, indeed, the obligation to construe and apply a statute relevant to the issues to be decided. The authority on this had not been at all clear up to that point, but Chief Justice Laskin obviously felt that, for an administrative tribunal to do its job properly, it must have such a power. Today's decisions (and they are relatively commonplace) that give tribunals the authority to answer questions of law, and to interpret and apply not just other statutes but the *Charter of Rights and Freedoms* itself, find their origins in the *McLeod v. Egan* judgment.

To summarize briefly, Chief Justice Laskin's main legacy in administrative law is his view that tribunals must have the tools to do their job, and they must be given the freedom by the courts, within broad parameters of reasonableness, to do that job as assigned to them by the legislature.

But there is a second part that I want to discuss briefly and that is Chief Justice Laskin's view that what is also clearly required of tribunals is that if they are to be given this space, they must deal fairly with those whose interests they affect.

An early example of this issue came up in 1967 during Justice Laskin's time on the Ontario Court of Appeal in a case called *Bradley and Ottawa Firefighters*.[15] Writing for the court, he decided that, in cases where the result of a labour arbitration in favour of one employee could strip another employee of benefits, the latter is entitled to notice so that he or she has the opportunity to participate. So, in the context of a job competition where an arbitration has been brought on behalf of the loser, the unsuccessful applicant should give notice to the one who succeeded in getting the job since the latter might be displaced by the decision. Justice Laskin viewed this as simply requiring the board to be fair to those who might be significantly and adversely affected by the result. However, the board must not only *be* fair, it must also be vigilant to ensure that it *seems* fair.

In the same vein, he wrote a number of important decisions on the law of bias. For instance, his reasons in *Law Society of Upper Canada v. French*,[16] in 1974 set a course that the benchers here continue to take seriously. He found that the appearance of impartiality was put at an unacceptable level of risk if the same benchers who sit on the discipline committee also participate in convocation when that body considers an appeal from the committee. While that seems obvious today, at the time it was a minority view. In a 1984 tribute article to Chief Justice Laskin, Professor Janisch described Laskin's reasons in *French* as a "glorious dissent."[17]

Two years later, Chief Justice Laskin's view on the appearance of impartiality being essential to the integrity of administrative decision making got majority support in *Committee for Justice and Liberty v. Canada (National Energy Board)*[18] – the *Marshall Crowe* case. Chief Justice Laskin concluded for the majority that Crowe's previous involvement with the pipeline proposal his board was required to consider gave rise to a reasonable apprehension of bias, making it unfair for him to sit. He said in clarion language that this principle is "grounded in a firm concern that there be no lack of public confidence in the impartiality of adjudicative agencies."[19]

To complete this story, let me turn to the seminal case of *Nicholson*.[20] It's as famous in its own way as *New Brunswick Liquor* because it introduced the concept of fairness into our jurisprudence. Chief Justice Laskin oversaw the birth of the concept by applying it to the exercise of discretion by administrative decision makers. While it requires less than the full scope of natural justice, it entitles those affected by the exercise of discretion to be treated fairly and not arbitrarily. In that case, a provisionary constable had been discharged without being told why or without being given the chance to make submissions on his own behalf. In Chief Justice Laskin's opinion, imposing a duty of fairness on the Board of Police Commissioners would promote better decision making by the board, accord fair treatment to the constable, and justify the board's right or power to dismiss without being interfered with by the courts. As he said:

> In my opinion, the appellant should have been told why his services were no longer required and given an opportunity, whether orally or in writing as the Board might determine, to respond. The Board itself, I would think, would wish to be certain that it had not made a mistake in some fact or circumstance which it deemed relevant to its determination. Once it had the appellant's response, it would be for the Board to decide on what action to take, without its decision being reviewable elsewhere, always premising good faith. Such a course provides fairness to the appellant, and it is fair as well to the Board's right, as a public authority to decide, once it had the appellant's response, whether a person in his position should be allowed to continue in office to the point where his right to procedural protection was enlarged.[21]

From this beginning, the duty of fairness has matured into what is now a central concept in our administrative law. It's yet another legacy from Chief Justice Laskin, and perhaps as important in its own way as judicial deference. Certainly, it is central to his view that administrative decision makers must proceed fairly, overall.

For Chief Justice Laskin, fair treatment and deference are very much complementary concepts in administrative law. The public interest is best served when administrative decision makers are allowed by the courts to do the tasks expected of them and, in doing so, act fairly to those they affect. While each notion is itself of fundamental importance, the power of the two acting in concert is perhaps the greatest lesson he left with us.

In the words of my law clerk, Caroline Libman, who helped me in preparing this essay, Chief Justice Laskin's legacy in administrative law is unparalleled. His approach to deference gave administrative bodies the room they needed to live; his approach to fairness gave them the legitimacy they needed to thrive. We are all enormously in his debt.

NOTES

1 Bora Laskin, "Certiorari to Labour Boards: The Apparent Futility of Privative Clauses" *Canadian Bar Review* 30 (1952): 986 at 1003.
2 Ibid. at 990–91.
3 *Regina v. Ontario Labour Relations Board, Ex parte Hannigan et al.*, [1967] 2 OR 469 (CA).
4 *Regina v. Ontario Labour Relations Board, Ex parte Metropolitan Life Insurance Co.*, [1969] 1 OR 412 (CA).
5 *Anisminic Ltd. v. Foreign Compensation Commission and Another*, [1969] 2 WLR 163 (HL).
6 *Regina v. Tarnopolsky, Ex parte Bell*, [1970] 2 OR 672 (CA).
7 *Bradburn v. Wentworth Arms Hotel Limited*, [1979] 1 SCR 846.
8 Ibid. at 849.
9 *Canadian Union of Public Employees Local 963 v. New Brunswick Liquor Corp.*, [1979] 2 SCR 227.
10 Ibid. at 242.
11 Ibid. at 235–36.
12 *International Brotherhood of Teamsters, Chauffeurs, Warehousemen and Helpers of America, Teamsters Union Local 938 v. Massicotte*, [1982] 1 SCR 710.
13 *Canada (Labour Relations Board) v. International Longshoremen's Assn., Local 269*, [1983] 1 SCR 245.
14 *McLeod v. Egan*, [1975] 1 SCR 517.
15 *Re Bradley et al. and Ottawa Professional Fire Fighters Association et al.*, [1967] 2 OR 311 (CA).
16 *Law Society of Upper Canada v. French*, [1975] 2 SCR 767.
17 H.N. Janisch, "Bora Laskin and Administrative Law: An Unfinished Journey" *University of Toronto Law Review* 35 (1985): 557 at 575.
18 *Committee for Justice and Liberty v. Canada (National Energy Board)*, [1978] 1 SCR 369.
19 Ibid. at 391.
20 *Nicholson v. Haldimand Norfolk (Regional) Police Commissioners*, [1979] 1 SCR 311.
21 Ibid. at 328.

◀ 12 ▶

Laskin's Contribution to Labour Law

CHRIS G. PALIARE[1]

LABOUR LAW WAS ONE of Bora Laskin's passions, where he was both a labour relations visionary and a pragmatist. He was committed to a system of labour law that reflected the reality of labour relations in the plant and promoted practical, balanced solutions for the efficient resolution of industrial conflict. He recognized the importance of implementing a viable and credible alternative dispute resolution mechanism (long before the phrase ADR was coined) in order to resolve industrial strife.

Laskin took a nascent labour relations statutory scheme and made it work. He brought to it his commitment to social justice and fairness, his labour relations experience and his legal expertise – so much so that both labour and management, regardless of the result, could stand back and say his arbitration decision was fair and just. In one of his earliest awards, he set out his philosophy of arbitral decision making in these terms: "As I see my duty in this case, it is to find a basis of decision which will be conducive to orderly collective bargaining and which can consistently with that objective find support in the facts of this case as revealed by the evidence, and in accepted principles and practices prevailing in similar situations in organized industry."[2]

Laskin believed that the amalgam of these values was central to protecting the newly created postwar collective-bargaining regime. These values were essential to ensure bilateral acceptability of the arbitration process, which, by legislation, was now a final and binding determination of disputes at the workplace.

There were at least three phases to Laskin's contribution to labour law: Laskin as theorist, as arbitrator, and as judge. With respect to Laskin as theorist, he promoted a new approach to labour law in Canada that sought to oust the old common law doctrines of individual employment contracts, all of which failed to recognize the collective aspect of labour. Rather, he advocated an approach that reflected the new social reality of industrial relations – collective action – and he argued that the old, libertarian, common law principles of individual employee contracts were inapplicable in the face of the newly recognized inequality of bargaining power between employer and employee.[3] For that reason, he said, only a collective-bargaining regime (enacted through legislation) could sufficiently protect the workers' legitimate interests. Laskin was responding to the perceived lack of regulation that permitted the capitalist excesses at the root of the Great Depression.

For Laskin, the centrepiece of redressing the imbalance between capital and labour was through legislation akin to the *Wagner Act*, which was passed as part of the New Deal in 1935 in the United States. Before the passage of similar legislation creating a collective-bargaining regime in Ontario in 1943, Professor Laskin wrote articles about his vision of labour law. His view was informed by his studies at Harvard University in 1936–37, where he was exposed to the intellectual rigours of Felix Frankfurter, Roscoe Pound, Oliver Wendell Holmes, and Benjamin Cardozzo.

It also must be remembered that, while Laskin was at Harvard, President Roosevelt's New Deal was being implemented in the context of trying to formulate a recovery for the devastation caused by the Great Depression. A central topic at the time was determining a mechanism for accommodating the interests of labour within a capitalist economy. As a result of his experience in the United States, Laskin wrote a number of articles setting out his views once he returned to Canada. In a 1938 *Canadian Bar Review* article, six years before collective-bargaining legislation was passed in Ontario, Laskin wrote about the inequality of bargaining power for vulnerable people in our society:

> The legislation therefore, in coming to the aid of the workman, widow, infant or lunatic, is lending its support to those who, in the opinion of the community as a whole, are incapable of self-care because of their greater susceptibility to exploitation, sharp practices, fraud or economic

pressure, or because such near-helpless classes represent interests which the public policy of the state deems essential to preserve.[4]

In addition to economic justice in the workplace, Laskin viewed the collective agreement as a tool for ensuring the meaningful participation of employees at work. In a 1940 article in the *Canadian Bar Review*, he talked about ensuring that employees had a voice in the ordering of their employment relationship – a revolutionary concept at the time.[5]

LASKIN AS ARBITRATOR

ONCE A LEGISLATIVE COLLECTIVE-BARGAINING mechanism was in place, Laskin acted as an arbitrator in hundreds of arbitration cases, approximately 137 of which are reported. Consistent with the views about which he had written, Laskin refused to interpret collective agreements using outmoded common law principles applicable to individual employment contracts. Rather, he stated: "The acceptance of a collective bargaining regime involves the acceptance by the parties of assumptions which are entirely alien to an era of individual bargaining."[6]

In those early days of collective bargaining, many of the arbitrations were decided by County Court judges mechanically applying principles of interpretation that had no place in a collective-bargaining regime. Those County Court judges developed a "reserved rights theory" that favoured management by holding that all powers not specifically assigned in the collective agreement remain vested in the employer. Laskin fought the reserved-rights theory. He maintained a commitment to a reasonable approach that would make the system work. That is not to say that Laskin favoured labour over management. For example, he held in one of his cases that "unilateral action by the employer is still open if it is compatible with the integrity and preservation of the bargaining unit."[7] In addition, in another case he decided that an employee did not have an unchallengeable right to refuse to perform overtime because the employee "is part of the enterprise."[8]

In acting as an arbitrator, Laskin took seriously the legislative mandate that arbitration was to offer final and binding resolutions for labour disputes. This logic led him to his famous *Polymer Corporation* award, in which he concluded that arbitrators had the right to award damages for breach of a collective agreement, a proposition that, in a post-*Weber* context, we now take for granted. But, before the *Polymer* decision, most arbitrators took the position that even though a breach of a collective agreement had been established, the arbitrator had no jurisdiction to award damages for the breach unless the terms of the collective agreement expressly gave the arbitrator that jurisdiction.

Laskin held that awarding damages was not a matter of jurisdiction but, rather, part of the board's remedial authority in making a final and binding award. Simply to give a declaratory award that a collective agreement had been breached was, to Laskin, an illusory and hollow victory. For him, where there was a breach, there had to be a remedy. Ironically, in *Polymer*, where the union had engaged in a wildcat strike, the award of damages was against the union for breach of the "no strike" provision of the collective agreement.

Awards such as *Polymer* were part of Laskin's larger mission to actualize the legislative goal of an independent and efficient labour arbitration system. Not only was his approach groundbreaking but also it has prevailed. For proof, we need only look at the enormous influence he had on two arbitrators who continued this work after Laskin's appointment – Harry Arthurs and Paul Weiler.

LASKIN AS JUDGE

FINALLY, AS PROFESSOR LASKIN became Mr. Justice Laskin, he continued to support the pre-eminence of collective bargaining as a fundamental right and principle of our labour relations scheme.

Harrison v. Carswell is a perfect example, although Justice Laskin was writing in dissent. The issue was simple. Could a picketer who was engaged in peaceful picketing during a lawful strike be convicted under the *Petty Trespass Act* because she refused to leave the front of the store where she was picketing? The store happened to be located in a shopping centre. The action was commenced by the owner of the shopping centre, not the tenant who was being struck. In fact, it is unlikely that the tenant would have been able to bring any action against the lawful picketer.

Justice Laskin's dissent was both powerful and passionate. It embraced the principles he had espoused in the early days of seeking an appropriate dispute-resolution mechanism in a new collective bargaining regime in the 1940s and 50s. He said, in dealing with the intersection of the principles of trespass and the lawful right to picket: "[T]he present case involves a search for an appropriate legal framework for new social facts which show up in the inaptness of an old doctrine (trespass) developed upon a completely different social foundation."[9]

Laskin would have upheld the quashing of the conviction of the picketer.

Then, in a second case, *Hoogendorn*, regarding a "religious objector" who refused a compulsory checkoff for union dues, when he was in the Court of Appeal, he made this observation:

> I find nothing admirable in the applicant's stand. Our society secures to everyone the right to adhere to a religion of his choice and to hold to a self-determined political creed. It does not, however, give liberty to insist on religious conviction or political creed or both in a context which the law does not regard as relevant to their free enjoyment and as a ground for thwarting agreements binding on all irrespective of religious or political persuasion. This is presently the case of labour relations.[10]

Although speaking for the majority in the Court of Appeal, this case was overturned in the Supreme Court of Canada on a natural justice issue related to whether Hoogendorn had received proper notice of the arbitration.

Finally, any discussion of Justice Laskin and the impact he had on labour law as a judge would not be complete without a brief mention of his view that significant deference should be paid to the decision of arbitrators. With all the attendant temptation to overrule an arbitrator's clumsily worded award, Justice Laskin was consistent in his approach to the judicial review of labour-arbitration awards. He maintained his belief in the deference that ought to be accorded to labour arbitrators and explained this principle:

> [I]f the general law of arbitration and reviewability of awards is to be applied to labour-management arbitrations under collective agreements, where the Courts have no original jurisdiction, it appears to me to be plain sense to confine interference to what, for want of precise definition, I would call gross error. Especially in a situation of ongoing collective bargaining relations, where the parties themselves legislate for the common enterprise and provide their own supervisory and admin-

istrative machinery without judicial oversight, they should be equally left pretty well alone with their adjudicative machinery."[11]

NOTES

1. I would like to acknowledge the great assistance I received from Danny Kastner (a summer student) and my partner, Robert Centa, on the research and preparation of this essay.
2. Laskin in *McQuay-Norris Manufacturing* (1947), 1 LAC 81, at 85.
3. Brian Langille and David Beatty, "Bora Laskin and Labour Law: From Vision to Legacy," *University of Toronto Law Journal* 35 (1985): 672 at 680–85.
4. Bora Laskin, "The Protection of Interests by Statute and the Problem of 'Contracting Out,'" *Canadian Bar Review* 16 (1938): 669 at 674.
5. Bora Laskin, "Right of a Union Officer to be Present at Employer's Investigation of Employee's Breach of Discipline" *Canadian Bar Review* 18 (1940): 810 at 811.
6. *Peterboro Lock Manufacturing* (1953), 4 LAC 1499 at 1502.
7. *Falconbridge Nickel Mines Ltd.* (1958), 8 LAC 276 at 282.
8. *Re United Packinghouse Workers and Toronto Abattoir Ltd.* (1963), 13 LAC 339.
9. Laskin, in dissent, *Harrison v. Carswell* (1975), 62 DLR (3d) 68 (SCC) at 75.
10. *Re Hoogendorn & Greening Metal Products & Screening Co.*, [1967] 1 OR 712 (Ont. CA) at 723 (*contra, Bradley v. Ottawa Firefighters*).
11. *Bell Canada v. OPEIU (local 131)* 37 DLR (3d) 561 (1973) at 570–71.

◄ PART SIX ►

Constitutional Law, Federalism, & Individual Rights

◂ 13 ▸

Laskin and the Constitutional Protection of Rights and Freedoms[1]

ROBERT J. SHARPE

BORA LASKIN, A GREAT scholar and a great judge, is remembered for the contribution he made to the constitutional protection of rights and freedoms. It's interesting to compare what he said about the subject, first as a legal scholar, and then as a judge.

Throughout his career, Bora Laskin was a passionate defender of civil liberties. He was a founding member of the Canadian Civil Liberties Association; he taught and wrote on civil liberties before it was fashionable to do so; and, in his judicial work, he made an enormous contribution, courageously giving life to the *Canadian Bill of Rights*. As both a legal scholar and a judge, Bora Laskin was consistent in his belief in the need to protect fundamental rights and freedoms under the Constitution. He saw these rights and freedoms as an essential underpinning of democratic government. However, we will discover a dramatic change in his views about how the Constitution could best protect those rights and freedoms as he proceeded from the academy to the bench.

Laskin, the legal scholar, advocated a federalism-based theory of civil liberties that placed the most important rights and freedoms within exclusive federal competence and beyond the reach of the provinces. As a scholar, he accorded a limited role to the courts for the protection of fundamental human rights and resisted the idea of an entrenched charter of rights. As a judge, he was the author of powerful, passionate, and persuasive opinions, almost always in dissent, giving full effect to the *Canadian Bill of Rights*. He elevated that statutory instrument to "quasi-constitutional status,"[2] which made it capable of overriding federal legislation, and insisted, against the prevailing views of timid and conservative colleagues, that the *Bill of Rights* provided objective, manageable standards against which to measure federal laws.

These changes in Laskin's thinking parallel Canada's constitutional evolution from our pre-1982 preoccupation with federalism, through the transitional *Canadian Bill of Rights* phase, and into the post-1982 *Charter* era. Regrettably, Laskin did not live into the era of the *Canadian Charter of Rights and Freedoms*, but his vision of protecting fundamental rights and freedoms as a constitutional matter, whether under federalism or under the *Canadian Bill of Rights*, had significant influence on Canada's decision to adopt the *Charter*. Despite his academic opposition to the *Bill of Rights*, in both his academic and his judicial work, especially his *Bill of Rights* dissents, Bora Laskin laid the foundation for the *Charter*. In many ways, he made the *Charter* possible.

LASKIN THE SCHOLAR

THE CENTRAL FEATURE OF Bora Laskin's academic work in this area was his distinctive federalism-based theory of civil liberties.[3] He saw civil liberties as a "matter" for the purposes of analyzing the constitutional competence of the federal and provincial governments. When it came to the protection of civil liberties (as with other matters), Laskin had enormous confidence in the Parliament of Canada and was sceptical about giving too much power to the provinces. In his view, there was a category of civil liberties that fell within exclusive federal competence and beyond the jurisdiction of the provinces.

Laskin's federalism-based theory was never accepted, and however unorthodox it might seem today to argue that civil liberties were exclusively within federal competence, he believed it with passion. How, he asked, could Canada have a Constitution that did not protect civil liberties? In a 1955 article, he wrote that to suggest that civil liberties was not a discrete matter within exclusive federal competence would be "repellent to our institutions and to our political and social traditions, and thus alien to the very sources of our constitutional law. It would amount to a rejection of civil liberties as an independent group of values in our society and reduce them to a parasitic position."[4]

In the pre-1982 era of Canadian constitutional law, Laskin's method for protecting civil liberties under the Constitution was to consider them to be a matter for constitutional analysis and place them within exclusive federal competence, under the control of the level of government he trusted. Several shocking invasions of civil liberties at the provincial level only bolstered his belief that it was safer to trust Parliament than the provinces to protect political civil liberties and legal rights.[5]

So strong was Laskin's confidence in protecting civil liberties by establishing exclusive federal power over the subject that, as an academic, he actually opposed the idea of an entrenched charter of rights. He did not accept the "implied Bill of Rights theory," which placed certain fundamental rights and freedoms beyond the reach of both the federal and the provincial governments.[6] He resisted any limitations on federal power because he believed that positive measures which could only come from legislation were required to achieve economic justice and to protect equality. His federalism-based theory already protected civil liberties from what he perceived to be the real threat, the provinces, and he feared that entrenching civil liberties against federal incursion would unduly limit and constrain the power of Parliament to achieve social justice.

Surprising as it may seem to those more familiar with his judicial work, as an academic Bora Laskin was quite hostile to the *Canadian Bill of Rights*, the very document he made so much of as a judge. As Laskin the academic saw it, the *Bill of Rights* turned his idea of how best to protect civil liberties on its head. It applied only to federal laws and did not limit the powers of the provinces. By binding only itself and leaving the provinces untouched, Parliament was abdicating its plenary power over the matter of civil liberties.[7]

The second central feature of Laskin's scholarly writing on civil liberties I wish to consider is his identification and ranking of four categories of civil liberties.[8] These categories are essential to understanding his federalism-based theory of civil liberties.

The first category, and to Laskin the most important, is what he called political civil liberties. These are the rights and freedoms associated with the operation of our parliamentary institutions, rights and freedoms that are the necessary underpinnings of parliamentary democracy – freedom of expression, freedom of association, freedom of the press, freedom of conscience and religion.

The second category encompassed the civil liberties he associated with the legal order – what we tend to refer to now as legal rights: freedom from arbitrary arrest, right to counsel, right to impartial adjudication, right against self-incrimination, and the like. Laskin gave these first two categories high value and, applying his federalism-based theory, he argued that they were a matter within exclusive federal competence and beyond the reach of the provinces.

His third and fourth categories were contrasting and to some extent conflicting. The third was economic civil liberty. I have never entirely understood why he included economic liberty as a class of civil liberty worthy of protection. He identified it with the philosophy of laissez-faire economics, to which he was, if anything, hostile. In the end, I think that he was just being honest, recognizing that, as the courts tended to protect economic civil liberty, he had to include it. He did make it clear that the protection of economic civil liberty was not something he encouraged and that, indeed, he tended to favour an active government role to constrain powerful economic forces in order to bring about economic justice.

Laskin called his fourth category "liberty in a human rights or egalitarian sense."[9] He gave this category wide definition. It extended beyond anti-discrimination to include matters such as unemployment insurance, state medicare, and state-provided education. Laskin recognized that there was a strong tension between his third and fourth categories of civil liberties. He described equality rights as "the antithesis of the economic individualism that deprecated state interference in business or social relations."[10]

Although Laskin gave "liberty in a human rights or egalitarian sense" high value, he was decidedly unenthusiastic about according any significant role to the courts to ensure its protection. Rather, he assigned the courts a very limited role in protecting equality, quite unlike what we have come to expect of the courts under the *Charter* and even from what Laskin himself would later advocate as a judge under the *Canadian Bill of Rights*. There are several reasons why Laskin the scholar minimized the judicial role in the quest for equality. He was a social democrat at heart, and he simply did not trust the courts in the quest for social and economic justice. In his scholarly writings, he did not isolate legal equality from the broader panoply of social welfare rights. Given the nature and breadth of the matters included in his fourth category, it is hardly surprising that he did not look to the courts to advance the values it embraced.

Laskin's distrust of the courts as a suitable vehicle for fostering economic justice or equality was also the product of other factors. He had an active career as a labour arbitrator and was all too familiar with the dismal record of the courts in the area of collective bargaining. He had also been closely involved in litigation challenging the validity of racist restrictive covenants and knew that the record of the courts in this area was far from pristine.[11] Laskin was also strongly influenced by his experience as a graduate student at Harvard University in the 1930s. There he had been exposed to Felix Frankfurter and other leading American scholars who fought against the judicial activism of the United States Supreme Court which had threatened to undo the New Deal's post-Depression plan for economic social justice. All these factors combined to make Laskin reluctant to place too much power in the hands of judges. He believed that progressive and positive measures were needed to bring about equality, and he thought that those measures could be achieved only through legislation, not adjudication. His experience as a scholar and as an activist led him to distrust the courts in this area, and he feared that an enhanced judicial role would equip the courts with the power to interfere with progressive legislation.

Laskin's relegation of equality to an inferior position in the hierarchy of civil liberties values, despite his passionate belief in the value of equality itself, was also driven in part by his core theory that civil liberties were a matter for purposes of constitutional analysis under sections 91 and 92 of the *British North America Act, 1867*. As a matter of legal doctrine, his federalism-based theory of civil liberties simply could not embrace equality. It was plain beyond argument that a wide range of social and economic issues, as well as anti-discrimination legislation in relation to housing, employment, and provincial public services, fell squarely within provincial competence.

To some extent we are all the product of our times, and Laskin was no exception. In the 1950s, when he was developing his academic theory for the protection of civil liberties, several factors led him to trust Parliament over the provinces with respect to the first two categories – political civil liberties and legal rights – and to trust Parliament over the courts with respect to the third and forth categories – economic liberty and equality.

Although Laskin's federalism-based theory was never accepted, it did present a coherent process-based vision of how best to defend and advance civil liberties and social justice. The courts, as defenders of the legal and constitutional framework, would enforce the fundamental values necessary for a free, orderly, rational, and tolerant democratic debate. Parliament and the legislatures would be assigned the primary role of resolving the substantive issues of equality and of economic and social justice through the democratic process.

As a legal scholar, Laskin did not write at great length about the idea of an entrenched bill of rights, but he made it clear that it was a development he did not favour. When he reviewed *Civil Liberties and Canadian Federalism*[12] by F.R. Scott, another dominant constitutional scholar of his era, he disagreed with Scott's argument that rights and freedoms should be specifically entrenched in the Constitution. He wrote that not all civil liberties are "equally deserving of constitutional enshrinement. Those that are – for example, the political freedoms – fall within federal competence."[13] In his 1959 article, provocatively entitled "An Inquiry into the Diefenbaker *Bill of Rights*," Laskin attacked the *Canadian Bill of Rights* as an irresponsible abdication of federal responsibility because it failed to remove civil liberties from the reach of provincial legislation. He treated the notion that the *Bill of Rights* could override federal legislation with contempt: "Will the Bill as a later enactment be regarded as modifying all pre-existing inconsistent legislation which must be 'applied' to conform with the provisions of the Bill? ... It would be a hardy court, indeed, that would so treat existing legislation."[14]

LASKIN THE JUDGE

BY THE TIME OF Laskin's appointment to the bench, the *Bill of Rights* had been adopted, the *Drybones* case[15] had been decided, and Laskin had accepted that the law had changed. His academic theory had not prevailed, and he scrupulously refrained from attempting to enforce judicially the federalism-based theory he had advanced as a scholar.[16]

Laskin accepted that he was now called upon to work within a changed and changing legal framework. As he saw it, his passion for civil liberties could flourish within this framework, although in a manner different from that he had advocated as an academic. He wrote a long list of powerful and courageous *Bill of Rights* dissents in which he sought to elevate to quasi-constitutional status the very document he had ridiculed as a scholar. At the same time, however, Laskin insisted upon discipline and principle, with an emphasis on a tightly reasoned approach that stressed the need for manageable judicial standards for *Bill of Rights* interpretation and application.

Laskin the judge was even prepared to give full force and effect to the *Bill of Rights* equality guarantee, a development few would have predicted from his academic writings. In *Lavell*,[17] he described the denial of "Indian status" to an Aboriginal woman who had married a non-Aboriginal man as the "statutory excommunication of Indian women,"[18] and he decried the abandonment of *Drybones* by the majority: "I have no disposition to reject what was decided in *Drybones*," he wrote, "that the *Canadian Bill of Rights* was more than a mere interpretation statute whose terms would yield to a contrary intention; it had paramount force when a federal enactment conflicted with its terms, and it was the incompatible federal enactment which had to give way."[19]

Lavell was but the start of a series of strong dissents insisting that the courts had the power to strike down discriminatory legislation and reading the promise of equality in the *Bill of Rights* as being more or less the equivalent to a fully fledged and entrenched equal protection clause. In *Burnshine*,[20] Laskin railed against the majority's notorious "valid federal objective" approach, which essentially gave Parliament a free hand to adopt whatever classifications it deemed necessary to gut equality rights of any meaning. In *Canard*,[21] a case dealing with federal legislation that disqualified "Indians" from acting as the administrators of their deceased spouses' estates, Laskin departed from the majority view that this restriction was nothing more than a scheme for the administration of "Indian" property. He labelled it as offensive racial discrimination. Laskin adopted the opinion of the Manitoba Court of Appeal, where Justice Dickson had written that the legislation "placed a legal road-block in the way of one particular racial group, placing that racial group in a position of inequality before the law."[22] The majority view, he concluded, was directly contrary to the *Bill of Rights* and could not be justified as a proper exercise of federal legislative competence with respect to "Indian" property. Again, in *MacKay*,[23] Laskin dissented from a majority opinion premised on the "valid federal objective" approach and would have struck down legislation providing for a trial by court martial of military personnel: "I cannot conceive that there can be in this country two such disparate ways of trying offences against the ordinary law, depending on whether the accused is a member of the armed forces or is not."[24]

But Laskin did not entirely abandon the deferential attitude reflected in his scholarly writing. In particular, he took a decidedly "hands-off" and protective approach when it came to challenging the authority of statutory human rights commissions charged with the responsibility for enforcing anti-discrimination legislation and the advancement of equality.[25] Perhaps most notable in this regard is his decision in *Bhaudauria*,[26] refusing to recognize a common law tort of discrimination, a move that in his view would have undermined the regime established by the legislature to protect against discrimination.

Laskin also wrote forceful opinions favouring vigorous judicial protection of legal rights. In *Brownridge*,[27] he held that the denial of the accused's right to consult legal counsel before complying with a police demand for a breathalyzer sample amounted to a reasonable excuse to refuse the sample. In *Hogan*,[28] without the benefit of section 24(2) of the *Charter*, Laskin advocated a departure from the common law rule permitting the admission of illegally obtained evidence to vindicate the rights guaranteed by the *Bill of Rights*: "The contention that it is the duty of the courts to get at the truth has in it too much of the philosophy of the end justifying the means."[29] He defended the presumption of innocence against legislative incursion in *Appelby*[30] and *Shelley*,[31] resisting the narrow majority view that the *Bill of Rights* did nothing more than reflect the common law rule that allowed for statutory exceptions.

In *Miller and Cockriell*,[32] Laskin gave "cruel and unusual punishment" meaningful content. Although he rejected the argument that capital punishment for murder of police officers or prison guards constituted cruel and unusual punishment, he also rejected the majority's simplistic frozen-rights theory that denuded the *Bill of Rights* of meaning: "[T]he legislation of Parliament falls to be tested as to its operative effect by what the *Bill of Rights* prescribes; otherwise, the *Bill of Rights* becomes merely an interpretation statute, yielding to a contrary intention in legislation measured against it."[33] He insisted that it is "the duty of the Court not to whittle down the protections of the *Canadian Bill of Rights* by a narrow construction of what is a quasi-constitutional document."[34]

Laskin cautioned, however, that there were limits on the reach of the *Bill of Rights* and that, without "objective and manageable standards by which a Court should be guided,"[35] deference to the will of Parliament was appropriate. His passion for civil liberties was a legal one – measured and controlled. In *Curr*, he flatly refused to read the *Bill of Rights* "due process of law" guarantee as an invitation to monitor the substantive content of legislation, and he cautioned against entering "the bog of legislative policy-making."[36] In *Morgentaler*,[37] Laskin dismissed a *Bill of Rights* challenge to the *Criminal Code* abortion prohibition, rejecting arguments virtually identical to those that would succeed ten years later under the entrenched *Charter of Rights and Freedoms*.[38] Here, as in *Curr*, we see Laskin adhering to the view he held as an academic: the courts should act as the referees for democracy to ensure that we have the necessary ingredients for healthy and lively debate, leaving the substantive outcomes to be determined by Parliament.

BORA LASKIN AND THE *CHARTER OF RIGHTS AND FREEDOMS*

BORA LASKIN LIVED TO see the entrenchment of the *Charter of Rights and Freedoms*, but, unfortunately, we do not know what he would have made of the *Charter* as a judge. His example teaches us, however, that one's thinking must necessarily change with the times. There can be little doubt that Laskin's own thinking would have continued to evolve and that he would have been a superb interpreter of the *Charter*.

What we do know is that Laskin's work as a legal scholar and as a judge had an important influence on Canada's decision to entrench the *Charter of Rights* in the Constitution and on the vigorous interpretation his successors on the Supreme Court of Canada have afforded the rights and freedoms it secures. His passionate commitment to the values of fundamental human rights and freedoms, and the need to ensure their protection under the Constitution, was a vision to which he remained faithful and committed throughout his career. Both as a scholar and as a judge, Laskin was courageous. He fearlessly took positions that ran against the prevailing conservative legal thinking of his times. His commitment to fundamental rights and freedoms was tied to and controlled by his insistence on adherence to principle, to objective and manageable judicial standards.

For Laskin, rights did not exist in isolation. They existed as part of a process – and that process was democracy. Laskin the legal scholar and Laskin the judge argued that the constitutional protection of fundamental rights and freedoms was not only consistent with democracy but the essential underpinning of democracy. Throughout his life, he strove to achieve a central role for the courts in ensuring an open democratic process, in protecting the individual dignity of every citizen, and by ensuring the right to be treated fairly and without discrimination. For Laskin, the constitutional protection of rights also respects the central role of both Parliament and democratic choice to achieve substantive justice.

Bora Laskin was a man capable of changing with the times. His thinking evolved as Canada proceeded from its constitutional preoccupation with federalism, to the transitional era of the *Canadian Bill of Rights*, and finally to the *Charter of Rights and Freedoms*. In the final analysis, Laskin presented Canada with an attractive and appealing constitutional vision for the protection of fundamental human rights and, in the end, Canada accepted the Laskin vision. The enactment of the *Charter* represented a clear repudiation of the narrow formalism of the Supreme Court's majority judgments under the *Bill of Rights*. Read against Laskin's powerfully persuasive dissents, those majority opinions, although perhaps justified in part by the *Bill of Rights*' lack of constitutional pedigree, were disappointing and discouraging to those committed to the protection of civil liberties in Canada. The enactment of the *Charter* can be seen as an embrace of Laskin's dissenting *Bill of Rights* opinions. Laskin's disciplined, tightly reasoned approach, based on "objective and manageable standards," fuelled with his passion for human dignity under the law, made an irresistible case for the constitutional protection of fundamental rights and freedoms. We owe him a great deal.

NOTES

1. This essay draws freely on R.J. Sharpe, "Bora Laskin and Civil Liberties," *University of Toronto Law Journal* 35 (1985): 632, where many of the points made here are developed more fully.
2. *R. v. Hogan*, [1975] 2 SCR 574.
3. Bora Laskin, "Our Civil Liberties – The Role of the Supreme Court," [1955] *Queen's Quarterly* (1955): 455.
4. Ibid., 463.
5. See, for example, *Reference Re Alberta Legislation*, [1938] SCR 100; *Saumur v. Quebec (City)*, [1953] 2 SCR 299; *Switzman v. Elbing*, [1957] SCR 285; *Roncarelli v. Duplessis*, [1959] SCR 121.
6. See *Switzman v. Elbing*.
7. Bora Laskin, "An Inquiry into the Diefenbaker *Bill of Rights*," *Canadian Bar Review* 37 (1959): 77.
8. See ibid.; Bora Laskin, *Canadian Constitutional Law*, 2nd ed. (Toronto: Carswell, 1960), 942.
9. Laskin, "An Inquiry into the Diefenbaker *Bill of Rights*," 81.
10. Ibid., 81–82.
11. *Noble v. Alley*, [1951] SCR 64; *Re Drummond Wren*, [1945] OR 778.
12. F.R. Scott, *Civil Liberties and Canadian Federalism* (Toronto: University of Toronto Press, 1959).
13. Bora Laskin, review of F.R. Scott, *Civil Liberties and Canadian Federalism*, in *University of Toronto Law Journal* 13 (1959–60): 289.
14. Laskin, "An Inquiry into the Diefenbaker *Bill of Rights*," 132.
15. *R . v. Drybones*, [1970] SCR 282.
16. See *Nova Scotia Board of Censors v. McNeil*, [1978] SCR 662, and *Canada (Attorney General) v. Montreal (City)*, [1978] 2 SCR 770, where Laskin refrained from advancing his academic views, a point discussed at greater length in Sharpe "Bora Laskin and Civil Liberties ," 651–55.
17. *Lavell v. Canada (Attorney General)*, [1974] SCR 1349.
18. Ibid., 1386.
19. Ibid., 1382.
20. *R. v. Burnshine*, [1975] 1 SCR 693.
21. *A.G. Canada v. Canard*, [1976] 1 SCR 170.
22. Ibid., 177.
23. *R. v. MacKay*, [1980] 2 SCR 370.
24. Ibid., 380
25. See *Gay Alliance Toward Equality v. The Vancouver Sun*, [1979] 2 SCR 435.
26. *Seneca College of Applied Arts and Technology v. Bhadauria*, [1981] 2 SCR 181.

27 *R. v. Brownridge*, [1972] SCR 926.
28 *R. v. Hogan*, [1975] 2 SCR 574.
29 Ibid., 597.
30 *R. v. Appleby*, [1972] SCR 303.
31 *R. v. Shelley*, [1981] 2 SCR 196.
32 *Miller and Cockriell v. R.*, [1977] 2 SCR 680.
33 Ibid., 686.
34 Ibid., 690.
35 *R. v. Curr*, [1972] SCR 889 at 899–90.
36 Ibid., 902.
37 *R. v. Morgentaler*, [1976] 1 SCR 616.
38 *R. v. Morgentaler*, [1988] 1 SCR 30. For a detailed discussion of the relationship between the two *Morgentaler* cases, see Robert Sharpe and Kent Roach, *Brian Dickson: A Judge's Journey* (Toronto: University of Toronto Press, 2003), 6–24.

◀ PART SEVEN ▶

Contract, Tort, & Fiduciary Obligations

◀ 14 ▶

The Laskin Legacy in Private Law:
The Judge as Custodian of the Common Law

JOHN D. McCAMUS

MUCH ATTENTION HAS BEEN given to Bora Laskin's achievements in the field of public law. He is justly renowned as a constitutional scholar and jurist. His reputation as an expert in labour relations and various other public law fields preceded him to the bench. Public law is at the centre of the agenda of the Supreme Court of Canada, and it was obviously a major professional preoccupation during his years on the bench. The Laskin legacy in public law is self-evidently of major significance. But is there a similarly substantial Laskin legacy in the field of private law? Any consideration of his contributions to both tort law and contract law will show that there is such a legacy – one likely to endure for years to come.

Before I turn to this subject, however, I would like to record a few recollections of my own about Bora Laskin. Many years ago I had the privilege to serve as his law clerk during his first full year as a member of the Supreme Court of Canada. I can confirm his warmth, kindness, and good humour, as well as his extreme care, indeed fastidiousness, in the use of the English language. On one occasion I discovered in one of his drafts a word that appeared not to be a word at all. I checked the Oxford English Dictionary, then, remembering his time at Harvard, in Webster's. With something bordering on glee, I reported that the only concern I had about his current draft was one word – a word that was, in fact, not a word known to the English language. Apparently not overwhelmed by this objection, Laskin asked me if I initially thought that I understood what the word might mean. I offered a definition. "Exactly," said he, and he asked whether I could come up with a synonym in current English usage. I responded that a phrase would be required to capture the idea. "Exactly," said he again. "Well," he continued after a moment's reflection, "I think I'll leave it in. That is, after all, how words come into the English language." I had not expected my duties as law clerk to include being present for or, indeed, participating in the invention of new words for the English language. I was impressed.

On another occasion, when Justice Laskin invited me and my fellow clerks to dinner, he asked us about the nature of our work experience and our impressions of the Court in action. Some of the clerks felt comfortable enough to express their reservations with respect to the linguistic capacities of the anglophone members of the Court. Those were, after all, the early days of Trudeau's bilingual and bicultural Canada. Conceding the point that the anglophone judges typically did not wear headsets during the course of argument in French, Laskin observed that, in his case at least, he felt it was important for him to listen to the argument in French, unaided by simultaneous translation, with a view to increasing his understanding of the French language. "And in any event," said he, "tomorrow I will be asking my first question of counsel in French. At an appropriate point in argument, I plan to ask, 'Quelle page, maintenant'?"

What I remember most about Bora Laskin, however, was his devotion to his work and his consummate professionalism. The almost daily conversations with him in his chambers were quite focused and seldom strayed from the Court's current agenda. He believed passionately in the importance of law as an instrument of social justice. His enthusiasm for his work and the work of the Court was palpable and infectious. The quality and quantity of his judicial opinions – invariably drafted in long hand and the apparent product of long evening hours at his desk – set a new standard for the contribution that could be made by a member of the Court. His sense of professionalism was evident in many ways. Although Laskin never discussed his personal circumstances with me, it was not an easy year for him both professionally and personally. He was separated from his family, geographically speaking, and it was evident from the work product of the Court that he was not warmly welcomed by some members, at least in an intellectual sense. His early opinions were frequently in dissent. In our conversations, however, there was never a hint of any of these difficulties, either personal or professional.

I do not remember a critical or unkind word spoken of any of his colleagues on the bench. As close as he came to this was an occasion on which, after reviewing one of his draft opinions together, he remarked, "I wonder what the four horsemen will think of this?" – a reference to the four members of the Court who normally composed the majority against him. I laughed appreciatively, wondering which of the Four Horsemen of the Apocalypse – Pestilence, War, Famine, and Death – were to be matched with which of his judicial colleagues. It was only decades later when I told this story to my Osgoode colleague, Professor Jamie Cameron, an expert in U.S. constitutional law, that she advised me that Laskin was obviously referring to the expression used by many, including members of the American media, to refer to the conservative block that carried the conservative majority on the US Supreme Court during the Chief Justiceship of Charles Evans Hughes. President Roosevelt's infamous 1937 court-packing plan had been inspired by his frustration with the rulings of the Court led by the four horsemen. As 1937 was the year of Laskin's Harvard LL.M, Professor Cameron is undoubtedly correct in her assessment. Unfortunately, Laskin's wisecrack was more clever (and more gentle) than I was able to appreciate at the time.

Turning to the question of a Laskin legacy in private law, one way of measuring such a legacy would be to consult the standard Canadian casebooks in contracts and torts and consider whether Laskin is a visible presence in them. Is Laskin a figure in the minds of current law students? Any such survey will reveal that Laskin is, indeed, a presence in the classroom in this way. Several of his contracts and torts opinions, not necessarily majority judgements, appear in the various casebooks on these subjects used in Canadian law schools. The contract books typically contain excerpts from his opinion in *Barnett v. Harrison*,[1] the famous debate between Justice Laskin and Justice Dickson on the subject of "true conditions precedent." Students also typically read *AVG Management Science Ltd. v. Barwell Developments Ltd.*,[2] reversing the traditional rule for calculating damages in a real-estate transaction, as well as the decision in *Highway Properties Ltd. v. Kelly, Douglas & Co. Ltd.*,[3] overruling the traditional approach to the calculation of damages for breach of a covenant to pay rent. They also read *H.F. Clarke Ltd. v. Thermidaire Corp.*,[4] adjusting the traditional approach of the common law to the analysis of stipulated remedies clauses.

Students are also likely to read opinions written during his tenure on the Ontario Court of Appeal, cases such as *Finelli v. Dee*,[5] on anticipatory repudiation, and *Parrish & Heinbecker Ltd. v. Gooding Lumber Ltd.*,[6] on frustration. A similarly impressive presence is to be found in the torts casebooks: *Horsley v. MacLaren*,[7] the opinion concerning the duty to rescue on the ill-fated *Ogopogo*; *Harrison v. Carswell*,[8] the great debate between Dickson and Laskin concerning the application of trespass law to picketing within the premises of a shopping centre; *Seneca College v. Bhadauria*,[9] on the existence of a tort of racial discrimination; *Reibl v. Hughes*,[10] on consent to medical treatment; *Rivtow Marine Ltd. v. Washington Iron Works*,[11] on manufacturer's liability and the duty to warn; and *Jordan House Ltd. v. Menow & Honsberger*,[12] on the duty of care owed by an innkeeper to an intoxicated patron. In short, Laskin's role as a classroom teacher continues in this modified form to the present day, and I am confident it will remain so for a long time into the future. But why does Laskin's judicial work appear so frequently in these casebooks? What do students learn from reading Laskin? What, indeed, is his legacy as a private law jurist?

Bora Laskin had a clear vision of the role played by the courts, especially appellate courts, in the growth and development of the common law. In all areas of law, the courts must strive to find an appropriate accommodation between the conflicting interests of stability or certainty of doctrine and, at the same time, the need of the law to adjust to changing social and economic conditions and to evolving professional attitudes to determining the just result. But the weight of these competing demands for stability and reform surely vary from one field to the next. The creative or law-making role for the judiciary in the context of fields that are essentially based on statute law that is frequently visited by legislatures may be considered more constrained than it is, or should be, in other areas of the law. In Laskin's view, the courts, and especially the appellate courts, are the custodians of the common law of obligations. The common law is fundamentally and essentially judge-made law. The judges are its original architects, and the common law has evolved dramatically over time as a result of judicial innovation. As Lord Goff observed, "Judicial development of the common law is inevitable. If it had never taken place, the common law would be the same now as it was in the reign of King Henry II; it is because of it that the common law is a living system of law, reacting to new events and new ideas, and so capable of providing citizens of this country with a system of practical justice relevant to the times in which they live."[13]

Laskin did not, to my knowledge, explicitly express similar sentiments in his academic or extra-judicial writings, but views of this kind are plainly manifest in many of his decisions, such as the one he wrote as Chief Justice in *AVG Management Science Ltd. v. Barwell Developments Ltd.*,[14] a decision that overruled the venerable rule in *Bain v. Fothergill*.[15] That rule held that a vendor of land who was unable to make title, in the absence of fraud or bad faith on the vendor's part, would be protected by the rule, in the sense of being exposed only to a liability to return the purchaser's deposit and to compensate the purchaser for any transaction costs incurred such as lawyer's fees or the cost of a survey undertaken for purposes of completing the transaction. On the facts of *AVG Management*, the vendor had disabled itself from making good title by accidentally entering into two separate transactions to sell the same parcel. The plaintiff was the disappointed intending purchaser that did not obtain the parcel. The plaintiff then sought the full measure of contract damages, including the loss of bargain – the difference between the contract price and the market price of an equivalent parcel. The defendant vendor relied on the rule in *Bain v. Fothergill*, urging that its accident did not amount to either fraud or bad faith.

The British Columbia courts had held that perhaps a new exception to the general rule could be recognized in order to accommodate this situation or, alternatively, perhaps the Supreme Court of Canada should be invited to consider whether the rule in *Bain v. Fothergill* ought to be overruled in a more general way. Justice Laskin found this invitation impossible to resist. In his decision for the Court, he indicated his agreement with the British Columbia Court of Appeal that a new exception could be drafted to deal with this situation, thereby exposing the vendor to the harsh winds of the full expectancy principle. He was not, however, content to let the matter rest there. He further reasoned that the rule in *Bain v. Fothergill* was unsatisfactory and, accordingly, ought to be considered to be overruled. In reaching this conclusion, he briefly described the factual context of mid-nineteenth-century England that gave rise to the rule in *Bain v. Fothergill*. The original rationale for the rule rested in the difficulties of that time in determining title to land with accuracy. Registration of title documents was a voluntary matter, and proof of title was for this and other reasons notoriously difficult. In the intervening century, much had changed and, in Canada in particular, various provincial compulsory registration systems for title documents had been implemented. The rationale for the rule had simply vanished. Laskin also noted that the rule had been trenchantly criticized by the British Columbia Law Reform Commission and that the province of British Columbia, acting on the commission's advice, had introduced, but not yet proclaimed in force, legislation abrogating the rule. Further, Laskin noted that the rule had been rejected in most American states. Accordingly, the rule should be considered to be overruled as a matter of common law.

The reasoning in Laskin's opinion in the *AVG Management* case provides support for a number of observations concerning his vision of the role of appellate courts, and especially the role of a final court of appeal, in matters of private law. First, for Laskin, the court had a responsibility to monitor and occasionally provide refreshment to doctrines of common law that are no longer defensible. In this respect, I think there can be little doubt that Laskin would have agreed with the following observation of Australia's Chief Justice Mason in a decision in which the Australian High Court overruled the traditional doctrine precluding the recovery of monies paid under the mistake of law: "[I]t is the *responsibility* of this court to reconsider in appropriate cases, [whether] common law rules operate unsatisfactorily and unjustly."[16]

Moreover, although we may surmise that Laskin would have agreed that such changes to the law are normally of an incremental nature, extending an existing rule to a new fact situation that is embraced by the rule's rationale, crafting a new exception to a general rule which unsatisfactorily applies to the particular circumstance before the court, and so on, it also appears that he thought even more radical surgery was occasionally required. The rule in *Bain v. Fothergill* was well established and had no doubt been applied in many cases. The change to the form of liability being imposed on vendors of real estate, though consistent with more general principles of the law of contract, represented a sharp break with past doctrine. Again, Lord Goff appears to be in agreement: "Occasionally, a judicial development of the law would be of a more radical nature constituting a departure, even a major departure, from what has previously been considered to be established principle, and leading to a realignment of subsidiary principles within the branch of the law."[17]

Second, it was plainly Laskin's view that the Court, in exercising its oversight role with respect to the doctrines of private law, was entitled to look at a much greater variety of sources than Canadian courts had been examining in recent practice. In his opinion in *AVG Management,* Laskin referred not only to the predictable run of English and Canadian case law but also made reference to a law reform commission report, to an enacted but unproclaimed statute, to the experience in American jurisdictions, and, as well, to American literature. Obviously, Laskin was very familiar with and admiring of American materials. In remembering his time as a student in Dean W.P.M. Kennedy's program in law at the University of Toronto, he indicated that students in the program became familiar, to some extent at least, with the work of Holmes, Brandeis, and Cardozo.[18] Laskin's time at Harvard University no doubt gave him greater familiarity with American material than would likely have been the case with judges who had not had the benefit of such exposure. Certainly, in the Harvard of the late thirties, the American Law Institute's *Restatement of the Law of Contracts*[19] had been freshly minted, and the work of its co-reporters, Professor Samuel Williston of Harvard University and Professor Arthur L. Corbin of Yale University, would have been well known to Laskin. References to the *Restatement* and to the monumental treatises of Williston, Corbin, and other American sources are sprinkled throughout Laskin's private law jurisprudence. One major feature of Laskin's legacy in both private law and other fields is that he opened the Canadian judicial door widely to the richness of American jurisprudence and legal scholarship.

In retrospect, of course, it may appear obvious that courts, in discharging their onerous responsibilities, should be free to draw whatever assistance they might find from a broad range of earlier cases and legal scholarship, including foreign materials of both kinds. At the present time, this view is now widely accepted by the Canadian judiciary and has attracted increasing support in other Commonwealth jurisdictions. Lord Goff recently observed that a judge, when contemplating an adjustment to the common law, will drive "much assistance from academic writings ... and he has regard, where appropriate, to decisions of judges in other jurisdictions."[20] It should be remembered, however, that such views were not commonplace in Laskin's time. Two courtroom exchanges I observed as a law clerk capture the then prevailing mood on such questions.

On one occasion, the legendary J.J. Robinette, appearing on behalf of a taxpayer in a much publicized tax prosecution, sought to invoke for his client the protections, such as they were, of the *Canadian Bill of Rights*. When he attempted to rely on American authority concerning the U.S. *Bill of Rights* on an analogous point, the presiding judge interjected, "Mr. Robinette, you cannot expect us to entertain American authorities. They have riots in the streets down there." Robinette moved on to his next point. If the presence of "Chicago 67" was relatively new to the Canadian judicial mind at that time, the judicial reluctance to examine American authority was not. On another occasion, somewhat nervous and, it seemed, inexperienced counsel indicated that he wished to quote from "Lord Laskin's well-known casebook on constitutional law." A few smiles were provoked by the inappropriate reference. The presiding judge, the same one as it happens, interjected to remind counsel that the Court followed the English practice of refusing to entertain or listen to the words of a living author. This reluctance to openly acknowledge judicial reliance on academic writing was, indeed, the convention at the time. The presiding judge was apparently unaware, however, of the exception to the general principle applicable to authors who are subsequently appointed to the bench. Upon elevation, the previously authored works of the judge become authority and can be cited as such.[21] Be that as it may, Laskin's extension of the range of sources relevant to the Court's deliberations was a boldly innovative and important contribution.

Third, the *AVG Management* decision suggests a vision of the relationship between the legislature and the judges with respect to the oversight of private law that would not necessary be shared by all his colleagues. For a jurist of a more conservative demeanour, reform of the private law of obligations is more properly the responsibility of the legislature. Accordingly, the fact that a law reform commission might have studied a particular subject and recommended reform of the private law doctrine in question, and, further, the fact that a legislature, acting on that advice, had introduced legislation to that end, might be considered as strong support for the proposition that reforming the law in this area ought to be left to the legislature. For Laskin, however, the fact that a law reform commission had so pronounced and that the legislature had so enacted merely strengthened the case for judicial reform of the doctrine. In my view, at least, Laskin has a more satisfactory view of the role of the courts, as opposed to that of the legislature, with respect to the reform of private law for a number of reasons. First, the more conservative position – that it is for the legislature rather than the courts to reform private law – ignores the reality that legislatures simply do not engage in systematic reform and adjustment of the private law. That is in part, no doubt, because legislatures have more important matters to attend to. It may also result from the fact that, in the common law system at least, it is widely believed that the more flexible instrument of judicial modification of doctrine is a more satisfactory instrument of reform than the enactment of a statutory rule with resulting inflexibility and imperviousness to further judicial modification. The argument for a generous view of the responsibility of the judiciary in this regard is strengthened by the nature of a federal system. Just as it is true that provincial legislatures have demonstrated little interest in the reform of private law doctrine, it is also the case that, when legislatures have intervened, they have typically done so on a sporadic and individual basis, thus undermining the uniformity of common law doctrine throughout the Canadian common law provinces.

A stark illustration of the contest between these competing visions of the role of the courts in formulating doctrines of private law – on the one hand the judiciary as the architect and custodian of the common law and, on the other, the legislature as the principal, if not exclusive, instrument of reform of private law, with the courts left beholden to the doctrine of *stare decisis* – is to be found in the 1976 decision of the Supreme Court in *Barnett v. Harrison*,[22] a case in which the Court had an opportunity to reconsider the infamous rule in *Turney v. Zhilka*.[23] In the 1959 decision in *Turney*, the Court was faced with a dispute over a contract for the purchase and sale of land which, by its terms, was made subject to a condition precedent – that is, a term requiring that certain circumstances must exist if the agreement is to be enforceable – requiring that the subject matter of the sale "can be annexed to the Village of Streetsville and a plan is approved by the Village Council for subdivision." In the event, the Village Council was unaccommodating and the condition was not met. Nonetheless, the purchaser wished to proceed, having concluded, we may assume, that the property was worth the purchase price even in the absence of such approvals. An untutored lay person might be forgiven for thinking that, in such circumstances, the purchaser would be entitled to waive a condition that was obviously inserted for the purchaser's own benefit and would be able to require the vendor to proceed with the transaction.

In *Turney*, however, Justice Judson, writing for a unanimous Court, held that the condition concerning annexation was a "true condition precedent" and could not be waived by the purchaser. The vendor was therefore excused from the transaction. The critical feature that rendered the provision a "true condition precedent," in Judson's view, appeared to be that fulfilment of the condition was dependent on an exercise of the will of a third party, the Village Council. The rule in *Turney v. Zhilka* had attracted a good deal of criticism over the years since its invention in 1959. Indeed, provincial appellate courts appeared to be particularly incredulous and narrowly distinguished the rule in a series of cases. Two such decisions were appealed to the Supreme Court of Canada in 1969, and the Court used the occasion, again in opinions written by Justice Judson, to confirm the existence of the rule. By the time this issue returned to the Court in the *Barnett* case in 1976, it is fair to speculate that the Supreme Court generally, and the four horsemen in particular, may have felt deeply committed to the rule in *Turney v. Zhilka*.

Against this background, the opening salvo in Laskin's dissenting opinion may seem unnecessarily blunt. He began as follows: "This case raises the correctness and, if correct, the applicability of the judgments of this court in *Turney v. Zilka, FT Developments Ltd. v. Sherman*,[24] and *O'Reilly v. Marketers Diversified Inc.*"[25] If somewhat direct, the remark also reveals something of Laskin's conception of the growth of the common law. Laskin would agree with Cardozo's observation that the growth of the law proceeds by a process of trial and error.[26] If error has crept in, it should be corrected. In *Barnett*, the offer to purchase was subject to a set of conditions relating to planning approvals of various kinds rather more complex than the condition at issue in *Turney*. The majority of the Ontario Court of Appeal had dutifully taken the position, over the dissent of Justice Jessup, that the rule of *Turney v. Zilka* applied and that the purchaser was therefore unable to force the vendor to complete the transaction. This decision was affirmed by the Supreme Court of Canada. The dissenting opinion, however, is vintage Laskin. Properly understood, in his view, the rule in *Turney v. Zilka* did not apply to a case where the condition precedent had, as its object, protection of the interests of the purchaser who wished to waive its fulfilment. The apparent holding in *Turney v. Zilka* – that the mere fact that fulfilment of the condition was dependent on the will of a third party – was not a satisfactory explanation for the result in that case. Moreover, the case law in England, Australia, New Zealand, and the United States – including a decision of Justice Cardozo – was unsupportive of a rule of this kind. Accordingly, *Turney v. Zilka* must be construed to be a case in which the Court considered that the condition precedent was intended to benefit both parties and, understood in this way, would not preclude relief on the facts of *Barnett v. Harrison*. In effect, the decision in *Turney* was confined to its particular facts – and diplomatically, we may note, not directly overruled – and the more general and traditional principle, to the effect that provisions inserted for the benefit of one party can be waived by that party, was effectively restored.

The *Barnett* majority rejected Laskin's approach, however, and relied in part on the proposition that because the rule in *Turney v. Zilka* had been in effect since 1959 and had been applied many times, the rule should endure in the interests of certainty and predictability in the law unless compelling reasons for change could be shown. Dickson, writing the majority opinion, conceded that a number of American and English authorities appeared to be inconsistent with *Turney v. Zilka*. Nonetheless, he was of the view that the decision could be defended on the basis that it avoided the necessity for the courts to make a difficult determination as to whether a condition precedent had been inserted for the benefit of one party alone rather than for the benefit of both parties. Moreover, to enable the purchaser simply to waive non-fulfilment of the condition precedent in cases of this kind essentially conferred a non-bargained-for option on the purchaser to withdraw or affirm the transaction in the circumstances prevailing at closing, an option for which the vendor had not paid. Laskin's convincing reply to this second point was that there is nothing either offensive or prejudicial in the fact that, in circumstances where terms of this kind are present in an agreement, a vendor may not know whether a contract is to be performed until the moment for performance.

I suspect that few observers have found convincing the reasons offered by the *Barnett* majority for preserving the doctrine in *Turney v. Zilka*. The critical consideration appears to have involved a simple and perhaps mechanical application by the majority of the doctrine of *stare decisis*. Indeed, it is somewhat surprising that Dickson should appear in the role of defender of a rule that is both anomalous in the common law world and difficult to defend on grounds of legal logic or legal policy. His strong reaffirmation of the importance of *stare decisis* surprises in part because, in due course, Dickson acquired a much more muscular view of the role of the Supreme Court of Canada in private law matters and did not refrain from overruling well-established doctrine in circumstances where he felt it to be the Court's responsibility to do so. Among the evidence that might be cited in support of this proposition are his majority opinion in the Court's decision in *Pettkus v. Becker*,[27] effectively overruling the Court's decision in *Murdoch v. Murdoch*[28] (which had been rendered a mere five years before), and the boldly innovative decision in *Air Canada v. British Columbia*.[29] The latter decision reversed the venerable mistake of law doctrine, an overruling that appears to have exerted some influence in subsequent and similar decisions by the House of Lords[30] and the Australian High Court.[31]

One must be circumspect, of course, in ascribing to judges motivations or modes of thought that are not clearly articulated in their reasons for judgment. It may be that Dickson simply did not find the rule in *Turney v. Zilka* to be sufficiently offensive to require overruling. The better view, I suspect, is that his view of the role to be played by the courts as custodians or stewards of the common law aligned more closely with Laskin's views over time. When *Barnett* was decided, Dickson had been on the Court for only a few years. As others have noted, his jurisprudence during his early years at the Court was within the conservative mainstream and was marked by many disagreements with Laskin.[32] Perhaps the most famous of their debates is found in the 1976 decision in *Harrison v. Carswell*,[33] concerning picketing in a shopping plaza, a decision that continues to enjoy a long after-life in various subjects within the LL.B curriculum. At the risk of oversimplification of the issue, the basic question was whether picketing in a shopping plaza over the objection of the owner constituted trespass. Laskin, in dissent, favoured restricting the application of the law of trespass in the context of the quasi-public property of a shopping centre. The Dickson-led majority favoured traditional notions of private property. Again, the conservatism of early Dickson prevailed over Laskin's desire to mould the law in a new direction. There can be little doubt, however, that Dickson's view of the role of the Court evolved over time and, in doing so, it was much influenced by

Laskin. Indeed, I think it is plausible to claim that Laskin's apparent influence on Dickson in this regard may be considered an important aspect of Laskin's private law legacy.[34]

Laskin's vision of the role of the Court as the custodian of the common law was coupled with a personal mastery of the various branches of the private law of obligations. His knowledge of the common law was simply prodigious. In conversation, it was common for him to suggest that there might have been a Supreme Court of Canada case dealing with some point or other, followed by a successful search of the relevant volume of the Supreme Court reports. His familiarity with the architecture and substance of private law arose principally from his teaching and writing while still a member of the academic community. Professor Laskin, though perhaps better known for his scholarship in constitutional and other fields of public law, taught private law, including property law and the law of real-estate transactions. His knowledge of private law may well have been enriched by his activities as the author of notes on a great range of subjects, including private law, in the *Canadian Bar Review* and his activities as a arbitrator and editor of the *Dominion Law Reports*. His extensive knowledge of private law is manifest in the fact that his judgments on matters of private law seem very sure footed. When he leant against extension of an existing principle or the restriction or overruling of an established precedent, for instance, his instinct appeared to be sound. Thus, his attempt to subvert, if not overrule, the doctrine in *Turney v. Zilka* rested on a clear understanding on his part that the doctrine is not only anomalous in the common law world but simply difficult to defend on policy grounds.

Some of Laskin's opinions illustrated a willingness to hold well-established exceptions to general principles up to scrutiny in order to determine whether the exception had anything other than the historical circumstances of its invention as a basis for its prolonged life. The *AVG Management* and *Kelly, Douglas & Co. Ltd.* decisions illustrate the phenomenon of Laskin-led courts overruling traditional exceptions on the grounds that no contemporary justification for the exception exists. Laskin's intimate knowledge of the historical origins of the rules jettisoned in each of those cases no doubt provided a basis for his confident view that the time for their abolition was ripe. His extension of tort liability into novel fact situations appeared to be consistent with the general direction of the evolution of tort liability in the twentieth century. His willingness to restrict the scope of the flawed decision of the House of Lords in *White & Carter (Councils) Ltd. v. McGregor*[35] in *Finelli v. Dee*,[36] and his willingness to allow a trucker to escape liability in his obligation to deliver vegetables, notwithstanding a crop failure, on grounds of the frustration doctrine in *Parrish & Heimbecker Ltd.*[37] also ring true.

I confess, however, that for many years I thought the master had momentarily lost his touch in *H.F. Clarke Ltd. v. Thermidaire Corp.*,[38] a case in which Laskin, for the Supreme Court of Canada, significantly modified the traditional treatment accorded to liquidated damages and penalty clauses. In that case, a manufacturer sought to enforce a non-competition clause that was to apply for three years following the termination of its relationship with the defendant distributor. The clause provided that the manufacturer would be entitled to recover the "gross trading profit" secured by the distributor in breach of that provision. The evidence indicated that "gross" rather than "net" trading profit was chosen in order to provide compensation for losses that could only be estimated with some difficulty because of the loss of the manufacturer's good will and depreciation of the manufacturer's customer and trade relations. Under traditional doctrine, such a provision would appear to engage the rule that such clauses would be enforced if they represented a genuine attempt by the parties to pre-estimate loss in the event of breach. Under the traditional rule, such a clause would be categorized as a legitimate and enforceable "liquidated damages clause" as opposed to a mere unenforceable "penalty." Again, at the risk of oversimplification, the Laskin-led court took the view that the gross trading profits formula was an unreasonable one and, notwithstanding whatever the good intentions of the parties may have been at the time of formation of the agreement, it therefore constituted an unenforceable penalty. In contrast to the traditional rule, the decision appears to suggest that the enforceability of the clause is to be determined at the time of breach rather than in the light of the intentions of the parties at the time of formation.

My own view was that this approach reduced the capacity of the parties to stipulate remedies and, accordingly, imposed an unattractive restriction on the utility of liquidated damages provisions. It softened in later years, however, when I read an article by another of my heroes, Professor Mel Eisenberg, who persuasively argues that the very difficulty of predicting and quantifying consequential loss at the time of contract formation is such that a second look, at the time of breach, with respect to the reasonableness of the operation of the clause offers a sensible basis for determining the enforceability of the clause.[39] In the face of such support for what appear to be Laskin's views, I have retreated to the position that, at the very least, this point is one on which reasonable people can differ. I suspect that *Clarke v. Thermidaire* may nonetheless receive searching scrutiny in the contemporary classroom. More generally, however, I doubt that Laskin's opinions are used by particular instructors in the classroom as examples of judicial reasoning gone awry. My impression, rather, is that students come to them as illustrations of excellence in judicial craftsmanship.

For reasons such as these, then, I maintain that there is a substantial Laskin legacy in matters of private law as well as public law. The legacy in private law is transmitted to neophyte law students and lawyers by the fact that the case-law diet of the private law subjects in the LL.B. curriculum contains a healthy dose of Laskin's opinions. The most important element of that legacy is constituted by Laskin's vision of the role of courts in private law adjudication. The courts, as he plainly understood, are not only the principal architects of the private law of obligations but the custodians, and they bear the principal responsibility for its stewardship in the modern era. The more conservative view – that reform of the private law of obligations is essentially a matter for the legislatures – was rejected by Laskin, and it continues to be rejected by other like-minded jurists in Canada and in other common law jurisdictions. Our experience of the general and understandable lack of legislative interest in the reform of private law, one manifested by Canadian provincial legislatures over virtually all our legal history, suggests that Laskin's views on this important question are quite correct.

I wish to conclude on a different and perhaps surprising point. Some might suggest in response that Laskin's legacy in private law, however valuable, is dwarfed by his legacy in matters of public law. Though that may be so, it can nonetheless be argued that his gifts as a public lawyer rest to some extent on the strong analytical and conceptual foundation he developed as a private law scholar and jurist. The thought that a person's prowess as a public lawyer may well rest on a foundation of this kind may appear to be counter-intuitive. For a private lawyer such as myself to advance such a view may appear to be coarsely self-serving. Nonetheless, I have good authority for the proposition. In one of our conversations during my time as a law clerk, Laskin offered the view that whatever merits his work as a public law jurist may have, its success rested on the analytical abilities and insights into the general nature of law and legal methodology that he developed as a private law scholar. I find the point completely persuasive and, indeed, during my time as dean at Osgoode Hall Law School, I often recounted this incident in the course of trying to persuade budding young constitutional lawyers to include a section of contracts, tort, or property law within their teaching assignments. I am sure that some remain bitter about the experience, but I am unrepentant. Laskin's legacy as a private lawyer is not only substantial but the very foundation on which his enormous contribution as a public lawyer was constructed.

NOTES

1 *Barnett v. Harrison*, [1976] 2 SCR 531.
2 *AVG Management Science Ltd. v. Barwell Developments Ltd.*, [1979] 2 SCR 43.
3 *Highway Properties Ltd. v. Kelly, Douglas & Co. Ltd.*, [1971] SCR 562.
4 *H.F. Clarke Ltd. v. Thermidaire Corp.*, [1976] 1 SCR 319.
5 *Finelli v. Dee*, [1968] 1 OR 670, 67 DLR (2d) 393 (CA).
6 *Parrish & Heinbecker Ltd. v. Gooding Lumber Ltd.*, [1968] 1 OR 716, 67 DLR (2d) 495 (CA).
7 *Horsley v. MacLaren*, [1972] SCR 441.
8 *Harrison v. Carswell*, [1976] 2 SCR 200.
9 *Seneca College v. Bhadauria*, [1981] 2 SCR 181.
10 *Reibl v. Hughes*, [1980] 2 SCR 880.
11 *Rivtow Marine Ltd. v. Washington Iron Works*, [1974] SCR 1189.
12 *Jordan House Ltd. v. Menow & Honsberger*, [1974] SCR 239.
13 *Kleinwort Benson Ltd. v. Lincoln County Council*, [1998] 4 All ER 513 (HL) at 534.
14 *AVG Management Science Ltd. v. Barwell Developments Ltd.*, [1979] 2 SCR 43.
15 *Bain v. Fothergill* (1874), LR 7 HL 158.
16 *Trident General Insurance Company Ltd. v. McNiece Bros. Pty. Ltd.* (1988), 165 CLR 107 at 103 per Mason CJ (emphasis added).

17 *Kleinwort Benson Ltd. v. Lincoln County Council*, [1998] 4 All ER 513 (HL) at 535.
18 Bora Laskin, Interviews with Robin Harris, 1976, p. 16 (on file in the University of Toronto Archives).
19 American Law Institute, *Restatement of the Law of Contracts* (Philadelphia: ALI Publishers, 1932).
20 *Kleinwort Benson Ltd. v. Lincoln County Council*, [1998] 4 All ER 513 (HL) at 534.
21 Compare *Cordell v. Second Clanfield Properties Ltd.*, [1969] 2 Ch 9 at 16, where Justice Megarry, in response to an argument based on a passage from his well-known text on real property law, disclaimed any special status for the works of authors elevated to the bench and welcomed references to a variety of textbook sources.
22 *Barnett v. Harrison*, [1976] 2 SCR 531.
23 *Turney v. Zhilka*, [1959] SCR 578.
24 *Turney v. Zilka, FT Developments Ltd. v. Sherman*, [1969] SCR 203.
25 *O'Reilly v. Marketers Diversified Inc.*, [1969] SCR 741.
26 B.N. Cardozo, *The Growth of the Law* (New Haven: Yale University Press, 1924), 55.
27 *Pettkus v. Becker*, [1980] 2 SCR 834.
28 *Murdoch v. Murdoch*, [1975] 1 SCR 423.
29 *Air Canada v. British Columbia*, [1989] 1 SCR 1161, adopting Dickson's prior dissent in *Hydro Electric Commission of the Township of Nepean v. Ontario Hydro*, [1982] 1 SCR 347.
30 *Kleinwort Benson Ltd. v. Lincoln City Council*, [1999] 2 AC 349.
31 *David Securities Pty. Ltd. v. Commonwealth Bank of Australia* (1992), 175 CLR 353 (Aust. HC).
32 R.J. Sharpe and K. Roach, *Brian Dickson: A Judge's Journey* (Toronto: University of Toronto Press, 2003), chap. 7.
33 *Harrison v. Carswell*, [1976] 2 SCR 200.
34 It can be argued that the Supreme Court's recently articulated "incremental change" test represents the resurgence of a more conservative view of the courts' responsibilities as custodian of the common law. See P. Perell, "Changing the Common Law and Why the Supreme Court of Canada Incremental Change Test Does Not Work," *Advocate's Quarterly* 26 (2003): 345. It is to be hoped that Justice Perell's views rest on an unduly pessimistic view of the Supreme Court's vision of its role in private law adjudication. If not, his critique is warranted, in my view, and quite Laskinian in character.
35 *White & Carter (Councils) Ltd. v. McGregor*, [1962] AC 413 (HL).
36 *Finelli v. Dee* (1968), 67 DLR (2d) 393 (Ont. CA).

37 *Parrish & Heimbecker Ltd.* (1968), 67 DLR (2d) 495 (Ont. CA).
38 *H.F. Clarke Ltd. v. Thermidaire Corp.*, [1976] 1 SCR 319.
39 See M. Eisenberg, "The Limits of Cognition and the Limits of Contract," *Stanford Law Review* 47 (1995): 211.

◀ 15 ▶

Laskin and Fiduciary Duties

KATHRYN N. FELDMAN

IN 1982 I SPOKE at a dinner honouring Bora Laskin as the first recipient of the Distinguished Alumnus Award from the University of Toronto Faculty of Law. As a revered founding member of the faculty who went on to become the top jurist in Canada, not only in title but also in judicial stature, he was the obvious choice. He was held in enormous respect and awe by both the public and the legal profession. He was well known for the breadth of his legal knowledge as well as for his reputation for integrity, ethics, and perception of what was right and fair.

Normally at a tribute such as that one, the honouree listens while a procession of speakers praise the award recipient. But at that dinner we were asked to speak about our memories of our time at the law school and to make it funny. In a photograph I have of that dinner, there is the distinguished Chief Justice of Canada laughing and enjoying reminiscences of law-school days and of his colleagues and students at the school. It was typical of Laskin that he wanted the tribute to be not to him, but to all the professors and students who made the law school what it had become over the years.

In this essay I have been asked to consider Bora Laskin's significant impact on the branch of the law that teaches and requires people to do the right thing – fiduciary duties. As a member of the Supreme Court of Canada, Chief Justice Laskin wrote only one judgment on the law of fiduciary duties, but it was a big one, and in 1974 it set the tone for the corporate behaviour of directors and officers which became the precursor to today's demands for the strictest standards of corporate governance and corporate duties. That case is *Canadian Aero Service Ltd. v. O'Malley*, known as *Canaero*.[1]

Canaero was a Canadian subsidiary corporation of the US parent, Aero Service Corporation. Mr. O'Malley served as president and CEO of Canaero as well as a director, and Mr. Zarzycki, its chief engineer, was executive vice-president. The business of these companies involved identifying and executing topographical mapping and geophysical exploration, together with negotiating with the governments of the developing countries where this type of exploration was necessary, and negotiating with the governments of developed countries, such as Canada and the United States, that would fund the projects.

From 1961 Canaero had worked on the so-called Guyana project. Mr. Zarzycki was personally involved in the development of the project from both the technical and the financial perspectives. By 1966 it became clear that, after years of studies of the feasibility and cost of the Guyana project, the government of Canada was going to extend a loan to Guyana to fund it. However, if Canada rather than Guyana was to have the final say on the choice of contractor, it was less likely that Canaero, as a non-Canadian company, would be awarded the contract.

Fearing that they would lose this opportunity with Canaero, O'Malley and Zarzycki, along with others, incorporated a new company in August 1966, Terra Surveys Limited, in order to be able to bid on the Guyana project. They each resigned from Canaero a few days later. Terra bid on the Guyana project in September, in competition with Canaero. When the contract was awarded to Terra, Canaero sued O'Malley, Zarzycki, and Terra for conspiracy to convert a corporate opportunity for themselves, in breach of their fiduciary duties to Canaero.

The action was dismissed at trial. The trial judge believed that, because the defendants had already left the company before they sought to acquire the opportunity for themselves, they were no longer bound by a fiduciary duty, nor had they taken or used any confidential information. An appeal to the Ontario Court of Appeal was also dismissed. The appeal court felt that, because the defendants were under the control of the parent company for all decisions, they were officers of the company in name only and their true positions were only as employees. In that capacity, as long as they did not use confidential information, they were free to compete with their former employer to bid for the Guyana contract.

Chief Justice Laskin, however, saw the equities differently from the Court of Appeal. He referred to the defendants as "the faithless fiduciaries."

I digress here for a moment to point out that in his 2002 Dubin Lecture on Advocacy, Justice Binnie credited Canaero's eminent counsel, Charles Dubin, later Chief Justice of Ontario, for his skill in recasting the complexion of the case for the Supreme Court, so that the Court would view the equities in a different way. But today, the credit goes to Justice Laskin.

Laskin first rejected the idea that O'Malley and Zarzycki were merely employees and affirmed that they were senior officers who stood in a fiduciary relationship to the company. He virtually ignored the then recent 1966 Supreme Court decision in *Peso Silver Mines Ltd. (N.P.L.) v. Cropper*,[2] which had treated the good faith of a director who appropriated a corporate opportunity as a valid excuse. He stated that case law in Canada and in other like jurisdictions showed that the fiduciary duties of corporate directors and officers require a strict ethic that disqualifies a director or senior officer from usurping or diverting a maturing business opportunity that the company is pursuing, even if the company would never have been able to capitalize on that opportunity. And he further established that the fiduciary duty continues even after a director or officer resigns from the company if the purpose of resigning was to acquire the opportunity, or where it was the person's position with the company that led the former director or officer to that opportunity.

Although he described a strict standard for corporate fiduciaries, Laskin refused to define a rule for all circumstances, insisting instead on the need for flexibility. In a discussion that truly foreshadowed the functional, pragmatic, and contextual approach that the Supreme Court of Canada later developed for interpreting statutes and contracts, and for the standards of judicial review, Laskin rejected the formulation of a one-size-fits-all rule. Instead, he suggested an approach where contextual factors are to be assessed:

> In holding that on the facts found by the trial judge, there was a breach of fiduciary duty by O'Malley and Zarzycki which survived their resignations I am not to be taken as laying down any rule of liability to be read as if it were a statute. The general standards of loyalty, good faith and avoidance of a conflict of duty and self-interest to which the con-

duct of a director or senior officer must conform, must be tested in each case by many factors which it would be reckless to attempt to enumerate exhaustively.[3]

He then went on to list many factors that have proved to be very helpful in subsequent cases.

Along with the proper test for breach of fiduciary duty, the remedy for breach of fiduciary duty is also an extremely important part of the *Canaero* decision. It did not depend on what profit Canaero might have made or even whether the company would have been awarded the contract. Rather, the remedy was restitutionary – an accounting of the profits that the defendants made on the Guyana project – because those profits were considered an unjust enrichment in their hands.

So, how much impact has the *Canaero* decision had on the law of corporate fiduciary duties since 1974? Regrettably, the shelf life of judgments, including very significant ones by some of the giants of our jurisprudence such as Chief Justice Gale and Justice G. Arthur Martin, is becoming very brief indeed. Case law develops and changes so rapidly that many historic judicial pronouncements have quickly become obsolete. *Canaero*, however, remains fresh as the leading authority on the nature and extent of the duty owed by corporate directors and officers not to appropriate corporate opportunities. A recent Quickcite search of Canadian cases citing *Canaero* disclosed 452 references right up to the present time and from courts at all levels across Canada.

One of the most recent references was by the Supreme Court in its important 2004 decision in *Peoples Department Stores Inc. (Trustee of) v. Wise*.[4] In that case the Court had to distinguish between two types of corporate duty. It referred to the settled law from *Canaero*: the strict obligation of directors and officers to account for personal profits made by appropriating a corporate opportunity, even if that opportunity was not available to the corporation. But the Court then pointed out that when directors and officers are conducting their corporate management function in good faith, although there may be an apparent self-interest there, they are normally entitled in that circumstance to keep any personal gain they make – for example as shareholders, if the value of their shares goes up, or in their compensation package.

The influence of the *Canaero* decision is not limited to Canada but extends to England and Australia. The High Court of Australia has relied on *Canaero* in three of its leading decisions on fiduciary duties in the corporate context. And, in a 2001 judgment of the English High Court called *CMS Dolphin Ltd. v. Simonet*, the Court referred to the issue at the opening of its reasons as defined by the *Canaero* case as follows:

> The case raises (among other questions) the existence and applicability of the principle (extending *Regal (Hastings) Ltd. v. Gulliver*, [1942] 1 All E.R. 73; [1967] 2 A.C. 134n.) developed by the Supreme Court of Canada in *Canadian Aero Service Ltd. v. O'Malley* (1973), 40 D.L.R. (3d) 371, 382 ....[5]

Besides imposing a strict ethic of corporate honesty and the avoidance of any conflict of duty and self-interest for directors and officers, Justice Laskin also foresaw, with an almost uncanny insight, the problems that would arise in the late 1990s and into this millennium because of lax standards of corporate governance. This excerpt from his judgment in *Canaero* explains why the new rules on corporate governance are so necessary, and it could, in addition, be taken from any contemporary discussion of the *Sarbanes-Oxley Act* and related legislation:

> Strict application against directors and senior management officials is simply recognition of the degree of control which their positions give them in corporate operations, a control which rises above day-to-day accountability to owning shareholders and which comes under some scrutiny only at annual general or at special meetings. It is a necessary supplement, in the public interest, of statutory regulation and accountability which themselves are, at one and the same time, an acknowledgment of the importance of the corporation in the life of the community and of the need to compel obedience by it and by its promoters, directors and managers to norms of exemplary behaviour.[6]

Three months after penning the Supreme Court's unanimous decision in *Canaero*, Justice Laskin extended his imprint on the law that requires people to treat others fairly in his famous dissent in the case of *Murdoch v. Murdoch*.[7] In that case he sought to extend the constructive trust remedy, which he had used in *Canaero* to recover directors' and officers' profits that belonged to the company, to allow Mrs. Murdoch to receive her rightful share of her husband's ranch property, which he had acquired and maintained using some of her money and a lot of her physical work. The majority considered the wife's many years of work as a ranch hand on the husband's various properties to be just the normal role of a wife. As the parties had no common intention that the wife's contribution would give her any interest in the properties, the majority concluded that she had no remedy.

But Justice Laskin would have granted relief to the wife on the basis of a constructive trust to prevent the unjust enrichment of the husband. In words that are a testament to his judicial courage and his willingness to advance the law, he said:

> No doubt, legislative action may be the better way to lay down policies and prescribe conditions under which and the extent to which spouses should share in property acquired by either or both during marriage. But the better way is not the only way; and if the exercise of a traditional jurisdiction by the Courts can conduce to equitable sharing, it should not be withheld merely because difficulties in particular cases and the making of distinctions may result in a slower and perhaps more painful evolution of principle.[8]

Ultimately, the law followed the direction set by Laskin. Just a few years after *Murdoch*, in the case of *Pettkus v. Becker*,[9] the Supreme Court adopted and applied what Laskin saw as the fair result between a husband and wife by granting the constructive trust remedy to a common law spouse.

The initial constructive trust remedy used in *Canaero*, then expanded in Laskin's dissent in *Murdoch*, has since spread beyond the corporate opportunity and matrimonial contexts to many situations where, in the opinion of the Court, a constructive trust provides more adequate relief for a deserving plaintiff. For example, the Ontario Court of Appeal in *Waxman v. Waxman*[10] recently upheld the application of a constructive trust in the context of the appropriation not simply of a single corporate opportunity or contract but of an ongoing family business.

From just these two cases, *Canaero* and *Murdoch*, it is apparent that Bora Laskin was a pioneer in developing the law of fiduciary duty and constructive trust, two legal doctrines that embody the concept of fair and honest dealing among people. He led the way in this area as in so many others. These two decisions are an enduring testament to Bora Laskin's unfailing insistence on honourable behaviour, and a wonderful legacy for this great man, as a judge and as a person.

NOTES

1 *Canadian Aero Service Ltd. v. O'Malley,* [1974] SCR 592 [*Canaero*].
2 *Peso Silver Mines Ltd. (N.P.L.) v. Cropper,* [1966] SCR 673.
3 *Canaero* at 620.
4 *Peoples Department Stores Inc. (Trustee of) v. Wise,* [2004] 3 SCR 461.
5 *CMS Dolphin Ltd. v. Simonet,* [2001] EWJ No. 4021 at para. 2.
6 *Canaero* at 610.
7 *Murdoch v. Murdoch,* [1975] 1 SCR 423.
8 Ibid. at 450–51.
9 *Pettkus v. Becker,* [1980] 2 SCR 834.
10 *Waxman v. Waxman* (2004), 186 OAC 201.

◆ PART EIGHT ▶

Laskin in Dissent

◀ 16 ▶

Chief Justice Bora Laskin:
The Great Dissenter

NEIL FINKELSTEIN

CHIEF JUSTICE LASKIN IS Canada's great dissenter. He holds that distinction not so much by the number of his dissents, although the number was substantial, but by the impact of his dissents on the subsequent development of the law. During his tenure on the Supreme Court of Canada, he sat on 965 cases and wrote reasons in 456, or 47 percent, of them. Of those 456 written judgments, fully 108 – or 24 percent – were dissents.[1] Further, that number does not include cases where he may have written for the majority or been in the majority in the result, but dissented on a key point. For the purposes of this essay, I shall refer to the latter type of decision as well to illustrate various points. For example, in the *Anti-Inflation Reference*,[2] where Laskin wrote for the majority in the result, he dissented (with four of nine judges) on the critical issue of the scope of the national dimensions doctrine under the Peace, Order and Good Government power. I will return to the *Anti-Inflation Reference* later.

A year-by-year analysis of Laskin's judgment writing reveals that his power to sway the Court increased over time. Although he was a member of the Supreme Court from 1970 to 1984, he wrote only one decision in 1970 and none in 1984.[3] This essay therefore considers only the thirteen years between 1971 and 1983. If we break this period roughly in half, we see a striking change in his ability to bring a majority of the Court with him.

In Chief Justice Laskin's first six years, from 1971 to 1976, he wrote 174 judgments, of which sixty-three (or 36 percent) were in dissent. In the second seven years, from 1977 to 1983, his overall production increased to 281 judgments. However, only forty-five of those judgments were in dissent. The total number of judgments written by the Chief Justice thus increased from 174 in the first half of his tenure on the Supreme Court to 281 judgments in the second half, for an increase of 61 percent, yet his dissents dropped in absolute terms from sixty-three between 1971 and 1976 to forty-five between 1977 and 1983. What do these numbers tell you? They demonstrate that, even though he wrote significantly more judgments in the second half of his tenure than in the first, his dissents dropped both in absolute terms (sixty-three down to forty-five) and as a percentage of judgments written (36 percent to 16 percent). Put differently, Laskin wrote for the majority only 64 percent of the time from 1971 to 1976, and 84 percent of the time from 1977 to 1983. In this sense, he was far more influential with other members of the Court in the second half of his tenure than in the first.[4]

What is not apparent from a review of the statistics alone is the degree to which Laskin's dissents later became law. It is therefore useful to understand the philosophy that guided his judicial career.

In 1959, six years before his appointment to the Ontario Court of Appeal, Professor Laskin wrote an article on the Diefenbaker *Bill of Rights*.[5] In this article, he divided liberty into four categories: political liberty (free speech, religion); legal liberty (freedom from arbitrary arrest, search and seizure, and so on); economic liberty (which was essentially the entitlement to national standards in health, education, and welfare); and egalitarian liberty. In 1987, after I had clerked for the Chief Justice (1980–81) and edited/written the last edition of his seminal work, *Laskin's Canadian Constitutional Law*,[6] I wrote an article in the *Canadian Bar Review* entitled "Laskin's Four Classes of Liberty."[7] There I explored the relationship between Laskin's philosophy of liberty as expressed in the 1959 article and his subsequent jurisprudence. It was my theory then – and it remains so today – that the strong centralism espoused by the Chief Justice in both his academic and his judicial careers was rooted in his practical conception that only a strong central government can set national standards for health, education, and welfare programs. Only a strong central government can garner the resources to redistribute income from wealthy provinces to poor ones, and only the central government has the power to set national standards or create national programs. It was, accordingly, that utilitarian view of economic liberty (access to national health, education and welfare programs) expressed in his 1959 article that drove his vision for a strong central government for Canada. Understanding that, one has a better picture of the practical reasons the Chief Justice was considered such a strong federalist.

As to the political liberties of free speech and freedom of religion, Chief Justice Laskin made the following comment in his 1959 article, which could just as well have been written today:

> History and tradition have hallowed what may be termed political civil liberty which is associated with the operation of our parliamentary institutions and which makes parliamentary democracy possible and tolerable. The substance of this kind of liberty is freedom of association ... freedom of press (or of the use of other media for dissemination of news and opinion) and freedom of conscience and of religion. Crucial as any of these may be to the preservation of the nature of our polity, they are not absolutes. As will be shown below, freedom of association and of assembly have been qualified by propriety (and in the result, legality) of purpose and by a duty to keep the peace. Freedom of speech does not on a level of public order and law cover incitement to crime or seditious utterances; and, on a private level, it is limited by the law of defamation. This is equally true with freedom of the press which, moreover, cannot be invoked to support publications that are in contempt of court. Freedom of religion and of conscience will not, in the views of the courts of the common-law countries, justify human sacrifice or polygamy or the practice of medicine without proper certification or refusal to obey compulsory school attendance laws.[8]

Laskin went on to discuss the need to balance various rights against one another – almost twenty-five years before section 1 of the *Charter of Rights and Freedoms* came into existence.

Not only did the words of the Chief Justice foreshadow the *Charter* by decades but they were written during a period of extreme judicial conservatism. For at least the first half of his tenure on the Supreme Court of Canada, Laskin sat on a very conservative bench. In contrast to the Rand Court in the 1950s, which struck down Quebec's *Padlock Act* in *Switzman v. Elbling and Attorney-General of Quebec*[9] and imposed damages on the most powerful premier in Quebec's history in *Roncarelli v. Duplessis*,[10] the 1970s Supreme Court upheld provincial censorship legislation in *Nova Scotia Board of Censors v. McNeil*[11] and a content-based restriction on freedom of assembly in the *Dupond*[12] case.

The Chief Justice, following the theories and philosophies of his 1959 article, wrote powerful dissents in both *McNeil* and *Dupond*. Those dissents now represent the law under the *Charter*. In both cases, he used a vocabulary that is commonplace today under the *Charter*, but was unfamiliar then. In the 1970s, the vocabulary was that of the division of powers and of civil law concepts of property and contracts. The analysis of political liberties issues had to be reshaped in these restricted conceptual boxes – akin to the proverbial square pegs into round holes. Laskin dealt with them directly, using the language of political liberties. Similarly, he did so without a legal standard such as exists today in the *Charter of Rights*. He had nothing to use but a toothless statutory *Canadian Bill of Rights* and the *British North America Act, 1867* (now the *Constitution Act, 1867*), which divided the totality of legislative power (with minor exceptions) between the federal and provincial levels of government and had no constitutionally protected individual rights at all. He thus enunciated legal standards that did not exist in any written legal instrument as they do today under the *Charter*, while using a civil liberties vocabulary that also did not exist.

In his 1959 article, Laskin spoke about liberties connected with the legal order, again using language of rights that is commonplace today but was not commonplace then:

> Closely associated with political liberty, if not in truth particular projections thereof, are liberties connected with the legal order. Among these are freedom from arbitrary arrest, or arbitrary search and seizure of person, premises and papers; and protection of impartial adjudication, involving notice and hearing, an independent judiciary and access to counsel; and protection against compulsory self-incrimination. It is well to note that while these values emerged in the political struggles that helped fashion our basic criminal procedure, they have in recent years been adapted in part as a means of curial control of administrative adjudication.[13]

This concept of legal liberty is expressed in Laskin's dissent in the *Canadian Bill of Rights* case of *Mitchell v. The Queen*.[14] In *Mitchell*, the accused had been convicted, imprisoned, and released on parole. A week before his sentence was due to expire, the National Parole Board revoked his parole without giving any reasons. In its denial of reasons, the board was, in effect, shielding itself from review because, in the absence of reasons, the majority of the Supreme Court held that it had no foundation for determining whether the revocation of parole was arbitrary. Thus, one week before his scheduled release date, Mitchell was taken back to prison and lost all credit for time spent outside on parole. As Laskin wrote in his dissent, "The uncontested facts on which the application was based tend to shock from their mere narration." This comment reveals that it was often the human element that drove the Chief Justice's decisions. He said that a revocation of parole without reasons, in these circumstances, with those consequences, was arbitrary and thus inconsistent with the *Bill of Rights*. As he stated in his dissent in *Mitchell*:

> The plain fact is that the Board claims a tyrannical authority that I believe is without precedent among administrative agencies empowered to deal with a person's liberty. It claims an unfettered power to deal with an inmate, almost as if he were a mere puppet on a string. What standards the statute indicates are, on the Board's contentions, for it to apply according to its appreciation and without accountability to the Courts. Its word must be taken that it is acting fairly, without it being obliged to give the slightest indication of why it was moved to suspend or revoke parole.

The majority decided the case the other way on the basis of an old notion of rights versus privileges. Laskin's dissent is now the law under the *Charter* following *R. v. Miller*.[15]

His dissent in *MacKay v. The Queen*[16] is also relevant here. In *MacKay*, a member of the Canadian Armed Forces was charged with a breach of the *Narcotic Control Act*, which is not military law but ordinary criminal law. Because the offence in question was not a military offence but an ordinary criminal offence, its prosecution and adjudication did not require special military expertise. Nonetheless, the accused was convicted by a Standing Court Martial of charges that were laid by the accused's commanding officer. The court martial was ordered by a senior commander, and both the prosecutor and the presiding officer who adjudicated the case were part of the Office of the Judge Advocate General. So MacKay was entirely in the hands of his superiors in respect of the charge, the prosecution, and the decision.

Justices Ritchie and McIntyre wrote separate decisions concurring in the result that this procedure did not violate the fair-hearing provisions of the Canadian *Bill of Rights*. The accused was in the military, and proper military procedure was applied. Laskin disagreed. He reasoned as follows:

> In my opinion, it is fundamental that when a person, any person, whatever his or her status or occupation, is charged with an offence under the ordinary criminal law and is to be tried under that law and in accordance with its prescriptions, he or she is entitled to be tried before a court of justice, separate from the prosecution and free from any suspicion of influence or of dependency on others. There is nothing in such a case, where the person charged is in the armed forces, that calls for any special knowledge or special skill of a superior officer, as would be the case if a strictly service or discipline offence, relating to military activity, was involved. It follows that there has been a breach of s. 2(f) of the Canadian *Bill of Rights* in that the accused, charged with a criminal offence, was entitled to be tried by an independent and impartial tribunal.

Laskin's dissent is now good law under the *Charter*, following the 1992 decision of *R. v. Généreux*.[17]

There are many other areas where Laskin's dissents have become law. For example, in the famous case of *Murdoch v. Murdoch*,[18] the Chief Justice, as a lone dissenter, found that the constructive trust doctrine allowed for the recognition of the right of a spouse who had contributed to family property through unpaid labour to share in that property upon divorce. His dissent is now good law following the 1980 Supreme Court of Canada decision of *Pettkus v. Becker*.[19]

In *Rivtow Marine*,[20] Laskin dissented on the availability of damages for repairs to negligently manufactured equipment. His commentary on the issue of economic loss was first adopted explicitly by the House of Lords in *Anns v. Merton London Borough Council*.[21] In fact, Lord Wilberforce wrote, "On the question of damages generally I have derived much assistance from the judgment (dissenting on this point, but of strong persuasive force) of Laskin J. in the Canadian Supreme Court in the case of *Rivtow Marine Ltd v. Washington Iron Works*." Laskin's dissent later became the law in Canada in *Winnipeg Condominium*.[22]

Laskin's decision in the *Anti-Inflation Reference*[23] is one of my favourites. It shows the Chief Justice as a legal tactician. To appreciate his decision in *Anti-Inflation*, it is important to understand the background. Laskin's views on the division of powers were driven by the necessary (as he saw it) scope of the major federal powers, those that could be used by a centralized government to secure economic entitlements on a national basis, and, in particular, the trade and commerce power and the national dimensions doctrine of the Peace, Order and Good Government (POGG) power. His was a utilitarian, functionally based approach to federal and provincial legislative jurisdiction.

The trade and commerce power is one of the central economic powers, and it is textually very broad. Unlike the equivalent power of "*interstate* commerce" considered in the *U.S. Constitution*, the Canadian power in relation to trade and commerce was drafted without limitation. The trade and commerce power was interpreted expansively by the Supreme Court when it was first considered in *Severn v. The Queen*[24] and *City of Fredericton*.[25] It was subsequently attenuated (and attenuated and attenuated!) until, in 1922, the Privy Council, in the *Board of Commerce* case,[26] relegated it to the status of an ancillary power. It could be used in aid of some other power, but not on its own. Laskin's goal was to rebuild it to a meaningful level.

He also wanted to establish that there is a federal power to prosecute criminal offences. Generally speaking, criminal offences are prosecuted by the provincial attorneys general, and, until approximately twenty years ago, there was a dispute as to whether it was even constitutional for the federal attorney general to prosecute criminal offences. The Chief Justice believed that there had to be such a federal power.

Chief Justice Laskin wanted to establish two propositions: that there is a broad trade and commerce power as well as a federal power to prosecute criminal offences. Against this background, the *Anti-Inflation Reference* arose.

In the *Anti-Inflation Reference*, there were three judgments. Laskin wrote for four justices, Martland for three, and Beetz for two. On the issue of whether the *Anti-Inflation Act* could be sustained as a response to a peacetime emergency pursuant to the Peace, Order and Good Government power in the opening words of section 91 of the *Constitution Act, 1867*, Justice Martland concurred with Chief Justice Laskin that it could.

Hence, the Chief Justice wrote for a seven to two majority on the scope of the emergency power, the majority decision on the ultimate result of the validity of the Act. However, the Chief Justice could not draw majority support for the position that the Act could be upheld on a permanent basis under the national dimensions branch of POGG. He drew only four of nine votes on this issue. Beetz, writing in dissent in the ultimate result for two justices, received the support of Martland and accordingly formed a five to four majority on the issue of the scope of the national dimensions doctrine. In addition, in his judgment, Laskin made comments in *obiter* interpreting the trade and commerce power in section 91(2) of the *Constitution Act, 1867,* expansively. Those comments did not receive support from either Martland or Beetz.

Chief Justice Laskin continued his efforts to bolster the trade and commerce power one year later, in 1977, in *MacDonald et al. v. Vapor Canada Ltd.*,[27] where he struck down a provision in the *Trade Marks Act* on the grounds that it would have provided a free-standing federal civil right of action. However, in the course of his reasons, he commented that if there had been an overarching regulatory scheme in place that met certain conditions, rather than leaving enforcement to private individuals bringing suit on an ad hoc basis, the result would have been different. In so doing, he laid the groundwork for the *General Motors* case, a case decided in 1989, five years after his death, but ultimately based on his *Vapor Canada* opinion (*obiter*).

The *General Motors* case would uphold the *Combines Investigation Act,* not on the criminal law power in section 91(27) of the *Constitution Act, 1867* (as had been the law since *Board of Commerce*), but on the trade and commerce power. The difference in the constitutional basis for broadly based federal competition legislation is not merely technical. Where such a law is based exclusively on the criminal law power, its enforcement must be subject to all the protections of the criminal law. Proof must be made which goes beyond a reasonable doubt, the case must be heard by a judge rather than an expert tribunal comprised of lay and judicial members, those subject to investigation and enforcement must be afforded a right to remain silent, and so on. All these provisions make competition law, which at its heart is economic regulation, very difficult to enforce.

By contrast, if the law could be upheld as economic regulation pursuant to the trade and commerce power in section 91(2), such a result would have a huge practical significance, given the less onerous standards of proof and enforcement available to administer civil regulatory regimes. Upholding the *Combines Investigation Act* under the trade and commerce power would have allowed a vibrant competition law regime similar to the one we have in place today. Chief Justice Laskin's comments in *Vapor Canada* were merely opinion, not a decision.

Continuing the story, in 1979, in the *Hauser* case,[28] the Supreme Court of Canada considered whether the federal government could prosecute violations of the *Narcotic Control Act*. The Court – Chief Justice Laskin not sitting – held that the federal government could prosecute *Narcotic Control Act* offences, but, based on the surprising reasoning that the *Narcotic Control Act* was founded on the POGG, not the criminal law power. The Court supported its decision with the odd claim that narcotics were a "new matter" (another branch of the POGG, after the emergency and national dimensions branches) that did not exist at Confederation in 1867. Historians would no doubt find it surprising that narcotics were not a criminal problem in 1867 and earlier. Clearly the Supreme Court took this position to avoid having to decide that there was a federal power to prosecute criminal law offences.

Four years later, in 1983, the *CN Transportation* case[29] came before the Supreme Court of Canada. The case raised both the scope of the trade and commerce power and the federal prosecutorial power: Can the *Combines Investigation Act* be upheld on the trade and commerce power, and is there federal power to prosecute? Chief Justice Laskin clearly would have loved to answer both questions in the affirmative. However, he could not garner the majority support to do so. Instead, he took a strategic position and obtained majority support for federal power to prosecute by abstaining from commenting on the trade and commerce power. Justice Dickson dissented on the issue of the scope of the federal prosecutorial power but adopted Laskin's opinion from *Vapor Canada* in support of an expansive interpretation of the trade and commerce power to support the validity of the *Combines Investigation Act*. Laskin must have loved this endorsement, though he could not join in Dickson's judgment without losing majority support on federal power to prosecute.

So the Chief Justice was forced temporarily to abandon his fight for a definitive expansion of the trade and commerce power in order to secure a victory on the scope of the federal prosecutorial power. His decision to do so was likely eased by a belief that Dickson would continue to lead the way on the trade and commerce power issue, as indeed he did. In 1989, in *General Motors of Canada Ltd. v. City National Leasing*,[30] five years after Laskin's death in 1984, Chief Justice Dickson wrote the majority decision for the Supreme Court of Canada in which Laskin's opinion in *Vapor Canada* on the scope of the federal trade and commerce power in relation to the regulation of competition on a nationwide basis finally became law. Thus, ultimately, Chief Justice Laskin's judicial campaigns in relation to the scope of both federal power to prosecute criminal offences and Parliament's jurisdiction to legislate an effective scheme of competition regulation based on the trade and commerce power were successful. As this case study based on the progression from the *Anti-Inflation Reference* (1976) to *General Motors* (1989) demonstrates, the Chief Justice applied his judgments sensitively and strategically to shape the law in accordance with his vision of a strong central government.

Turning to the nature of dissents in general, Chief Justice Charles Evans Hughes of the United States Supreme Court wrote: "A dissent in a court of last resort is an appeal to the brooding spirit of the law, to the intelligence of a future day, when a later decision may possibly correct the error into which the dissenting judge believes the court to have been betrayed."[31] And U.S. Supreme Court Justice Ruth Bader Ginsburg commented: "Dissents speak to a future age. It's not simply to say, 'My colleagues are wrong and I would do it this way.' *But the greatest dissents do become court opinions and gradually over time their views become the dominant view.*"[32] As we have seen in *Mitchell, McKay, McNeil, Murdoch*, and others, that is certainly the case in relation to Chief Justice Laskin. His dissents in these cases have become the dominant view under the *Charter of Rights*.

This final quotation was written about Oliver Wendall Holmes Jr. and Louis Brandeis, but the same could certainly be said of Chief Justice Bora Laskin: "Their dissenting opinions cast beams that lighted the subsequent ways of the law."[33]

NOTES

1 Statistics are taken from Neil Finkelstein and Jennifer Marston, "Chief Justice Laskin, 1970–1984: Supreme Court of Canada Judicial Statistics," in "Laskin in Dissent: Introduction to the Future," Laskin Legacy Symposium, May 2005 (unpublished); the values are borrowed from the *Osgoode Hall Law Journal*, which, during the relevant period, published an annual statistical analysis of Supreme Court of Canada decisions.
2 *Re: Anti-Inflation Act*, [1976] 2 SCR 373.
3 Finkelstein and Marston, "Chief Justice Laskin."
4 Ibid.
5 Bora Laskin, "An Inquiry into the Diefenbaker *Bill of Rights*," *Canadian Bar Review* 37 (1959): 77.
6 Bora Laskin and Neil Finkelstein, *Laskin's Canadian Constitutional Law*, 5th ed. (Agincourt, Ont.: Carswell, 1986).
7 Neil Finkelstein, "Laskin's Four Classes of Liberty," *Canadian Bar Review* 66 (1987): 227.
8 Laskin, "An Inquiry into the Diefenbaker *Bill of Rights*," 80.
9 *Switzman v. Elbling and Attorney-General of Quebec*, [1957] SCR 285.
10 *Roncarelli v. Duplessis*, [1959] SCR 121.
11 *Nova Scotia Board of Censors v. McNeil*, [1978] 2 SCR 662.
12 *Attorney-General (Canada) and Dupond v. Montreal*, [1978] 2 SCR 770.
13 Laskin, "An Inquiry into the Diefenbaker *Bill of Rights*," 81.
14 *Mitchell v. The Queen*, [1976] 2 SCR 570.
15 *R. v. Miller*, [1985] 2 SCR 613.
16 *MacKay v. The Queen*, [1980] 2 SCR 370.
17 *R. v. Généreux*, [1992] 1 SCR 259.
18 *Murdoch v. Murdoch*, [1975] 1 SCR 423.
19 *Pettkus v. Becker*, [1980] 2 SCR 834.
20 *Rivtow Marine Ltd. v. Washington Iron Works*, [1974] 2 SCR 1189.
21 *Anns v. Merton London Borough Council*, [1978] AC 728.
22 *Winnipeg Condominium Corp. v. Bird Construction Co.*, [1995] 1 SCR 85.
23 *Re: Anti-Inflation Act*, [1976] 2 SCR 373.
24 *Severn v. The Queen* (1878), 2 SCR 70.
25 *City of Fredericton v. The Queen* (1880), 3 SCR 505.
26 *In re the Board of Commerce Act, 1919, and the Combines and Fair Prices Act, 1919*, [1922] 1 AC 191.
27 *MacDonald et al. v. Vapor Canada Ltd.*, [1977] 2 SCR 134.
28 *The Queen v. Hauser*, [1979] 1 SCR 984.
29 *Attorney General (Canada) v. Canadian National Transportation Ltd.*, [1983] 2 SCR 206.

30 *General Motors of Canada Ltd. v. City National Leasing*, [1989] 1 SCR 641.
31 Charles E. Hughes, *The Supreme Court of the United States* (New York: Columbia University Press, 1928), 68.
32 National Public Radio interview, May 2, 2002.
33 Percival Jackson, quoted in Claire L'Heureux-Dubé, "The Dissenting Opinion: Voice of the Future?" *Osgoode Hall Law Journal* 38 (2000): 495 at n. 6.

◀ PART NINE ▶

Reassessment: The Next Generation

◂ 17 ▸

Bora Laskin:
Lifting the Legacy from the Legend

ELLEN SNOW

BORA LASKIN IS, WITHOUT doubt, one of Canada's foremost jurists, and his impact on the development of the law in general, and the Supreme Court of Canada in particular, is significant. That Mr. Justice Laskin is an important figure for further study may mark the end of the consensus, however. The precise nature and scope of his legacy in Canadian law and on the Canadian judiciary continues to be debated.

To date, this debate has remained obscured. Laskin's judicial contribution has become shrouded behind the language of laud and honour and confused by a kind of historical reductionism. Often, his legacy is conceived of through the use of axioms – the "great dissenter" or the Court's "most vocal dissenter," for example, caricatures that attempt to reflect his desire to affect reform and his willingness to break with traditional modes of thought. In addition, many critics also credit Laskin with modernizing the Supreme Court and, through the office of Chief Justice, leading it fully out of the shadow of the Privy Council and bringing it into its own right.[1] Yet, while there are elements of truth in these characterizations of the former Chief Justice, none accurately speak to the lasting impact that Laskin had on Canadian law. Without testing these popular conceptions through rigorous explanation and debate, the nature of Laskin's legacy will likely remain elusive.

One does not have to probe deeply to realize that there is no overarching unanimity regarding Laskin's lasting impact as Chief Justice. Perhaps the most notably divergent assessments of his judicial career are offered, respectively, by Ian Bushnell and Peter McCormick. In tracing the history of the Supreme Court, Bushnell's 1992 study, *The Captive Court*, depicts Laskin's early years on the Court as his most influential but argues that, by the late 1970s and early 1980s, the Chief Justice had been relegated to a marginal position.[2] It is unclear exactly what Bushnell means by the phrase "marginal." He seems to suggest that Laskin was, from 1976 onwards, no longer leading the Court towards innovative solutions to legal dilemmas and, in the end, failed to live up to the promise for change.

In contrast, following extensive empirical research into the decision-making patterns of the Supreme Court during Laskin's membership, Peter McCormick concludes that Laskin's reputation as the "great dissenter" may be merited during his early years on the Court but inaccurately describes the latter half of his tenure. Beginning around 1976, but particularly from 1979 onwards, Laskin exerted a strong influence in the Court's decision making, finding himself more often in the majority than in dissent. Moreover, after 1979, he wrote majority reasons more often than any other justice on the Court.[3] McCormick concludes that Laskin's judicial legacy emerged in his final years on the bench: in these later years he was most effectively able to shape the reasoning and holdings of the Court.

In viewing the work of both McCormick and Bushnell, it becomes obvious how labels such as the great dissenter can obscure, rather than encapsulate, Laskin's legacy. These books raise the question of when, and to what extent, Laskin was a dissenting voice on the Supreme Court and, even more important, what was the nature of his contributions to Canadian jurisprudence while he sat on the high court.

Initially, it would seem either one or the other of these views of Laskin, but certainly not both, must be a more supportable interpretation of Laskin's impact. Was Laskin relegated to the margins of the Supreme Court in his final years on the bench, or was he exerting considerable influence over his fellow judges and actively shaping the law up until the end of his career? However, an alternative view is also possible – that neither Bushnell nor McCormick has accurately accounted for Laskin's effects while on the Court and that his legacy lies somewhere in between the conceptions posited by these two scholars. Both McCormick and Bushnell reflect on Laskin's contributions during his latter years on the Court, but a precise assessment of his impact on Canadian law and its legal institutions requires a more nuanced approach than presented by either author. The position asserted in this essay is that, while Laskin was exerting a great deal of influence in the second half of his appointment to the Court (1976–84), as suggested by McCormick, an accurate characterization of his legacy must look beyond mere empiricism and the frequency with which he joined the majority position or was in dissent. Rather, the content of his judicial opinions must be taken into account when assessing what influence Laskin was in fact exercising. When the substance of those opinions is considered, there is a discernible shift in his views from his earlier to his later days on the Court. In the second half of his term at the Court, Laskin demonstrates more reserve and conservatism than he had previously. Thus, while Bushnell is not accurate in stating that the frequency of Laskin's dissents increases in the latter portion of his career,[4] his assertions that Laskin's "promise" – his reforming zeal – was not maintained throughout his judicial tenure may be more persuasive. The Laskin of 1976–84 did indeed express different attitudes and approaches to the law than the early Laskin of 1970–75, and, although he effected change right up to his last days on the bench, his influence was more moderate than it had been with the kinds of changes he envisioned and advocated in his initial days on the Court.

This essay is divided into in six parts. Part I will provide a brief background to Laskin's legal career and his appointment to the Supreme Court. Part II considers how Laskin's career has been assessed by his contemporaries and by legal academics. In particular, this section will outline McCormick's and Bushnell's characterizations of Laskin's legacy. Once these competing visions of Laskin have been detailed, the accuracy of these depictions will be evaluated, beginning in Part III, through a survey of Laskin's judicial opinions, which demonstrate a noticeable shift in outlook towards judicial conservatism. Part IV will undertake a similar analysis with regard to Laskin's extra-judicial writings during his period on the Supreme Court and will note a similar trend to more moderate views regarding law and the judicial function generally. Part V will then synthesize the changes in thought that are perceptible from a comparison of Laskin's earlier and later periods, and Part VI will canvas several factors that may explain the change in Laskin's stance towards the law. Finally, the essay will end with a broader discussion of the significance of this study on the general understanding of Laskin's judicial legacy.

PART I: THE LIFE AND TIMES OF BORA LASKIN

BORA LASKIN WAS BORN on October 5, 1912, in Fort William, Ontario, a rural northern mining community that is now known as Thunder Bay.[5] His roots were modest – his parents had emigrated from Russia to Canada in order to escape persecution in the pogroms and, after a failed attempt to outcrop in the harsh climate of northern Ontario, they opened a second-hand store. Along with his brothers, Laskin was raised in a devout Jewish home.[6]

Encouraged by his parents, Laskin embarked on a successful academic career, graduating with a B.A. from the University of Toronto in 1933 and going on to obtain his M.A. (1935) and LL.B. (1936) from the same institution. He then pursued his LL.M at Harvard Law School and had the opportunity to study under such legal icons as Felix Frankfurter.

After graduating from Harvard University in 1937, Laskin decided to return to Canada and settled in Toronto. However, establishing a legal career in the city proved difficult, despite his impressive academic background. For all his academic credentials, Laskin remained a Jew and, in the 1930s, most Toronto law firms held strict quotas on the number of Jews they hired. Consequently, Laskin took a job writing headnotes for a legal reporter at fifty cents per note.

The adversity Laskin faced in joining a law firm was perhaps not the primary source of his disappointment and frustration. Legal practice was not his ideal; rather, he hoped to be employed as an academic at a Canadian law school. However, he faced substantial hurdles in this ambition too. Again, his Jewish heritage presented difficulties to his being accepted. When Laskin attempted to secure employment at the University of Manitoba, for instance, Cecil Wright offered the following reference:

> Unfortunately [Laskin] is a Jew. This may be fatal regarding his chances with you ... His race is, of course, proving a difficulty facing him in Toronto so far as obtaining a good office is concerned ... Laskin is not

one of those flashy Jews, and the highest recommendation which I could give him is to say that, in the absence of any overwhelming prejudice and if I had control of a decent faculty, I would have no hesitation in placing Laskin.

Even this offensive avowal by Wright could not break down the barriers for Laskin. Finally, in 1940, W.P.M. Kennedy managed to place Laskin at the University of Toronto, but only after assurances were given that he was a loyal British subject and that he disavowed any allegiances or sympathies to Communism. Laskin remained at the Faculty of Law at the University of Toronto until 1965, except for a brief sojourn at Osgoode Hall from 1945 to 1949.

Laskin left academia when he was appointed to the Ontario Court of Appeal. He spent five years on the appellate court before being appointed by Prime Minister Pierre Trudeau to the Supreme Court of Canada in 1970. It was a watershed moment in Canada history – Laskin was not only an outspoken academic, rather than a trial or corporate lawyer, but the first Jew to sit on the Court. His appointment was generally regarded as a harbinger of change.[7]

Three years later, despite being junior to five members of the Court, Laskin was named Chief Justice. Until this time, automatic promotion of the senior-most justice on the bench had been nearly inevitable. On only two previous occasions had such promotion failed to occur – once in 1906 and again in 1924.[8] Laskin remained on the Court and as Chief Justice until 1984 when, after on-going health problems, he passed away.

PART II: ASSESSING LASKIN'S LEGACY:
VARIOUS VIEWS ON LASKIN'S CONTRIBUTIONS

WITHOUT DOUBT, THE VACANCY Bora Laskin left on the Supreme Court was sorely felt. Brian Dickson, Laskin's successor as Chief Justice and a personal friend, wrote: "[Laskin] leaves us a legacy of judicial and personal greatness that will endure for many an age."[9] Similarly, Professors Risk and Pritchard opined that "[b]y any standard Bora Laskin was a great Canadian.... His contributions as a judge and scholar will no doubt contrive to influence our visions of law and courts. We miss him, but we celebrate his legacy."[10]

Yet, despite this agreement that Laskin played a pivotal role on the Court, such comments reveal little about the nature of the role he played. Nor does an assertion that Laskin will likely continue to influence the Court in coming years provide any insight into what form that influence will take. It is on these more difficult questions that different conceptions of Laskin's legacy emerge. Bushnell and McCormick have expressed the most divergent views to date, and Part II of this essay will present in greater detail how each of these scholars has interpreted Laskin's Court years.

The title of Bushnell's work, *The Captive Court,* derives from an article Laskin published before his judicial appointment, while he was a professor.[11] There Laskin roundly criticized the Court for its slavish adherence to precedent and characterized it as a prisoner of sorts, held captive and prevented from reaching its potential by the Privy Council. Drawing on this work, Bushnell outlines the history of the Supreme Court and argues that, despite the abolition of appeals to the Privy Council, the Court largely stagnated in the latter half of the twentieth century. The doctrine of *stare decisis* was applied too rigidly and the Court proved unwilling to undertake necessary law reforms.

In developing this larger thesis of the institutional nature of the Supreme Court, Bushnell considered Bora Laskin's place on, and his contributions to, the Court. In his estimation, Laskin's most significant years were those immediately after his appointment. Until 1975, he led the Court in a new activism, attempting law reform and breaking away from a slavish adherence to precedent and doctrine.[12] After 1975, however, roughly coinciding with his oft-noted dissent in *Harrison v. Carswell,*[13] Laskin's influence and promise of reform waned and ultimately remained unfulfilled. By the late 1970s and early 1980s he had been relegated to such a dissenting role on the Court that it was no longer proper to speak of a "Laskin Court."[14] Bushnell is joined in this framing of Laskin's career by Professors Snell and Vaughan.[15] Like Bushnell, they assert that even after becoming Chief Justice, Laskin was unable to infuse the Court with the kind of activism he had displayed in his earlier decisions – the Court remained decidedly traditional in its approach both to legislative deference and to decision making generally.

In contrast to this model of failed potential posited by Bushnell and by Snell and Vaughan, McCormick sees Laskin as having had a far greater impact on the Court and its decisions throughout his final days on the bench. In a series of articles and his book, *Supreme at Last*, he studies the patterns of judicial decision making on the Supreme Court under the leadership of numerous Chief Justices.[16] The focus of these texts is mainly empirical, and he devotes a large amount of his work to studying the frequency of majority, dissenting, and concurring judgments among the justices, as well as the presence of coalitions on the bench. Through this study of judicial patterns in decision making, McCormick has drawn various conclusions regarding Laskin's influence while on the Court. He argues that the "Laskin Court" emerged during the last half of the Chief Justice's time on the bench (1976–84).

In these later years, Laskin was wielding tremendous sway over his judicial brethren through the office of Chief Justice and was able to use this privileged position to build hitherto unprecedented consensus on the Court. Acknowledging the tension in attributing the achievement of this consensus to Laskin – the great dissenter – McCormick explains that, to a large extent, Laskin's honour is unearned. Noting that Laskin signed more majority judgments than either of his contemporaries Justice Fauteux or Justice Kerwin, McCormick attributes Laskin's legacy as a dissenter to the fact that his independence in the delivery of his reasons in his first years (1970–76) stands out only because they sharply contrast with the increasing solidarity in the delivery of the Court's reasons under his leadership as Chief Justice.[17]

Employing a rigorous methodology,[18] McCormick notes that the frequency with which Laskin dissented or wrote separate concurring judgments decreases near the end of his career[19] and that he dominated the Court more than any previous Chief Justice.[20] In his earlier terms on the Court, he was often found in dissent; in his first six terms as Chief Justice he joined in, or wrote, eighty-seven dissents (1970 to 1973).[21] However, in his last four terms on the Court, he joined in or wrote only eight dissenting judgments. McCormick takes these figures as evidence that, by the end of his tenure on the Court, Laskin was in firm control. Specifically, he pinpoints 1979 as the crucial term in the consolidation of Laskin's influence on the Court. After 1979, Laskin, who had agreed with the majority judgment in a smaller proportion of cases with divided reasons than any other member of the Court, now joined in the majority more often than any other justice.[22] Even more important, beginning with the 1979 term, Laskin even wrote the majority reasons disproportionately more often than anyone else.

McCormick contemplates Bushnell's very different interpretation of Laskin's impact and argues that the statistical evidence does not bear out Bushnell's assertion that Laskin sank into the role of dissenter in his latter career.[23] Responding specifically to Bushnell's claims that Laskin's early decisions in cases such as *Murdoch v. Murdoch*[24] demonstrate a reforming zeal and the promise of change, but that this promise had evaporated by the mid to late 1970s, McCormick simply states, "I can only say that I see it differently."[25]

One possible explanation for this divergence in their assessments of Laskin is that Bushnell and McCormick are not studying precisely the same periods. Bushnell focuses on Laskin's entire tenure and compares his "failure" in later years to his first days on the Court, before he became Chief Justice. McCormick, in contrast, focuses on Laskin's years as Chief Justice and begins his study of the Laskin Court in 1973. However, these different time frames cannot completely explain the differences in viewpoint. Bushnell sees Laskin as failing in 1976 and notes a decline in his subsequent years on the Court. Yet McCormick views 1976 and onwards (although particularly 1979) as years when Laskin came into his own right on the Court, wielding a great deal of influence and effecting change through ever more majority judgments. The scope of the two studies may account for some discrepancies in their assessments of Laskin, but it does not go to the heart of explaining the fundamental differences in these views.

Nevertheless, in both assessments, Laskin emerges clearly as an important figure on the Court. Part III now turns to the question of which portrayal more accurately reflects the scope and effect of Laskin's impact.

PART III: THE JUDICIAL OPINIONS

IN EVALUATING THE MERITS of McCormick's and Bushnell's understandings of Laskin's years on the Supreme Court in terms of his judicial opinions, this survey does not purport to be an exhaustive study of the Laskin case law; rather, it is a sampling of his judicial opinions while on the Court.

This broad survey will examine several of Laskin's decisions, offering a characterization of the substance of the judgment and suggesting what implications may be drawn about his conception of the judicial function from those decisions. Of lesser importance for this discussion is whether Laskin was in the majority or in dissent with respect to his reasons. No dispute is taken with McCormick's statistical analysis of Laskin's opinions, and, on a strictly empirical analysis, Laskin was more often in dissent in 1970–76, with the frequency in these minority opinions decreasing from 1976 to 1979, at which time he is most often in the majority. Greater consideration and emphasis will have to be given, then, as to whether the spirit of Laskin's judgments remains consistent throughout his judicial terms.

The discussion will be divided into two parts: first a sampling of Laskin's early judgments on the Court, followed by a discussion of the decisions he rendered in his final years on the bench. Laskin's dissent in the *Harrison* case in 1976 will mark the dividing line. There are multiple reasons for discussing 1970 to 1975 as the "early" years and 1976 to 1984 as the "later" years. First, Bushnell takes 1976 as the year that marks Laskin's transition from a powerful voice on the Court to that of marginal dissenter, so adopting that same division for evaluating Laskin's judgments permits a testing of Bushnell's thesis. Also, it is around this time that McCormick views Laskin as having more impact over the Court, although he sees 1979 at the zenith of Laskin's influence. In addition, a more practical reason exists for adopting the *Harrison* case as the dividing point in this assessment: it marks the mid-point of Laskin's career. Appointed to the Court in 1970 and sitting on the bench until 1984, Laskin had, by 1976, nearly reached the half-way point in his tenure. Given that his final years were marked by poor health that did not permit him to be as involved on the Court as in his earlier days, that year seems to be a justifiable dividing line for the purpose of this discussion.

The Early Decisions, 1970–75

ONE OF LASKIN'S EARLIEST judgments, *Highway Properties Ltd. v. Kelly* (1971),[26] demonstrates his reputation for innovation and his penchant for reform. Although the case was heard only three months after Laskin was appointed to the Supreme Court, he delivered the reasons for judgment and introduced a significant measure of law reform in so doing.[27] The dispute in question arose out of a commercial tenancy where a landlord had entered into a long-term lease with a commercial tenant to carry on business in one of the store units in a strip mall. The tenant's business floundered, and eventually he ceased to conduct business from the location any longer. The landlord, accepting the repudiation of the lease, sought to find another tenant and notified the previous one that he intended to seek damages for any losses sustained as a result of this repudiation.

Previous to this case, a decision of the Ontario Court of Appeal in *Goldhar v. Universal Sections & Mouldings*,[28] in which damages were recoverable only until the time that the repudiation was accepted, was considered to be good authority and binding law. However, Laskin rejected such a formal adherence to precedent where valid policy reasons militated towards a contrary result. Speaking for the majority of the Court, he wrote:

> It is no longer sensible to pretend that a commercial lease, such as the one before the court, is simply a conveyance and not also a contract. It is equally untenable to persist in denying resort to the full armour of remedies ordinarily available to redress repudiation of covenants, merely because the covenants may be associated with an estate in land.[29]

Thus, Laskin crafted a hybrid approach between traditional property principles and standard contract law; the landlord was allowed to terminate the lease and seek a new tenant without sacrificing his abilities to recover damages flowing from the tenant's breach. As Professor Arnold Weinrib has noted, while this decision may not be revolutionary, it is certainly innovative and demonstrates a new emphasis on policy considerations that, previously, had not been present in the Court's decisions.[30]

Decided in the same year, *Rivtow Martine Ltd. v. Washington Iron Works*[31] is a case that displays similar invention in the private law sphere. In this decision, Laskin wrote a separate judgment, dissenting in part from the majority, on whether damages for economic loss could be recoverable under tort law principles. The case dealt with a claim for damages by a barge operator against a manufacturer and distributor of barge cranes. The barge operator learned of the faulty design of the barge crane it had purchased from the manufacturer and distributor when an identical crane, owned by a third party, collapsed. Instead of waiting for a similar collapse of their own crane, the plaintiff sued for the cost of making the crane safe and for losses consequent to the barge being out of operation for the repair period. The majority held that the only recoverable head of damage was for losses flowing from a breach of the manufacturer's duty to warn – pure economic loss occasioned by the faulty manufacture was not recognized by tort law.

Laskin rejected this formalistic view and would have found the repair costs recoverable, thereby extending the law to cover claims for economic loss. He reasoned that to deny recovery for pure economic losses that would have been subject to a damage award had physical harm from the faulty design actually occurred was nonsensical and an absurd result for the law to sanction. Accordingly, the rationale of tort law ought logically to extend to cases where the threat of physical harm was present and could be avoided through the diligence of the plaintiff.

The significance of this case is that Laskin was not willing simply to apply existing tort law principles without regard to their surrounding circumstances. Traditionally, only harm for actual physical damage is recoverable at law; however, Laskin would have attenuated the rule in these circumstances and made available damages consequent to pure economic loss. Thus, quite early on in his career, Laskin demonstrated an aptitude for fitting the law to modern circumstances and rejecting a formalistic approach to legal doctrine.

In the same year as *Rivtow*, Laskin also gave a forceful dissent in *A.G. v. Lavell; Isaac v. Bédard* (1974).[32] This case followed in the wake of *Drybones v. The Queen* (1970),[33] which challenged a provision of the *Criminal Code* making it an offence to be intoxicated while on reserve lands as a violation of the equality guarantees of the Canadian *Bill of Rights*. The challenge was successful, and the Court in that case demonstrated a willingness to treat the *Bill of Rights* as a quasi-constitutional document.

In *Lavell*, challenges were brought against the *Indian Act* under the same equality guarantees. Lavell was an Aboriginal woman who forfeited her Indian status on her marriage to a non-status man. The *Indian Act* had no equivalent provision stripping men of their status should they marry a non-status female. The majority of the Court failed to accept the challenge and adopted a formal and mechanical reasoning in the process. Distinguishing this case from *Drybones* on a narrow basis, the majority held that the *Bill of Rights* could not override special legislation enacted with respect to Indians. Second, as all women under the *Indian Act* were treated in the exact same fashion, there was no violation of equality. According to the majority reasons, it was both permissible and necessary for Parliament to draw distinctions between different groups of people. The effect of this decision effectively undercut the equality provision – under the reasoning that, as long as there is consistent discriminatory treatment among a particular group, that discrimination is legal.

Laskin vociferously dissented in the case and held that the differential treatment of Aboriginal women sanctioned under the *Indian Act* contravened the equality provisions of the *Bill of Rights*. Rejecting the amount of deference the majority paid to the federal government's authority to legislate with respect to Aboriginal people, Laskin held that the Act resulted in Aboriginal women being alienated from their societies. Thus, he said, the authority to legislate cannot be construed so broadly as to enable Parliament to act in a manner that violates the equality guarantees of the *Bill of Rights*.[34]

The following year, in *Hogan v. The Queen*, (1975),[35] Laskin once again argued for a broader understanding of the *Bill of Rights* and of the judicial role in law reform. The accused in that case had argued that improperly obtained evidence ought to be subject to absolute exclusion under the *Bill of Rights*. The majority of the Court rejected this understanding and continued to adhere to the traditional common law approach that evidence, no matter how obtained, was only to be assessed according to its relevancy: If that evidence had probative value, it would be admissible. Laskin rejected this rigid adherence to the past, advocated an absolute exclusionary rule modelled on the approach of the United States Supreme Court, and once again demonstrated his divergence from most of the Court about the appropriateness of courts and judges introducing legal reform.

Rivtow and *Highway Properties* indicate a willingness on Laskin's part to expand the law in the realm of private law – which is largely common law based and consequently often considered an appropriate province for judges to be more activist.[36] *Lavell* and *Hogan* suggest that Laskin's reformist tendencies were not limited to the common law arena but were also present in the public law context; the existence of a statutory authority was not, in itself, a bar to Laskin to undertaking law reform. To the modern reader, the innovation displayed in Laskin's reasons in *Lavell* and *Hogan* may not be readily apparent. Modern jurisprudence relating to section 15 equality guarantees and the exclusion of evidence under section 24(2) of the *Charter* may make these cases seem simple to a modern audience. However, when taking a historical approach, it is important to remember that these issues and events must be viewed as the contemporary actors would have done, not as we do now. The *Charter* has likely changed our sense of what was and was not, for its time, a constitutional milestone.

Yet it must also be borne in mind that there was no constitutional authority or mandate on which to base this enunciation of individual rights. The *Bill of Rights* was a statutory document and, while it purported to be quasi-constitutional in nature, it had been enacted by the Diefenbaker government to guarantee citizens basic rights and freedoms. However, the courts were slow to recognize the document as anything other than a simple Act of the legislature.[37] As is apparent from the *Drybones* case, there are no instances of the Supreme Court giving full effect to the *Bill of Rights*. Thus, Laskin is noteworthy for his willingness to make the Act more than a mere statute and, moreover, for using it as a means to give effect to our more familiar modern-day notion of human rights.

Kienapple v. The Queen (1974)[38] provides a further example of Laskin's challenge to a traditional understanding of public law. However, his pioneering approach can only be appreciated with a discussion of *Doré v. A.G. of Canada* (1974).[39] The *Doré* case was heard in 1972, before Laskin became Chief Justice and prior to *Kienapple*. Laskin was not selected as a member of the bench in the former case. The decision in *Doré* was reserved, however, when the leave to appeal in the *Kienapple* case was granted. Essentially, the same issues were implicated in *Doré* as in *Kienapple*. The central question was whether an accused could be charged and convicted on two separate offences for the same action. The majority in *Doré* – Justices Fauteaux, Abbott, and Ritchie – concluded that such a result was indeed possible and that there was no principle to deny the multiple convictions for one action. The decision was not released immediately, however, but was issued on the same day that a contrary result was reached in *Kienapple*. Interesting events happened in the interim between the *Doré* and the *Kienapple* appeal – specifically, Laskin was named Chief Justice and Justices Abbott and Fauteux both resigned.

Writing for the majority in *Kienapple*, Laskin broke judicial ground by recognizing a new defence to criminal charges on the basis of a kind of *res judicata*. The accused in the case had been charged and convicted of both rape and having sex with a female under the age of 14 years. The two charges were laid in relation to the same incident and the same sexual act, and the Court was called on to consider whether it was lawful to convict an individual twice for essentially the same offence. Despite the presence of a strong dissent, Laskin found majority support for his argument that the law ought to be extended to recognize the principle that no one ought to be punished twice for the same offence.

However, Laskin's innovation and his willingness to expand the law can only be appreciated when considered in context. The decision in *Kienapple* was achieved by a narrow majority of 5 to 4, and there was considerable pull among the justices to adopt the more traditional view of the law that would allow for multiple punishments for the same transgression. The release of contradictory rulings was an embarrassment for the Court. *Kienapple* suggested change and law reform, while *Doré* signalled maintenance of the status quo. Although Laskin's view ultimately won out, a rehearing was ordered for the *Doré* case, and the finding in *Kienapple* was upheld. The contradiction in the results was personally embarrassing for Laskin because this kind of situation was one that a Chief Justice ought to avoid. The role requires a large degree of consensus building, and Laskin, in these early days, seemed generally more preoccupied with effecting change than in presenting a unified Court. Thus, these cases emphasize the progressive elements of Laskin's decisions and highlight that, in many respects, Laskin was waging a war in these early years against the Court's often conservative ideology.

In 1974, when both the *Kienapple* and *Doré* judgments were rendered, Laskin also wrote the majority opinion in *Thorson v. A.G. Canada*[40] – considered one of the most active law reform decisions of the Court during the era.[41] At issue was the question of when a party would have standing before the courts. The majority rejected the traditional grounds that a person must have to be specially affected or exceptionally prejudiced to have standing in cases where a declaration of constitutional validity was sought. Recognizing that to require a special interest for a grant of standing to occur would effectively immunize from judicial review a great deal of government legislation (which is, by nature, drafted in general terms), Laskin declined to uphold the strict historical rule that a special interest was required. Instead, he and the majority stretched the law to recognize that it was the right of every citizen to have Parliament act within its boundaries and, therefore, any citizen could challenge the constitutionality of a law. What was granted was not an unfettered right, whatever the circumstance, to challenge a law. However, the majority position articulated by Laskin significantly lowered the threshold for accessing justice. The reformulated rule was, where there was no person or class of persons more directly affected by the legislation, and the legislation in question would otherwise be immune from review, that the Court could exercise discretion and grant standing to an individual seeking to challenge the constitutional authority of the government.

Perhaps the best known of Laskin's early judgments is his dissent in *Murdoch* (1975), which caused him to be hailed as a "jurisprudential folk hero" by one CBC radio reporter.[42] The case centred on the division of property between two divorcing spouses who had operated a ranch in Alberta. The majority of the Court denied Mrs. Murdoch's petition for an equal division of the marital property. Mr. Murdoch had sole title to the ranch, and Mrs. Murdoch could not avail herself of the relevant trust doctrines because she had not made any direct contribution to the property. The Supreme Court upheld the finding of the trial judge that the "work done by any ranch wife" was not a "substantial contribution" to the matrimonial home.

Laskin rejected the majority position and would have awarded Mrs. Murdoch an equal share in the property through the development of trust law. He explicitly advocated taking an activist role, arguing that courts ought to become involved to fill the gaps in the existing law:

> No doubt, legislative action may be the better way to lay down policies and prescribe conditions under which and the extent to which spouses should share in property acquired by either or both during marriage. But the better way is not the only way; and if the exercise of a traditional jurisdiction by the Courts can conduce to equitable sharing, it should not be withheld merely because difficulties in particular cases and the making of distinctions may result in slower and perhaps more painful evolution of principle.[43]

Again, this decision marks Laskin as being separate and apart from the rest of the Court. Rather than apply clear and uncontroverted law, he preferred to shape and create new law to avoid a perceived injustice. This decision resonated with the general population and highlighted how out of step the existing law was with modern circumstances. Following reforms to the *Divorce Act, 1968*, and the subsequent decision of the Court in *Rathwell v. Rathwell*,[44] Laskin's dissent eventually would become the governing law.

It might be that Laskin's dissent in *Murdoch* is something of an anomaly; Professor Carol Rogerson has argued in the *University of Toronto Law Journal* collection of articles and essays on Laskin's jurisprudence that, generally, Laskin was not at the forefront of change in his family law decisions.[45] She notes that many of Laskin's later family law decisions fail to make the law respond as robustly to the needs of the family as he was able to do in the *Murdoch* dissent. Whatever the content of Laskin's other family law decisions, this does not detract from the innovation present in *Murdoch*. Recognizing both an injustice and a gap in the law, Laskin, in his early years on the Court, demonstrated willingness and an aptitude for construing and expanding the law to meet perceived needs.

The final case to be discussed in the early Laskin period is the *Harrison* (1976) decision itself. This case once again found Laskin in dissent. At issue was the right of Sophie Carswell to picket outside her employer's place of business, which, in this case, happened to be situated within a shopping plaza and constituted private property.

An earlier case, *Peters v. The Queen*,[46] decided by the Ontario Court of Appeal in the year after Laskin's departure, determined the issue and held that a property owner had the right to exclusive possession of his premises. Therefore, the shopping plaza owner in this case was within his rights to exclude Carswell from attending her employer's place of business to picket. The majority of the Supreme Court adopted the analysis of the lower court on this issue and found *Peters* to be a binding precedent. The shopping plaza was private property, and the landlord's right to exclude persons from it was absolute.

Again, Laskin dissented and wrote specifically with regard to the *Peters* decision: "This court, above all others in this country, cannot be simply mechanistic about previous decisions, whatever be the respect it would pay to such decisions."[47] To ignore the fact that Carswell was exercising her freedom of expression and interests as a worker was nonsensical and antithetical to Laskin's conception of the law and justice. For him, where social facts existed that ought to be noted, it was the responsibility of the Court to take them into account when rendering judgment.

For the dissent, it was clearly important that the social interest in allowing peaceful protest be balanced against the traditionally uncontested rights of owners to exclusive possession of property.

These examples of Laskin's early decisions on the Supreme Court, taken together, suggest that, regardless of the area of the law, Laskin was willing to change the law – either by expanding it to account for change (*Murdoch, Hogan, Rivtow, Kienapple*) or refusing to follow it when it was out of step with reality (*Harrison, Highway Properties*). These cases indicate a refusal by Laskin to be bound by the doctrine of *stare decisis* or by statutory authority. Implicit in these judgments is a belief in the validity of judicial creativity, justified by the perceived need for judges to respond to the circumstances of cases with a subtle and innovative application of the law. Thus, the Laskin of these early decisions appears to be both a pioneer and a non-traditionalist in his willingness to make the law fit the circumstances, rather than have the old forms and rules govern where sense would not be served or an injustice would be done.

The Later Decisions, 1976–84

IN 1976 LASKIN HAD been a member of the Supreme Court for six years and Chief Justice for half that time. As the cases discussed have shown, he assumed an activist position, frequently dissenting, and was generally unafraid to cause controversy when he thought it justified. This section will focus on whether a marked shift in the content and philosophy underlying Laskin's judgments exists from 1976 to 1984, one that sets them apart from the earlier cases.

In *Re Anti-Inflation (Canada)* (1976),[48] the Supreme Court was called on to determine whether the federal government had constitutional authority to legislate to combat rising inflation rates. The Court was severely fractured both as to the appropriate result and as to reasons but, ultimately, the *Anti-Inflation Act, 1974*, was found to be a valid exercise of federal authority under the emergency power reserved in the "peace, order and good government" (POGG) clause of the Constitution.

Laskin found himself in the majority on this case, and his reasons display both innovation and traditionalism. His readiness to undertake reform is evident in his treatment of the POGG clause, which allows the federal government to enact legislation in situations of emergency or national crisis. Throughout Canada's constitutional history, this residual power has been significantly reduced, owing mainly to the efforts of the Privy Council.[49] Before 1976, it was generally accepted that, for this provision to operate, there needed to be some kind of national emergency.[50] Laskin, however, reinterpreted the doctrine in his decision, moving away from the need to demonstrate a clear "emergency" but allowing the federal government to step in when it perceived a "crisis." Sky-rocketing inflation rates stood a better chance of constituting a "crisis" than a "national emergency." However, it was far from clear that rising inflation rates demanded any intervention by the federal government. A large body of social science evidence was tendered suggesting that the situation was not urgent. The previous jurisprudence seemed to make it clear that only "emergencies" were the proper subject matter for the POGG power, but Laskin refused to interpret the case law in this way. Instead, the decisions rendered by the Privy Council defining "emergency" were considered illustrative only of the kinds of situations where the POGG could be invoked; these earlier cases offered examples, but not a threshold, for the invocation of the residual power. There was no need to limit the POGG simply to "emergencies"; instead, there was scope for the application of the power in less dire circumstances.

Yet there is a second aspect to the judgment – that of legislative deference. In considering whether rising inflation rates could amount to a "crisis," Laskin ignored the large body of social science evidence, which suggested this was not the case. Instead, he deferred to the Parliament, holding that the proper standard for review was not whether there was actually an emergency, but whether the government could reasonably believe that the country was in such a state. That is a much laxer test, and far easier for the government to meet. Therefore, while Laskin still exhibited his inclination to adjust the law as demanded by the situation, there is a tension in this case as he is, concomitantly, distancing himself from too rampant an activism. Laskin's willingness to take account of social conditions is checked by legislative deference, and a limit emerges to Laskin's conception of judicial authority.

Paskivski v. Canadian Pacific Ltd. (1976)[51] suggests that Laskin was still committed to exercising judicial creativity in the realm of private law. This case involved the consideration of a common law rule that shielded railways from tort liability unless statutory requirements had been violated or extenuating circumstances were implicated in the events. The

Court divided on this issue, with the majority finding the railway liable but grounded liability in the "extenuating circumstances" exception to the traditional rule. Consequently, the rule exempting liability was not overturned despite *obiter* comments that such a rule may no longer serve a useful purpose. Laskin, concurring in the result, went a step further and explicitly stated that this rule ought no longer to be accepted, noting that the rule was crafted in very different circumstances – when governmental aid was given to railways to develop a fledgling economy – and that, in 1975, it no longer served any pressing purpose.

Continuing the examination of Laskin's treatment of private law, *Board of Governors of Seneca College of Applied Arts and Technology v. Bhadauria* (1981)[52] arguably represents a more conservative approach by Laskin. The case raised issues of the appropriate interplay between Ontario's new *Human Rights Code* and the common law. Bhadauria was attempting to have a new tort recognized – the tort of discrimination – alleging that she had been wrongly passed over for promotion on the grounds of race. This issue could have been dealt with under the provincial legislation, as the *Ontario Human Rights Code* provided remedies to those discriminated against on the basis of race. However, any application filed was subject to the minister's unfettered discretion whether or not to proceed. Thus, the Code offered no guarantee that one's claim would be heard, nor was compensation for harm suffered the objective of the legislation. Instead, the emphasis in the statute was to be on building conciliation between the parties.

The Ontario Court of Appeal found in favour of Bhadauria, expanding the law so as to provide relief under tort principles for those wrongfully discriminated against. The Supreme Court, however, led by Laskin, reversed this finding and refused to recognize a novel tort. According to Laskin, courts ought not to create by "judicial fiat" a new tort, particularly where the legislature had already responded to the situation. For Laskin, the existence of human rights legislation militated in favour of non-intervention by the courts. It seems that Laskin conceived of the provincial statute as "covering the field" and left little room for judicial creativity.

In one sense, this case could be seen as a progressive decision – a remedy is refused in favour of having the individual take recourse under the authority of an administrative tribunal, the Human Rights Commission of Ontario. This approach was certainly a marked change from the lack of deference courts have traditionally afforded such agencies and, perhaps in this sense, Laskin may be seen as breaking new ground. However, it is arguable that there was a definite conservative element to this judgment which was not present in some of Laskin's early decisions.

Presented with a gap in the common law which would allow wrongful, harmful conduct such as discriminatory treatment in the workplace to pass unchecked, Laskin failed to respond to the deficiency. In earlier cases, such as *Rivtow* and *Highway Properties,* he responded to deficiencies in the common law by extending it to cover the new circumstances and better accord with contemporary values and objectives. However, such incremental reform is refused here. The main reason for denying the reform seems to be the existence of the *Human Rights Code*. However, there was nothing in the Code which would preclude a common law remedy. Given Laskin's past strong judicial treatment of discrimination claims (e.g., *Lavell*), the decision in the *Bhadauria* case suggests that Laskin is espousing more moderate views, particularly in relation to the appropriate role of the judiciary in achieving law reform.

Laskin's decision in *Bhadauria* has been criticized for being both "bad law and bad policy."[53] Commentators have noted that the pre-emption of recognition of a new tort was not mandated by the legislation and was contrary to the ordinary principles of statutory interpretation. Generally speaking, a statute will not be considered to derogate from the common law unless it does so explicitly. In this case, the Code was silent about possible private law remedies for such discrimination and, in the ordinary course, this silence would not be taken to exclude intervention by the courts. Indeed, an alternative to statutory relief was generally considered desirable – the Code provided only for conciliation, not compensation; capped awards to complainants at $5,000; and was subject to the complete discretion of the minister.[54]

Professor Denise Réaume has argued that the *Bhadauria* case is reconcilable with Laskin's overall judicial philosophy because the nature of the decision in the case was precisely the kind of matter that "courts were relatively powerless to redress"[55] and one that is best left to the legislature to resolve. While there may be a coherent ideology underlying these decisions, it is difficult to understand Laskin's reserve in this case. In earlier private law cases, he demonstrated a willingness to expand and adapt the law to serve justice. In *Highway Properties* (1971) and *Rivtow* (1974) he expanded legal principles. In addition, when dealing with legislation, Laskin rejected a formalistic interpretation of the equality provisions in the *Bill of Rights* in the *Lavell* case (1974). The *Bhadauria* decision in 1981 seems to demonstrate more restraint and conservatism than Laskin had previously shown in his earlier period on the Court.

Given the deference shown to administrative agencies in *Bhadauria* in the private law context, it is useful to examine Laskin's treatment of similar agencies in cases where he dealt with public law matters.

The decision Laskin penned for the majority of the Court in *Nicholson v. Haldimand-Norfolk Regional Board of Commissioners of Police*[56] sparked what has since been termed the "fairness revolution" in administrative law.[57] Nicholson was a member of the police force who faced discipline under the Board of Commissioners, an administrative agency and not a court. The majority of the Supreme Court broke with tradition and held that, even in an administrative tribunal context, an individual was still entitled to some degree of procedural fairness. Until that time, individuals could only assert rights to fair procedures from the courts. In rejecting this traditional stance, the majority decision was effectively rejecting strict conceptual classifications of courts and agencies and of legislative and judicial functions.[58] Instead, Laskin stated, the resulting fairness to the individual was of greater importance than a strict observance of forum:

> What rightly lies behind this emergence is the realization that the classification of statutory functions as judicial, *quasi*-judicial or administrative is often very difficult, to say the least: and to endow some with procedural protection while denying others any at all would work injustice when the results of statutory decisions raise the same serious consequences for those adversely affected, regardless of the classification of the function in question ... [59]

Consequently, this decision introduced a vast change in this area of the law and – while it remained unclear precisely what an individual could now expect in terms of procedures – the general tenor of the Court was quite clear. It seems, therefore, that the judicial creativity present in so many of Laskin's early decisions was not absent in *Nicholson*, and the case demonstrates a willingness to undertake judicial reform of public law.

In *Canadian Union of Public Employees, Local 963 v. New Brunswick Liquor Corporation* (1979)[60] and in *Canada Labour Relations Board v.*

Halifax Longshoreman's Association (1983),[61] Laskin also displayed a great deal of deference for administrative agencies. In both cases, at issue was a consideration of the authority of Labour Relations tribunals and, in each instance, Laskin took the position that, to the greatest extent possible, courts ought to recognize and defer to the expertise of such agencies. In neither case was a privative clause present – an indication from the legislature that the administrative body is to have exclusive jurisdiction in the particular field. Thus, where no privative clause exists, Laskin took the contrary position to the traditional view that judges ought to police the administrative state, holding:

> It is rarely a simple matter to draw a line between a lawful and unlawful exercise of power by a statutory tribunal, however ample its authority, when there are conflicting considerations addressed to the exercise of power. The Court has, over quite a number of years, thought it more consonant with the legislative objectives involved in a case such as this to be more rather than less deferential to the discharge of difficult tasks by statutory tribunals.[62]

As Professor Hudson Janisch has noted, the *Halifax Longshoreman's* decision and the *CUPE* decision echo Laskin's earlier views on the nature of the administrative state in emphasizing the specialized expertise of administrative tribunals and the comprehensive nature of their legislative mandate.[63] However, Janisch does go on to note that, in rising to the bench, Laskin's views were subject to alteration. As a law professor, he rejected the utility of courts becoming engaged of questions of "jurisdiction"; specifically, if the courts should review administrative decisions on the basis of whether the issue in question properly fell within the agency's mandate and statutory authority.[64] For Professor Laskin, administrative agencies were entitled to be accorded considerable respect from the courts. During his academic tenure, Laskin endorsed the belief that such agencies were better suited than courts to deal with certain spheres – such as labour law – and, within these spheres, agencies ought to be seen as authoritative. His decisions on the bench, however, suggest a moderated view.[65]

While on the Ontario Court of Appeal, Laskin endorsed the conventional jurisdiction doctrines to determine matters in *Metropolitan Life Insurance Company v. International Union of Operating Engineers, Local 796* (1970).[66] Even in his initial days on the bench, he became more moderate acting as a judge than he had been in his role as professor. At that time, he conceived of a more autonomous role for the administrative state, a position generally not endorsed by the courts. Yet, once on the bench, Laskin granted less independence to agencies and tribunals than he had previously advocated.

The salient point for the purpose of this discussion is that, even in the latter part of his career, Laskin was articulating a fairly innovative position with respect to administrative bodies and challenging the former notions that they were owed little deference and that the courts were a more appropriate forum for the adjudication of rights and interests. Yet, in another important decision, Laskin displayed even more conservative and moderate thoughts in relation to administrative law.

One of the most significant decisions in this area is found in *Crevier v. A.G. Québec* (1981).[67] At issue in the case was whether an administrative agency could be completely immunized from judicial scrutiny by its enacting statute. Laskin, writing for the majority, held that section 96 of the Canadian Constitution prevented the legislature from establishing an appellate administrative mechanism because it would, in effect, be creating a section 96 court.

In many respects, this decision was a blow to the viability and autonomy of administrative agencies because it effectively held that courts were always to have some type of advisory role over administrative bodies, regardless of Parliament's intentions. This conservative view of judicial authority entrenches and safeguards the rights of review and is sharply juxtaposed to many of Laskin's earlier views on the relationship between administrative agencies and the courts. Writing as a professor in 1952, Laskin espoused the view, first, that the courts were not constitutionally mandated in Canada and, second, that administrative bodies did not have to be subject to judicial review:

> We may well feel that judicial supremacy is the highest of all values under a democratic regime of law, and a value to which even the legislature should pay tribute. *But we have not enshrined it in any fundamental constitutional law or in our political system.* On the contrary, the cardinal principle of our system of representative government, inherited from Great Britain, has been the supremacy of the legislature ... We must not

then delude ourselves that judicial review rests on any higher ground than that of being implicit in statutory interpretation.[68]

What had been a modest view of the role and scope of judicial review in the Canadian constitutional system in 1952 had, by 1981, been elevated so that its exclusion was constitutionally prohibited. Laskin seemed to adopt a more restrained view of administrative agencies and a more conservative and traditional conception of the judiciary as guardians over the administrative state, and he has been roundly criticized by many for taking this stance. Some commentators regard the *Crevier* judgment as something of a betrayal by the former champion of the administrative state, one that reinforced the notion that courts and agencies are bodies within the same structure, and that courts are always to be paramount to the tribunal.[69]

However, it is not entirely clear that *Crevier* is such a betrayal. Laskin's decisions also include *Halifax Longshoreman* and *CUPE*, with *Crevier* sandwiched in between, where a deferential approach to the administrative state was taken. Like Laskin's family law decisions, the cases do not all tell the same story. The tenor of the *Crevier* decision does, however, seem to suggest a different view. It appears to invoke something of the more traditional view that courts are more institutionally competent to adjudicate rights and, therefore, no matter what the area or how specialized the knowledge of the tribunal implicated, courts will have a gatekeeping role to play by reason of their very nature – a view that Laskin now anchored in the Constitution.

The final case to be discussed is that of *Leatherdale v. Leatherdale* (1982),[70] and it also indicates the emergence of a more restrained element in Laskin's judgments. Reminiscent of the *Murdoch* case, *Leatherdale* involved a claim by Mrs. Leatherdale for one-half of the matrimonial property. Differentiating the case from *Murdoch* was the fact that, since the public outcry at the inequities of divorce legislation, the Ontario legislature had taken action and enacted a statute governing the division of property between divorcing spouses.[71] Here, Laskin wrote for the majority rather than the dissent, and the *Leatherdale* decision, written in 1982, close to a decade after *Murdoch*, displays greater reserve and less reforming spirit.

Like Mrs. Murdoch, Mrs. Leatherdale claimed a half interest in the matrimonial property. However, instead of having to resort to trust arguments, Mrs. Leatherdale could rely on Ontario's *Family Law Reform Act*.[72] Where Laskin would have awarded Mrs. Murdoch a one-half interest in the matrimonial property as a result of her contributions to the work years earlier, Mrs. Leatherdale received only a one-quarter interest in the matrimonial assets. The assets in question in this case were corporate shares purchased during the marriage. Laskin held that Mrs. Leatherdale was entitled to a lesser interest on the basis that her contributions as a homemaker did not provide an argument for the equal sharing in the asset. However, because she had worked outside the home and earned an income for a portion of the marriage, this contribution formed the basis on which the one-quarter interest was merited.

In one sense, it is difficult to compare the *Murdoch* and *Leatherdale* decisions, because the former case was decided on the basis of common law principles while the latter result was ostensibly governed by statute. In *Leatherdale*, it is therefore arguable that the statute, rather than Laskin, directed the finding. However, it is important to note how Laskin reasoned from the statute. This process reveals a far more conservative approach and outlook to the matters in issue than had been demonstrated in his earlier dissent in *Murdoch*.

The Ontario legislation divided matrimonial assets into two categories – only one of which required equal division between the spouses. The corporate shares fell into the "non-family" asset category and were not automatically to be shared equally.[73] However, the Act did provide in section 4(6) and in section 8 for the sharing of a non-family asset on the basis of indirect contributions. Thus, as Professor Rogerson explained in her piece on Laskin and family law, two provisions in the legislation could have operated as a "statutory hook" to effect what might be considered a more equitable result in the case.[74] However, Laskin declined to decide in this way and refused to acknowledge that contributions in the form of domestic service could give rise to an equal sharing of non-family assets.[75] Interestingly, Justice Estey reached exactly this same result in his dissent. What, then, had happened to Laskin, "the great dissenter," by this period?

The *Leatherdale* decision witnesses Laskin demonstrating two kinds of conservatism. First, his reluctance to consider domestic contributions as possibly giving rise to an interest in a non-family – characteristically businesslike – asset indicates a conservative notion of family law and fails to take into account relevant social changes that he had been prepared to acknowledge in *Murdoch*. Laskin was more sensitive to the importance of women's contributions to the home and family life in 1975 than he was in 1982 – and to the idea that these contributions could come in various forms. One might well expect that kind of awareness to grow, rather than diminish, over time.

Second, *Leatherdale* also demonstrates a kind of institutional conservatism. Laskin's flair for judicial creativity as exercised in the *Murdoch*, *Rivtow*, *Harrison*, and *Hogan* cases is completely absent here. Instead of using the "easy answer" and drawing on the possibilities provided by the statute to create an equitable division of the property, Laskin took a literal and unimaginative approach to the words and intentions of the legislature, thereby marginalizing the social context in which the decision was being made. Thus, *Leatherdale* is a marked departure from the innovation present in *Murdoch* and, given that the issues raised in the two cases were nearly identical, suggests a moderation of Laskin's earlier reformist tendencies and signals a departure from some of the creative spirit of the 1970s.

Rogerson argues that the decision in *Leatherdale*, while more conservative, is not necessarily inconsistent with Laskin's earlier decision in *Murdoch*, since both emphasize economic obligations of support between spouses.[76] She notes that, in the intervening period between the judgments, the ideals of equitable sharing of matrimonial property became so entrenched that "anything less than an award of a one-half share to the housewife is seen as retrograde."[77] The point is well founded: there does not seem to be any implicit shift in Laskin's attitudes towards the division of matrimonial property. However, the *Leatherdale* decision represents a much more conservative approach to the law.

Where in *Murdoch* Laskin was able to see the direction the law ought to take, and he attempted to direct it there, in *Leatherdale* he seemed, rather, to focus on the limits of the law and passed on the opportunity to further expand and push for more equitable results. It would not have taken a great deal of innovation on the law to push the limits of the equitable division of martial property in the *Leatherdale* case, but he no longer seemed interested in expanding the law in this way. The unanswered question is, of course, why Laskin lost interest in pushing this change. It could be that, at the time of the *Murdoch* decision, he was more interested in agitating for change, primarily for the sake of change and only secondarily in actual reforms to the view of women's contributions to the home. Or it remains possible that Laskin did, in fact, change his mind on the substantive issue of property division. The third possibility is that Laskin had not lost interest in changing the law, but, rather, no longer viewed it as his primary role. As professionals approach the end of their careers, thoughts of their legacy are common. It could be, as McCormick suggests, that the legacy Laskin sought to leave from his Chief Justiceship was that of moderate conservative, instead of the "dissenter" as envisioned by Bushnell.

However, it seems to overstate the case to say, as Bushnell does, that Laskin failed to live up to the promises for change that his appointment heralded. Increasingly in the majority, as McCormick emphasized, Laskin continued to be a strong influence on the Court. An examination of the substance of the post-1979 period depicts something more akin to subtle, rather than dramatic, change. Laskin does not abandon all creativity in adjudication. Instead, the opinions rendered in *Paskivski* (1976) and the *Anti-Inflation Reference* (1976) signal his continuing commitment to law reform and adapting the law to a changed environment.

Yet, while these tendencies are still apparent in Laskin's judgments, there are also perceptible undercurrents in some of these cases which suggest an alteration of Laskin's views in one particular area – that of the role of the judge. In *Bhadauria*, the *Anti-Inflation Reference*, and *Leatherdale*, Laskin seems to give more deference to legislative authority and the limits to judicial creativity than he displayed in the first part of his tenure on the Supreme Court. However, the limitations on judicial authority in these later cases must also be considered against cases such as *Halifax Longshoreman*, *CUPE*, and *Crevier* which widen the adjudicative role of the courts in relation to the administrative state and entrench their existence and mandate in the Canadian Constitution.

These later decisions therefore tend to reveal, in matters of substantive law, the Laskin of old in terms of imaginative effort. However, there are hints that a growing conservatism has coloured his understanding of the judicial function. This perceptible change will be further discussed in Parts V and VI, along with intriguing questions of why such a shift may have occurred. Although, ultimately, a firm resolution of this question remains elusive, tentative assertions will be made about possible reasons for Laskin's newfound conservatism.

PART IV: LASKIN'S EXTRA-JUDICIAL WRITINGS

EVEN THOUGH LASKIN'S JUDICIAL opinions are the best source of determining whether a shift occurred in his decision making, his extra-judicial writings during this period, specifically after his appointment to the Supreme Court, may also prove useful. Canadian judges are generally prevented from commenting on their decisions, but Laskin's academic work can still provide some insights into his philosophies and into his conception of the role and sphere of authority of the judiciary. As with his decisions, consideration of his extraneous writings will be evaluated in two parts: the early writings (1970–75) and the later writings (1976–84).

The insights drawn from these writings are limited, and care must be taken not to infer too much from the opinions expressed. Judges are constrained by their offices – and, to avoid the perception of bias, are limited in what they may talk about in public. Political issues are generally inappropriate subject matter for public address and, quite often, judges are limited to speaking broadly of the nature of the law or the role of the judge when called upon to speak. Consequently, there is a danger in drawing firm conclusions from the frequency or the nature of these writings.

There is also the problem of uniformity. In the writings selected here, Laskin offers his views on the nature of the judiciary and its public mandate. However, these are Laskin's expressed views – it is nearly impossible to measure the extent to which these ideals guided him in his actual decision making. In short, the expressed philosophy may not actually have been practised, in much the same way that a person speaking on the philosophy of dancing might not actually dance as she says.

The Early Writings, 1970–75

IT IS CLEAR FROM even Laskin's first days of appointment to the Supreme Court that he did not consider himself bound by tradition. At his induction ceremony, Laskin clearly enunciated his conception of his judicial role:

> When I took my seat on the Supreme Court of Canada I told my colleagues ... that (1) I had no expectations to live up to save those I placed

upon myself; (2) I had no constituency to serve save the realm of reason; (3) I had no influences to dispel unless there was a threat to my intellectual disinterestedness; and (4) I had no one to answer to save my own conscience and my personal standards of integrity.[78]

This statement highlights Laskin's unwillingness to be bound by precedent or to give undue deference to the legislature. Indeed, Laskin indicates in this early part of his career that he holds a vision of judicial activism, a vision suggesting that the courts are in a "junior partnership" with the legislature and are like elected officials, charged with updating the law.[79] Such words signal the presence of a reformer and a non-conformist on the Court.

Indeed, Laskin made clear in his early writing the importance of judicial creativity in adjudication. He wrote in 1973 that the public ought to be able to expect a creative capacity in judges and that the courts must "keep the law in motion, to nudge it along through review and reassessment to make and keep it contemporary."[80]

Through these extra-judicial writings, Laskin makes it clear that his vision of "judicial creativity" involves two important components. First, judges ought not to adhere rigidly to the doctrines of *stare decisis* and, second, that in resolving disputes, due weight and importance must be given to social circumstances and conditions.

Speaking to the first element of judicial creativity, Laskin called *stare decisis* a "convenience" only and stated that, previously, the doctrine was "a generalization of experience raised to a self-limiting rule."[81] For him,

> principles stated by predecessor Judges have no eternal verity. Stability is only a factor, not an invariable in the judicial process. Questions of "when" and "how" to deal with a principle whose force is spent may remain as indicators of a social lag because, as I have said elsewhere, the law's pace is generally slower than society's march.[82]

Thus, where merited, Laskin wrote that a judge can and ought to depart from the settled law in order to bring about a desirable change.

The corollary of this rejection of strict adherence to precedent is the notion that judges are responsible for apprising themselves of social conditions and must not allow a strict application of the settled law to create injustice in modern circumstances. Laskin demonstrated this view in discussing the responsibility of the courts to keep the law in step with social reality:

> [T]he courts themselves have fashioned many of the rules, they have some responsibility for keeping the rules under surveillance with a view to modifying or changing them as changing conditions may at a particular time warrant. This is true even under a Code when the generality of its terms provides sufficient leeway …. [a legislature's] time is occupied with economic planning, with managing resources, with social welfare policies, with administering the province or country, as the case may be. They may, hence, properly rely on the courts to share in the burden of law-making in those areas congenial to judicial legislation.[83]

In sum, Laskin's earlier writings from this period evidence a tendency towards innovation and creativity. Rejecting formalism and "mechanical jurisprudence,"[84] Laskin saw the role of the judge as responding creatively to the law to make it reflect changing social contexts. Indeed, this interpretation bears out when viewed against the cases decided during this early period. In cases such as *Murdoch* and *Harrison*, he demonstrated this willingness to look beyond settled law and to craft decisions that may depart from precedent but met the needs of present circumstances.

The Later Writings, 1976–84

LASKIN'S WRITINGS IN THE later part of his judicial appointment decrease, making it more difficult to use them as a source to garner insights into possible shifts in his judicial philosophies. This decline is likely largely attributable to the ill health that Laskin experienced for a large part of his final years. However, while these later writings are not voluminous, they do offer a few insights into his philosophies in his later years, with the continued caveat that such writings are not necessarily reflective of his deep-seated personal beliefs.

Writing in 1980, Laskin once again offered his vision of the judiciary and commented on the role of judges in the legal system:

> [I]n the discharge of their duties, a judge is bound to obey the law and to administer it if it is statute law, in accordance with its terms. [Judges] can protect human rights and individual freedom under the law if there are constitutional imperatives that enable them to do so. If there are no constitutional limitations on legislative or legislatively authorized executive action, there may still be judicial check on arbitrariness through the judicial power to interpret and apply the law. If repressive or discriminatory

legislation which is validly enacted leave little or no room for protection of the individual, Judges may express their dismay but will nonetheless be bound to give effect to it. Judges cannot enter the lists and engage in social or political controversy whatever be their private feelings.[85]

By conceding the "reality" that judges "may express their dismay but will nonetheless be bound," Laskin is acknowledging the legitimate role of a more restrained approach to adjudication. It is difficult to imagine that he would have made a comment about judges not being able to enter the lists and engage in social or political controversy in the earlier period. There, Laskin focused on the reach of a judge's mandate, but, in this instance, the focus has shifted to the limits of that authority. This excerpt suggests a level of deference to the legislature that was not raised in Laskin's earlier writings. Here, the idea is not that judges are in a "partnership" with the Parliament – as earlier expressed – but, rather, that each has its separate sphere with its own internal limitations, and each must stay within that role. There is also much less emphasis on the desirability of taking into account social circumstance in reaching a result. While Laskin certainly does not suggest that circumstances are no longer relevant in adjudication, he now seems to indicate that there is a limit as to which circumstances may properly drive the judicial result. Consequently, Laskin appears to view the function of the judiciary in more moderate and less activist ways than he had previously articulated.

A similar modification can be seen in Laskin's views about administrative law. As a professor, Laskin held administrative agencies in high esteem and argued that there was no legal requirement why such agencies should automatically be subject to review by the courts.[86] However, in 1977, in writing a paper on the nature of the Canadian Constitution, he took a much more judicially conservative view of administrative agencies and their role in the legal system. As if foreshadowing *Crevier*, he wrote:

> On the administrative agency side of the problem under discussion, it is obvious that such agencies cannot escape making determinations of law in the course of their regulatory or quasi-regulatory operations, and to deny them such leeway would weaken considerably their utility. The reasonable compromise here is *to deny them unreviewable authority* to make such determinations, and equally *to deny them power to determine finally the limits of their jurisdiction.*[87]

Laskin's views as a law professor in 1952, when taken in tandem with his decisions in *Halifax Longshoreman* and *CUPE*, portray a more progressive approach to the administrative state and demonstrate a greater willingness to view such agencies as autonomous from judges and the courts than is evident in his article published in 1977 or his decision in *Crevier*. However, there is a substantial difference in freedom between a professor espousing his views on the law and a justice on Canada's highest court making similar pronouncements. As a professor, Laskin was not under any duty and could freely criticize aspects of the law. As a judge, however, he was not only obliged to keep himself untainted from any apprehension of bias but also charged with the protection and enforcement of the law. Therefore, criticism of the law in the role of judge must largely be contained within a written decision.

There is still some basis, however, to suggest that, as Laskin approached the end of his career, his views on the role of judges were becoming more moderate. The drive for reform is attenuated in these later writings, and the emphasis seems to have shifted to delineating the proper sphere of judges and articulating limits to their authority.

PART V: ASSESSING LASKIN'S CONTRIBUTIONS TO THE SUPREME COURT

AFTER SURVEYING BROADLY LASKIN's early and late judicial decisions as well as his extra-judicial writings while on the bench, what conclusions are suggested by this material? More narrowly, does the material presented here lend credence to either Bushnell's or McCormick's formulations of Laskin's legacy and impact?

The early decisions (1970–75) certainly bear witness to Laskin as an agitator for change within the Court. Often writing in dissent, as in *Lavell* and *Murdoch*, he demonstrated a willingness to undertake reform and a refusal to be bound by antiquated precedents. In both public and private law, Laskin attempted to make the law meet reality and respond to actual needs. This effort manifested itself through the creation of the constructive trust, the extension of liability for pure economic losses, and the recognition of new criminal defences.

The interpretation of Laskin as innovator bears out when his extra-judicial writings are also taken into consideration. He advocated the exercise of judicial "creativity" in adjudication and suggested that the judiciary ought not to become trapped in formalism but should properly decide cases with a view to social reality.

Thus, Bushnell's portrayal of Laskin as a force of change on assuming his position on the High Court seems well founded. Laskin immediately began to challenge the status quo, as in *Highway Properties*, and he continued to stretch the law to adapt to changing conditions. However, Bushnell's second contention seems to be less obvious. In light of Mc-Cormick's empirical analyses, which indicate that Laskin was in the majority more often after 1976, and particularly after 1979, Bushnell's claim that Laskin was limited to a marginal, dissenting role on the Court after the *Harrison* dissent is not persuasive. A review of only a few specific cases, such as the *Anti-Inflation Reference* and *Nicholson*, shows that Laskin carried the majority of the Court and effected substantial changes in the law even in these later years.

Yet the failure of Bushnell's view to bear out does not necessarily follow that Laskin continued to have the same kind of impact in his later years as he did in his earliest judgments on the Court. That Laskin was playing a central role on the Court, as propounded by McCormick, is accepted, but what kind of role was it? Was he, perhaps, asserting a much more conservative influence?

Many of Laskin's later decisions still indicate reformist tendencies. *Halifax Longshoreman*, *CUPE*, and *Nicholson* were all progressive decisions in administrative law. Cases such as *Paskivski* indicate a continued willingness to hone private law doctrines to meet contemporary trends. However, in these later years, more restraint and conservative strains of thought appear in Laskin's judgments.

Present in these later cases are hints that Laskin's attitudes towards the judicial function have altered. Yet this change is something of a paradox. In some sense, Laskin's later judgments seem to secure more authority and a greater role for judges. *Halifax Longshoreman* and *CUPE*, while advocating for deference to administrative bodies, nevertheless secure a role for courts to police their boundaries. *Crevier* is the culmination of this entrenching of the judiciary because it determines that judicial review of agencies is not only desirable but mandated by the Constitution. This approach is very different from the views Laskin held as a professor. In those years Laskin demonstrated less deference for courts, suggesting that members of the judiciary were not constitutionally mandated as a check on administrative agencies, nor did they act as such. Yet, even as Laskin was involved in cases that increased and secured the judicial province, he was also associated with those that demonstrated increasing deference to the legislature and acknowledged the limited scope of judicial decision making. Cases such as *Bhadauria* and *Leatherdale* evidence more restraint and greater respect for the legislature's role than others that came earlier in his career. This is not to say that Laskin was a "maverick" in his first days on the Supreme Court. However, in many of his earlier opinions, such as in *Kienapple*, he emphasized the desirability of having the law meet current needs rather than what the legislature intended in the enacting statute.

The limited extraneous material penned by Laskin also indicates a moderation in his views of the judges' role. He takes both an expanded and a more limited view of the judicial role – the judge can rightly preside over the administrative agency but, when faced by the will of Parliament, the courts cannot intervene to change the law without a constitutional document. Despite these variations, however, commentators should not place undue emphasis on these writings. Without access to Laskin's personal letters and journals, it is difficult to know to what extent his personal opinions about the judicial function are reflected in these pieces. The need for judicial impartiality necessarily restrains judges from stating opinions outside their decisions. These writings therefore provide some indications of Laskin's leanings but are by no means conclusive of them.

On balance, then, even with the limited utility of the Laskin's extra-judicial writings, a comparison of his earlier and later work does not reveal any significant shift in his doctrinal thoughts. The shift in Laskin's views seems to be entirely in relation to the appropriate role of the courts within the Canadian system of government. This changed conception of judicial function may account for Bushnell's perception of Laskin as failing to live up to the promise of change that had been implied with his appointment to the high court. Merely perceiving the scope of judicial authority to be narrowed will, alone, have an impact on the bounds to which Laskin was willing to push the law. It might not mean that Laskin's own thoughts as to what the law ought to be had changed, but, rather, his reflections on how far a judge might be permitted to make his vision a reality had altered.

The *Leatherdale* decision seems to typify this change. There is no suggestion in the judgment that Laskin's views on the division of marital property had altered significantly since the dissent in *Murdoch*; indeed, Laskin goes a long way to make sure that Mrs. Leatherdale's contributions are not unrewarded. In one respect, Laskin was quite progressive in awarding her a quarter interest in assets in which the enabling statute does not require sharing of any kind. However, the judgment does portray a preoccupation with the legislative scheme and parliamentary intent, and Laskin, in reading in an intention that is not self-evident in the Act, delivers a far more conservative opinion than he handed down in *Murdoch*. In that case, he was ahead of the law and directed it towards appropriate changes. Some eight years later in *Leatherdale*, however, he trailed the legislature and failed to interpret the family law statute in a way that would have been more in keeping with social changes. Thus, this newfound conservatism with respect to the appropriate judicial sphere impinges on the relief and the reform that Laskin deemed himself able to grant. Therefore, while his views may not have changed in relation to the ideas of substantive justice, the results delivered were made different by this altered perception of the judiciary.

This examination of Laskin's work supports the contention of Snell and Vaughan, who argue that, even after assuming the office of Chief Justice, Laskin was unable to move the majority of the Court towards a more active role, as the tradition of legislative deference remained staunchly intact.[88] Rather, it would seem that, in advancing in his career, Laskin became more wedded to the idea of judicial restraint and deferring to Parliament.

This amended view of the judicial function should also be considered when assessing McCormick's characterization of Laskin's legacy. Although his Laskin was more often found in the majority during his later years on the Court, and the majority opinions became more consolidated under Laskin's leadership, what kind of influence was Laskin exerting, and at what price did the increasing consensus come? The analysis presented here indicates that many of Laskin's later judgments adopt a conservative approach to decision making, and it may well be that these resurging elements of traditionalism were a factor in creating greater unanimity on the Court. However, this shift towards conservatism is not directly linked to Laskin's assumption of the office of Chief

Justice. In his first years in the role, Laskin was still offering controversial and creative decision making. Cases such as *Kienapple*, *Lavell*, and *Murdoch* suggest that he had as much daring assuming the Chief Justiceship as he had when he was first appointed to the Court. Initially at least, it does not appear that Laskin saw conservatism as an inherent feature of being Chief Justice or viewed himself as being more restrained while in this role. Laskin's reserve emerged later, sometime closer to the end of the 1970s, for reasons discussed in Part VI. The triumph of Laskin in creating greater unanimity while Chief Justice may not be the victory for innovation and reform that is suggested by McCormick. Indeed, consensus came largely with conservatism.

PART VI: CAUSES OF THE SHIFTING THOUGHT

THE MOST INTERESTING QUESTION to pose – perhaps because ultimately it is unanswerable – is why such a shift may have occurred in Laskin's outlook. The possible reasons raised here are speculative, for two main reasons. First, the analysis presented in this essay is a starting point only. To conclude definitively that Laskin's views on the judicial function altered in his final years on the bench would be premature, as a far more in-depth and comprehensive study of his decisions and his extra-judicial writing would be needed. Instead, this essay has suggested that it is possible to discern some modification in Laskin's perspectives which might colour assessments of his judicial legacy. Firmer conclusions on this topic would require a broader canvassing of his decisions and other writings.

However, even if an exhaustive analysis of Laskin's body of work while on the Supreme Court were completed, it would still be difficult to offer a definitive assessment. Without being privy to Laskin's personal documents or materials that provide more insight into his personal thoughts than either his judgments or his academic articles, it is difficult to say with any certainty that such a shift occurred and what the possible impetus for that change might be. Judicial decisions, as well as speeches and articles written while a member of the bench, are limited tools with which to work. In many senses, they are inscrutable documents that often fail to provide a glimpse into what factors and considerations are motivating the views taken in them. Laskin's letters, diaries, and personal documents may be able to fill in some of the lingering questions about the influences that shaped his thoughts and ultimately his resolutions on many of these weighty issues. Until more primary resources are available for study, Laskin's contribution to and impact on Canadian law will likely remain elusive.

Despite these important caveats, it is possible to discuss possible causes that may have influenced Laskin's views on the judicial function. Three potential factors stand out in particular: Laskin's pragmatism, Laskin as an outsider, and the general institutional character of the judge.

Turning to the first factor, a large degree of pragmatism could well have caused Laskin's conception of the judge to alter. His earlier decisions are imbued with the spirit of law reform and, quite often, he wrote in dissent. His rejection of "mechanical jurisprudence"[89] and his willingness to expand the law were often unpalatable to other members of the Court. McCormick notes that a contingent of judges, generally led by Justice Martland, regularly opposed Laskin's views and adopted a much more reserved approach to adjudication, including greater adherence to precedent and more deference to legislative authority.[90] Given that Laskin's championing for reform, while bringing both popular support and promotion, was effecting very little change among his judicial brethren, he may well have been tempted to moderate his views. Neither the government nor the public were the parties that Laskin needed to convince of the desirability of reform – without the aid and support of the other members of the bench, change would never be possible. Thus, he would certainly have had a pragmatic reason for shifting his view of the role of judge towards a more conservative model. Some change is better than no change, and in his opinions demonstrating a more restrained approach to the judicial function, Laskin was generally found to be in the majority.

Another possible pragmatic explanation for this shift may be found in Laskin's American counterparts, with whom he shared similar ideals. In particular, a comparison of Laskin with Roscoe Pound, the noted American legal academic, might prove useful. Pound is often considered to be the father of "sociological jurisprudence" – a school of thought that emphasized the need for judges to take account of social conditions in adjudicating cases. Indeed, as a young scholar, Pound formulated the crusade against "mechanical jurisprudence" – a mantle that Laskin would also take up. Although there are differences between the two men, Laskin is often considered to be a member of this school of thought.[91] Like

Cecil Wright and John Willis, whom Laskin joined in leaving Osgoode Hall to join the University of Toronto in 1949, Laskin went through the Harvard University graduate program in the 1930s. By that decade and into the 1940s, Pound had become deeply conservative, turning on the legal realists, whom he had inspired, and battling with New Deal Progressives such as Frankfurter and Brandeis.[92] Laskin was, to some extent, influenced by Frankfurter, so one might well expect to see some evidence of these progressive views. However, another possibility remains, that Laskin internalized the Pound model – that of the daring young scholar who grows conservative with age and establishment. A more in-depth study of these two figures is certainly warranted, though it is beyond the analysis offered here.

There is a third consideration under the general heading of "pragmatism" that may help to explain the changes in Laskin's thought. Realistically speaking, by the last years of his career, he was a man of advanced years. Although not universally the case, it seems to be human nature to endorse more moderate views then than in one's younger years. Age often brings with it a reserve that would have been unknown to a person's younger self, and the beliefs one holds in youth may change given the wider perspective offered by a longer life. This theory is likely to be testable only by referencing Laskin's private materials.

Further pragmatist considerations on shaping Laskin's judicial views are purely conjectural. Without being able to reference any of Laskin's personal documents, it is impossible to know how Laskin viewed the contributions he was making on the Court and whether it was necessary to change his views to build consensus and achieve some lesser degree of reform. It is equally impossible to guess what views, if any, Laskin may have held with regards to legal realism and its impact on the law or to know what the effects of age may have been. Examination of these more intimate materials would prove useful in assessing the extent these factors may have inclined Laskin to change, and they may even answer the more intriguing questions of whether any alteration was apparent to Laskin himself. Awareness of such a change would suggest that outside factors – such as a desire to affect some change – were the true motivation of this shift in thought. Conversely, a lack of regard for such a change would suggest that age and slightly changed internal ideals are perhaps responsible for Laskin's revised views.

The second possible factor in Laskin's modified views is his general position as an "outsider" on the Court. Throughout his career, Laskin had suffered from marginalization. His Jewish descent prevented his full acceptance in Toronto's legal community on his return from Harvard and delayed his entrance into Canada's legal academia. Laskin knew well the difficulties of being on the fringe. These difficulties were compounded on his appointment to the Supreme Court in 1970. Not only was he the only Jewish justice on the bench at that time but he was the first Jewish person ever to be appointed to the high court.[93] Adding further to his distinction against the panel was the fact that he was an academic and had not practised law. Indeed, Laskin had earned a reputation as an outspoken and occasionally political academic. Nearly twenty years previously he had engendered the disapprobation of the legal community for criticizing the Law Society of Upper Canada and its practice of training lawyers,[94] and he had spent much of his career criticizing the Court for its rigidity and slavish adherence to precedent.[95]

Although much of the press surrounding Laskin's appointment was favourable, there was an element of displeasure from within the Court. This status of outsider was exacerbated by Laskin's meteoric rise to the office of Chief Justice in 1973:

> [T]here were unconfirmed reports of discontent. Laskin was described as an "academic lawyer" by some members of the bar. The other justices were allegedly annoyed at not being consulted about the appointment. Justice Martland reportedly was given very little warning that he would be passed over and was upset. The finance minister, John Turner, was said to be furious at the break with tradition, and sensitive Albertans were reported to be taking the rejection of Martland as a slight against the west.[96]

It would be understandable that an "outsider" on the Court would seek to gain acceptance by bringing his personal views more closely in line with the majority's position on the Court.

Ascribing this motivation – a desire for increased acceptance – to Laskin is debatable. Certainly there seems to be a shift in his views, and this change appeared to garner more support from the Court, yet it is not completely persuasive to attribute this result to an attempt to "fit in," particularly as this shift in view emerges at the end of Laskin's career and approximately six years from the time he had assumed leadership of the Court. One would think that a desire to belong, acute enough to warrant a modification of personal philosophy, would have emerged much earlier in Laskin's career, when he was most often in the role of dissenter. In 1976 Laskin had already been on the bench for nine years, on the Supreme Court for six, and had served as Chief Justice for three of those years. One would expect a desire to "belong" to emerge early in his career rather than in its final stage.

It is more likely that, after this lengthy judicial career, Laskin no longer felt as much the outsider as he once did. The departure of Justice Ritchie in 1976 slightly weakened the contingent of judges who often ruled in opposition to Laskin[97] and seemingly lessened any feelings of alienation that may have existed before this perceptible shift in Laskin's thought.

Indeed, an examination of the decision in *Bhadauria*, decided in the latter portion of Laskin's career, does not seem to indicate any particular predilection for the marginalized individual. In that case, Laskin explicitly refused to give a tort remedy to an alleged victim of discrimination on the basis of race. Thus, considering the dynamics of Laskin's circumstances, the desire to "belong" as the motivating force in Laskin's growing conservatism, on its own, remains unconvincing.

The third factor that may have played a role in the changes to Laskin's views relates to the very nature of the judicial office. More precisely, once one actually becomes a judge, one's preconceptions about the nature of the role are subject to change. Laskin himself seemed to acknowledge this point:

> [The law teacher] was and is able to touch law at its raw edges, to limit his or her concern to the intractables, to the deficiencies in the law as he or she sees them. The Judge, be he or she a trial Judge or an appellate Judge, is obliged to deal with the cases that come forward; there is no choice open to the Judge to slough off the routine and to apply himself or herself *only to the exotic, to the marginal issues*, to those cases that may be used to express a philosophy of law or to exhibit a sociological examination of legal doctrine. Not every case provides an opportunity for this kind of reflection.[98]

Such a reflection indicates that Laskin no longer saw himself as dealing with the exotic and marginal issues and, perhaps, no longer saw himself as exotic or marginal either. On the basis of his decisions and his other writings, it seems plausible that his shifting philosophy is related to his experience in the role of judge. This suggestion is bolstered by the knowledge that Laskin's views on substantive law remain relatively consistent throughout his career. His treatment of labour law, federalism issues, and civil liberties do not show a dramatic change. The most perceptible shifts relate to the nature of the judiciary, an issue about which a judge's perceptions might well change after inhabiting the position for an extended period of time. By the 1980s Laskin had been on the bench for over fifteen years – a long time to be on the "inside" by anyone's account.

Laskin's changed notions about the judiciary could be ascribed to his own enjoyment and experience in the office of judge. Decisions such as *Crevier* affirm and entrench judicial authority in a manner that Laskin, before he was on the bench, did not consider tenable. However, this view does not account for Laskin's increased deference to the legislature, an attitude that is evident in cases such as *Leatherdale* and the *Anti-Inflation Reference*. This entrenchment of the judicial function and the increasing willingness to keep judges as a check on the administrative state must also be balanced against strands within Laskin's later thought which also circumscribe, and acknowledge limits on, the province of the judge.

Based on his decisions and his published work, however, the most likely cause of his altered conception of the judiciary is his experience within it. There is little to suggest that Laskin's views in regards to substantive issues became more moderate. The differences in thought discerned in this essay relate to form and procedure rather than to substance. Conservative tendencies are present in questions of how far the legislature ought to go and how much autonomy should be accorded to the administrative state. Moreover, these changes emerge as Laskin becomes increasingly settled in the judicial role and as he is afforded more power, but also more responsibility, as Chief Justice of the Court. Laskin may have begun to view part of his role in this office as one of consensus building, and perhaps he considered it no longer fitting to be the Court's maverick – it's lone dissenter. Taken together, his experience in office is likely the primary impetus for the reform of some of his views. In sum, the view of the cathedral is substantially different standing within it.

However, at present, speculation is all that can occur. Laskin may have been motivated by a desire to conform to the more conservative elements on the bench – to become more fully accepted by his peers – though that assumption seems unlikely, given the point in his career at which this change occurred. He may have modified his views to build consensus on the Court – a kind of brokerage and compromise to achieve change. Or his conservatism may arise from his affinity with Pound and sociological jurisprudence or, more simply, it could result as a product of increased age.

In the end, it is impossible to say with any certainty, or even mere probability, what factors brought about the suggested change in Laskin's views. It seems most realistic to say that any change that occurred was likely a result of myriad factors and that apportionment among them is nearly impossible.

PART VII: CONCLUSION

IT HAS BEEN OVER twenty years since Bora Laskin's death and, since that time, there has been a struggle to define and articulate the impact of one of Canada's most famous jurists. Lost behind labels such as the "great dissenter" or reduced to pockets of law – administrative law[99] or federalism[100] – the real effects of Laskin's judicial tenure remain unclear. These depictions capture only one aspect of Laskin's career and, in emphasizing a part instead of the whole, they result in a distortion. In some respect, the creation of a legend has obscured the lasting legacy.

This essay has advocated a more complex and nuanced account of Laskin and his judicial legacy while he sat on the Supreme Court of Canada. To reduce Laskin to the "dissenter" ignores the fact that, for the latter part of his career, he was most often writing for or joining with the majority, as McCormick rightly points out. Yet McCormick's positive account of Laskin's final years alone cannot be taken as the definitive statement of the judicial legacy. To do so would ignore the concerns raised by Bushnell – that Laskin failed to carry out the promise of change which his appointment to the high court had signalled.

A complete picture and assessment of the reality of Laskin's years on the bench necessarily requires a study of the frequency of his dissenting and majority opinions as well as an analysis of the content and views advanced in those decisions. To assert that Laskin's innovations eventually carried the day on the Court, simply because he rarely dissented, is to ignore the real possibility that the consensus of the Court may have been brokered through moderation, attenuation, and alteration of some of Laskin's reforming enthusiasm.

This essay makes no definitive statement as to whether, in his final years, Laskin sacrificed or shied away from his earlier law-reformist tendencies. However, this analysis, which compared periods in Laskin's work, suggests that some changes occurred with respect to his view of the appropriate role of the courts, and that this change, in turn, influenced the zealousness with which law reform could be, and was, undertaken. Further study is merited into the degree and extent to which Laskin's views changed over the course of his career. The ultimate question – posed but not answered here – is whether the dissenting spirit in Laskin's early years won out or waned in the autumn days of the Laskin Court.

NOTES

1 Appeals to the Privy Council were abolished in 1949, and the Supreme Court became the final appellate court in Canada. Many analysts, Professor Laskin included, were critical of the Court in the years following the change as operating slavishly under the doctrine of *stare decisis* and placing too much emphasis on House of Lords decisions. See, for example, Bora Laskin, "The Supreme Court of Canada: A final Court of and for Canadians," *Canadian Bar Review* 29 (1951): 1038.
2 Ian Bushnell, *The Captive Court: A Study of the Supreme Court of Canada* (Montreal: McGill-Queen's University Press, 1992), 407.
3 Peter McCormick, *Supreme at Last: The Evolution of the Supreme Court of Canada* (Toronto: James Lorimer, 2000), 95.
4 Bushnell, *The Captive Court*, 414.
5 R.C.B. Risk and J.R.S. Pritchard, Introduction, *University of Toronto Law Journal* 35 (1985): 321.
6 Irving Abella, "The Making of a Chief Justice: Bora Laskin, The Early Years," *The Law Society Gazette* (1990): 190–92, is the source for the personal information in Part I of this essay.
7 James G. Snell and Frederick Vaughan, *The Supreme Court of Canada: History of the Institution* (Toronto: Osgoode Society and University of Toronto Press, 1985), 223.
8 Ibid., 224.
9 Chief Justice Brian Dickson, "Bora Laskin: An Appreciation," *Supreme Court Law Review* 6 (1984): xxv.
10 Risk and Pritchard, Introduction, 323.

11　Laskin, "The Supreme Court."
12　Bushnell, *The Captive Court*, 407.
13　*Harrison v. Carswell*, [1976] 2 SCR 200.
14　Bushnell, *The Captive Court*, 414.
15　Snell and Vaughan, *The Supreme Court of Canada*, 223.
16　Peter McCormick, "Follow the Leader: Judicial Leadership and the Laskin Court, 1973–1984," *Queen's Law Journal* 24 (1998):237–77; Peter McCormick, "Assessing Leadership on the Supreme Court of Canada: Towards a Typology of Chief Justice Performance," *Supreme Court Law Review*, 2nd Series, 4 (1993): 409; Peter McCormick, "Career Patterns and the Delivery of Reasons for Judgment in the Supreme Court of Canada, 1949–1993," *Supreme Court Law Review*, 2nd Series, 5 (1994): 499–521.
17　McCormick, *Supreme at Last*, 89.
18　McCormick's empirical analysis is based on a statistical database of Supreme Court decisions which analyzes, among other things, the frequency of dissents, concurrences, and majority decisions of the justices on the Court between 1973 and 1984. McCormick also notes and analyzes the judging coalitions formed during this period.
19　McCormick, *Supreme at Last*, 90.
20　Ibid., 104.
21　Ibid., 95. During this period, critics speak of the "LSD" connection – Justices Laskin, Spence, and Dickson – who often formed a minority coalition.
22　Ibid., 91.
23　Ibid., 95.
24　*Murdoch v. Murdoch*, [1975] 1 SCR 423.
25　McCormick, *Supreme at Last*, 92.
26　*Highway Properties Ltd. v. Kelly*, [1971] SCR 562.
27　Bushnell, *The Captive Court*, 385.
28　*Goldhar v. Universal Sections & Mouldings*, [1963] 36 DLR (2d) 450.
29　*Highway Properties*, 572.
30　Arnold Weinrib, "Property, Precedent and Policy," *University of Toronto Law Journal* 35 (1985): 545.
31　*Rivtow Martine Ltd. v. Washington Iron Works*, [1974] SCR 1189.
32　*A.G. v. Lavell; Isaac v. Bédard*, [1974] SCR 1349.
33　*Drybones v. The Queen*, [1970] SCR 282.
34　*A.G. v. Lavell; Isaac v. Bédard*, [1974] SCR 1349 at 1386.
35　*Hogan v. The Queen*, [1975] 2 SCR 574.
36　See Denise Réaume, "The Judicial Philosophy of Bora Laskin," *University of Toronto Law Journal* 35 (1985): 447. Laskin considered that there was more scope for judicial creativity in relation to the common law than to statute-based law.

37 Joel Bakan, ed., *Canadian Constitutional Law* (Toronto: Emond Montgomery Publishing, 2003), 677.
38 *Kienapple v. The Queen*, [1975] 1 SCR 729.
39 *Doré v. A.G. of Canada*, [1975] 1 SCR 756.
40 *Thorson v. A.G. Canada*, [1975] 1 SCR 138.
41 Bushnell, *The Captive Court*, 396.
42 Snell and Vaughan, *The Supreme Court of Canada*, 241.
43 *Murdoch v. Murdoch*, [1975] 1 SCR 423 at 440.
44 *Rathwell v. Rathwell*, [1978] 2 SCR 436.
45 Carol Rogerson, "From *Murdoch* to *Leatherdale*: The Uneven Course of Bora Laskin's Family Law Decisions," *University of Toronto Law Journal* 35 (1985): 484.
46 *Peters v. The Queen* (1971), 17 DLR 128.
47 *Harrison v. Carswell*, [1976] 2 SCR 200.
48 *Re Anti-Inflation*, [1976] 2 SCR 373.
49 Peter Russell, Rainer Knopff, and Ted Morton, *Federalism and the Charter* (Ottawa: Carleton University Press, 1989), 162–63.
50 See, for example, *Re Board of Commerce Act, 1919 and The Combines and Fair Prices Act, 1919*, [1922] 1 AC 191 (PC); *Toronto Electric Commissioners v. Snider*, [1925] AC 396 (PC); *AG of Canada v. AG of Ontario* (*Employment and Social Insurance Act Reference*), [1937] AC 355 (PC).
51 *Paskivski v. Canadian Pacific Ltd.*, [1976] 1 SCR 687.
52 *Board of Governors of Seneca College of Applied Arts and Technology v. Bhadauria*, [1981] 2 SCR 180.
53 Ian Hunter, "The Stillborn Tort of Discrimination," *Ottawa Law Review* 14 (1982): 227.
54 Harry Kopyto, "The *Bhadauria* Case: The Denial of the Right to Sue for Discrimination," *Queen's Law Journal* 7 (1981–82): 161.
55 Réaume, "The Judicial Philosophy of Bora Laskin," 468.
56 *Nicholson v. Haldimand-Norfolk Regional Board of Commissioners of Police*, [1979] 1 SCR 311.
57 David Mullan, ed., *Administrative Law*, 5th ed. (Toronto: Emond Montgomery Publications, 2003), 721–22.
58 Hudson Janisch, "Bora Laskin and Administrative Law: An Unfinished Journey," *University of Toronto Law Journal* 35 (1985): 577.
59 *Nicholson v. Haldimand-Norfolk Regional Board of Commissioners of Police*, [1979] 1 SCR 311 at 325.
60 *Canadian Union of Public Employees, Local 963 v. New Brunswick Liquor Corporation*, [1979] 2 SCR 227.
61 *Canada Labour Relations Board v. Halifax Longshoreman's Association*, [1983] 1 SCR 245.

62   Ibid., 256.
63   Janisch, "Bora Laskin and Administrative Law," 569–70.
64   Bora Laskin, "Certiorari to Labour Boards: The Apparent Futility of Privative Clauses," *Canadian Bar Review* 30 (1952): 989–90.
65   Ibid.
66   *Metropolitan Life Insurance Company v. International Union of Operating Engineers, Local 796*, [1970] 11 SCR 425.
67   *Crevier v. A.G. Québec*, [1981] 2 SCR 220.
68   Laskin, "Certiorari to Labour Boards," 989–90. Emphasis added.
69   See, generally, Harry Arthurs, "Protecting Against Judicial Review," *La Revue du Barreau* 47 (1983): 277.
70   *Leatherdale v. Leatherdale*, [1982] 2 SCR 743.
71   *Family Law Reform Act*, RSO 1980, c.152.
72   Ibid.
73   Rogerson, "From *Murdoch* to *Leatherdale*," 508.
74   Ibid.
75   *Leatherdale v. Leatherdale*, [1982] 2 SCR 743 at para. 26.
76   Rogerson, "From *Murdoch* to *Leatherdale*," 539.
77   Ibid., 538.
78   Bora Laskin, "The Institutional Character of the Judge," *Israel Law Review* 7 (1972): 330.
79   Ibid., 341.
80   Laskin, "A Judge and His Constituencies," *Manitoba Law Journal* 7 (1976): 14. This article is based on a speech Laskin delivered in 1975.
81   Laskin, "The Institutional Character of the Judge," 341.
82   Laskin, "A Judge and His Constituencies," 14.
83   Laskin, "The Institutional Character of the Judge," 341–42.
84   Réaume, "The Judicial Philosophy of Bora Laskin," 447.
85   Bora Laskin, "Some Observations on Judicial Independence," *Provincial Judges Journal* 4 (1980): 20.
86   Laskin, "Certiorari to Labour Boards," 989–90.
87   Laskin, untitled, *Australian Law Journal* 51 (1977): 457. Emphasis added.
88   Snell and Vaughan, *The Supreme Court of Canada*, 223.
89   Réaume, "The Judicial Philosophy of Bora Laskin," 447. See also Roscoe Pound, *An Introduction to the Philosophy of Law* (New Haven: Yale University Press, 1954).
90   McCormick, *Supreme at Last*, 91.
91   Réaume, "The Judicial Philosophy of Bora Laskin," 48.
92   In Pound's case, this conservatism manifested itself in the form of virulent anti-Semitism and vocal denunciation of Communism.
93   Abella, "The Making of a Chief Justice," 8.

94 In 1949 Cecil Wright, John Willis, and Bora Laskin left Osgoode Hall to establish a professional school at the University of Toronto, angering the Law Society and causing them to be ostracized for a period of time.
95 Laskin, "The Supreme Court of Canada."
96 Abella, "The Making of a Chief Justice," 225.
97 McCormick, *Supreme at Last*, 91.
98 Laskin, "A Judge and His Constituencies," 11. Emphasis added.
99 Janisch, "Bora Laskin and Administrative Law," 70.
100 See also Katherine Swinton, "Bora Laskin and Federalism," *University of Toronto Law Journal* 35 (1985): 353–91.